The
Fundamentals
of Fashion
Management

BLOOMSBURY VISUAL ARTS

Bloomsbury Publishing Plc

50 Bedford Square, London, WC1B 3DP, UK
1385 Broadway, New York, NY 10018, USA

**BLOOMSBURY and the Diana logo
are trademarks of Bloomsbury Publishing Plc**

First published by AVA Publishing SA, 2011

This 2nd edition is published by Bloomsbury Visual Arts, an imprint of Bloomsbury Publishing Plc

© Bloomsbury Publishing Plc, 2018

Susan Dillon has asserted her right under the Copyright, Designs and Patents Act, 1988,
to be identified as Author of this work.

Cover design: Louise Dugdale

Cover image © ALBERTO PIZZOLI/AFP/Getty Images

A catalogue record for this book is available from the British Library.

Library of Congress Cataloging-in-Publication Data

Names: Dillon, Susan, author.
Title: The fundamentals of fashion management / Susan Dillon.
Description: Second Edition. | New York : Bloomsbury Visual Arts, [2017] |
Revised edition of the author's The fundamentals of fashion management, 2011.
Identifiers: LCCN 2017006380 | ISBN 9781474271219 (pbk. : alk. paper) |
ISBN 9781474271226 (ePDF)
Subjects: LCSH: Clothing trade—Management. | Fashion merchandising. |
Fashion merchandising—Study and teaching. | Fashion design—Study and teaching. | Advertising—Fashion.
Classification: LCC HD9940.A2 D55 2017 | DDC 746.9/2068—dc23
LC record available at https://lccn.loc.gov/2017006380

ISBN: PB: 978-1-4742-7121-9
        ePDF: 978-1-4742-7122-6

Typeset by Lachina
Printed and bound in India

To find out more about our authors and books visit www.bloomsbury.com and sign up for our newsletters.

The Fundamentals
of Fashion
Management

SECOND EDITION

SUSAN DILLON

BLOOMSBURY VISUAL ARTS
LONDON • NEW YORK • OXFORD • NEW DELHI • SYDNEY

Contents

Chapter 1	**Chapter 2**	**Chapter 3**	**Chapter 4**
The business of fashion	Fashion trend prediction	Getting a product to market	Fashion transition

Chapter 5

Fashion marketing and communication

Chapter 6

The fashion machine

Chapter 7

Fashion entrepreneurship and management

Introduction

Fashion is a world of illusion and glamour on one hand and a complex, multibillion-dollar business on the other. Its success relies on the talent and vision of those working in the industry, both in design and in management. Because the way we look, the image we select, is so important to the human psyche, fashion plays an astonishingly large part in our culture; it is the motivation behind the multifaceted process of fashion design, manufacture and distribution.

The fashion industry is attracting a new genre of fashion professionals with the interdisciplinary skills and techniques required to respond to the demands of the sensitive consumer and a competitive, global marketplace. There is great demand for new talent and many opportunities for graduates to be a valuable asset in a fashion company – even if you don't have a knack for design. Fashion careers, like clothing, can take many different forms: if you have a head for business and apply it to your love for fashion, there is a career in fashion management for you. *The Fundamentals of Fashion Management* is an introductory text that provides you with a first look into the myriad of roles and activities that take place within the evolving and contemporary fashion industry. Every chapter begins with bullet pointed learning outcomes list and gives a 'quick-glance' overview of the chapter's content for revision purposes and allows you to use the text as a useful study guide.

Chapter 1

This chapter is an introduction to the basics of fashion management, business concepts and the different types of fashion businesses. It offers an overview of the fashion industry and how the fashion system works.

Chapter 2

This chapter examines the areas of fashion forecasting and trend prediction and how they are used within the fashion industry, in particular in fashion design and retail.

Chapter 3

Chapter 3 outlines the basic management activities for the fashion manager in order to get the fashion product to market. It includes an overview of the roles and tasks necessary to meet the needs of potential customers and designers and deliver the request for garments.

Chapter 4

The transition of fashion is explored in Chapter 4; this relates to all the aspects of the supply chain, from fashion manufacturing and buying to promotion and retail formats.

Fashion East Meadham Kirchhoff Autumn Winter Fashion Collection on the runway during London Fashion Week, 22nd February 2011.
© Paul Cunningham via Getty Images

Chapter 5

The focus of Chapter 5 is fashion communication, the ways in which the media and cultural industries promote and portray fashion. This includes branding, marketing and promotion models.

Chapter 6

This chapter looks at the fashion calendar: the tool that facilitates the smooth running of the global fashion industry. It looks at the coordination of the industry, taking in the fashion capitals of the world, including Paris, Milan, New York and London.

Chapter 7

Chapter 7 examines the managerial tools and leadership skills needed to succeed as a fashion entrepreneur, encompassing the financial, marketing, business-development models and strategies necessary for running a successful business.

1

The business
of fashion

The following chapter provides an overview and looks at the evolution of the fashion industry within the context of fashion design and management. It explains the impact of technology and sustainability, and it outlines some of the key fashion global brands and their influence today.

The chapter will help you:

- Understand the evolution of fashion in its broadest sense by contextualising some of the key influencers in the design, creation and communication of fashion protects.

- Develop an understanding of the different market levels in the industry and what makes them different.

- Learn about the impact of technology and the internet and how this has developed the way we make, sell and communicate fashion.

- Appreciate the way the global fashion industry works.

- Recognise the key designers and brands operating in the fashion industry today and their influence on the fashion marketplace.

1.1
Couture style.
© George Rose via
Getty images

The fashion industry: An overview

The fashion industry is the design and manufacture of fashion garments and is primarily a product of the modern age. Prior to the middle of the nineteenth century, most clothing was custom made (meaning, made to a particular customer's order). Clothing was handmade and either produced at home or ordered from dressmakers and tailors. The tailor was known for his ability to create garments through the art of designing, cutting, fitting and finishing clothes. Dressmakers, on the other hand, were mainly women and their job was to copy or adapt the latest clothing ideas from Paris, London or other fashion centres using printed illustrations called fashion plates. The *Oxford English Dictionary* first recorded 'dressmaker' in 1803.

Throughout the nineteenth century – with the rise of new technologies such as the sewing machine, the increase of global capitalism, the development of the factory system of production and the growth of retail outlets such as department stores – clothing became mass-produced in standard sizes and sold at fixed prices. The current fashion industry's origins are in Europe and America, but it is now an international and a highly globalised industry, with clothing often designed in one country, manufactured in another, and sold worldwide.

The fashion industry consists of four levels:

1. The production of raw materials, principally fibres and textiles but also leather and fur

2. The production of fashion goods by designers, manufacturers, contractors, and others

3. Retail sales

4. Various forms of advertising and promotion

The levels consist of many separate but interdependent sectors including textile design, production, fashion design, manufacturing, fashion retailing, marketing, merchandising, fashion shows and media. Each sector is devoted to the goal of satisfying consumer demand for clothing under conditions that enable participants in the industry to operate at a profit.

Fashion management is a constantly evolving area of the fashion industry and concentrates on the promotion of apparel sales involving tasks that meet the needs of potential customers and designers. Fashion marketing and management professionals work throughout the industry and focus on marketing collections for designers, creating fashion advertising campaigns and filling the ranks of retail merchandising and management. Whether working for designers, ad agencies, fashion journals or retail establishments, their responsibility is to move fashion by developing campaigns, displays, advertisements, directing manufacturing, marketing, and creating sales strategies.

The industry is divided into three main categories of manufacture:

1. Haute couture

2. Ready-to-wear (RTW)

3. Mass-market

It is useful to know about these three production levels in order to understand the **supply chain** and the fashion industry as a whole.

Couture has its origins in dressmaking when it was considered an art form, but it wasn't until the mid-nineteenth century that the first couture design house was established by Charles Frederick Worth (1826–1895). Worth is widely considered to have invented fashion design, as he was the first to produce a collection of dresses and show them on live models, with each design

Haute couture

noun: **haute couture**; noun: **haut couture**;
plural noun: **haut coutures**

1. The designing and making of high-quality fashionable clothes by leading fashion houses, especially to order.

2. Expensive, fashionable clothes.

available to order in a limited choice of fabrics. In 1858, Worth set up his design house, enabling his customers to attach a name and a face to his designs; before then, clothing design was handled largely by anonymous seamstresses. Designer Paul Poiret continued this concept and so began the practice of putting the designer's name on garments; and the origins of the fashion design industry, as we know it today grew. Many designers followed in the footsteps of Worth, including Coco Chanel, Elsa Schiaparelli, Cristóbal Balenciaga and Christian Dior.

Haute couture collections are developed exclusively for private customers by a design house, and just as car manufacturers show off their expertise through the creation of concept supercars, fashion designers use couture as a statement of strength and technical ability. The clothes produced for the couture collections are of high quality and the finish is excellent. The design concepts, along with highly skilled and time-consuming labour, mean there may only be ten or twenty pieces in production and, as a result, haute couture garments are very expensive. The collections shown twice a year feature around thirty-five individual outfits, which are displayed on the catwalk or in private salons. These shows showcase a designer's most outrageous ideas, where budget is no limit to ambition.

Entry to the schedule is strictly managed by the *Chambre de commerce et d'industrie de Paris* – and in order to become a couture designer, fashion houses must meet stringent guidelines. To qualify, a design house must be invited to join the *Chambre syndicale de la haute couture*, governed by the French department of industry. There are around twenty members. In short, couture designers are the *creme de la crème*; fashion's richest, most accomplished designers.

It wasn't long ago when only the super rich were able to make such major fashion purchases. However, today, with customer access to social media, couture's fantastic images are available to the masses through the tweeted hashtagged and Instagrammed images sent across the world as soon as the garments hit the runway. In the age of the super rich, couture still sells well; according to an article in the *Guardian* 2014 July,

**1.2
Seamstresses in the House of Worth.**
Worth was a pioneer of the fashion show and the first designer to create dresses intended to be copied and distributed throughout the world.

© Heritage Images via Getty Images

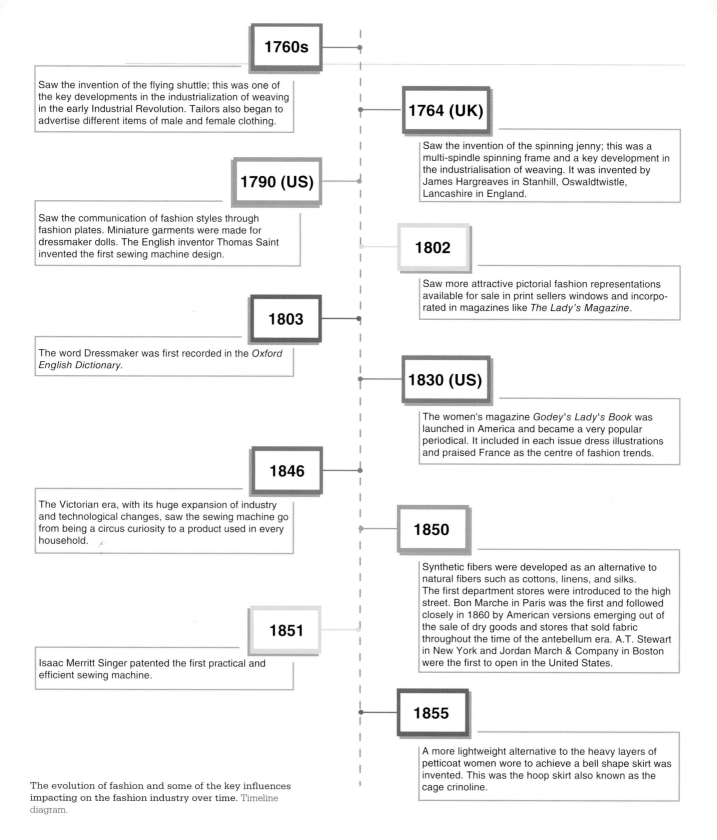

1760s

Saw the invention of the flying shuttle; this was one of the key developments in the industrialization of weaving in the early Industrial Revolution. Tailors also began to advertise different items of male and female clothing.

1764 (UK)

Saw the invention of the spinning jenny; this was a multi-spindle spinning frame and a key development in the industrialisation of weaving. It was invented by James Hargreaves in Stanhill, Oswaldtwistle, Lancashire in England.

1790 (US)

Saw the communication of fashion styles through fashion plates. Miniature garments were made for dressmaker dolls. The English inventor Thomas Saint invented the first sewing machine design.

1802

Saw more attractive pictorial fashion representations available for sale in print sellers windows and incorporated in magazines like *The Lady's Magazine*.

1803

The word Dressmaker was first recorded in the *Oxford English Dictionary*.

1830 (US)

The women's magazine *Godey's Lady's Book* was launched in America and became a very popular periodical. It included in each issue dress illustrations and praised France as the centre of fashion trends.

1846

The Victorian era, with its huge expansion of industry and technological changes, saw the sewing machine go from being a circus curiosity to a product used in every household.

1850

Synthetic fibers were developed as an alternative to natural fibers such as cottons, linens, and silks. The first department stores were introduced to the high street. Bon Marche in Paris was the first and followed closely in 1860 by American versions emerging out of the sale of dry goods and stores that sold fabric throughout the time of the antebellum era. A.T. Stewart in New York and Jordan March & Company in Boston were the first to open in the United States.

1851

Isaac Merritt Singer patented the first practical and efficient sewing machine.

1855

A more lightweight alternative to the heavy layers of petticoat women wore to achieve a bell shape skirt was invented. This was the hoop skirt also known as the cage crinoline.

The evolution of fashion and some of the key influences impacting on the fashion industry over time. Timeline diagram.

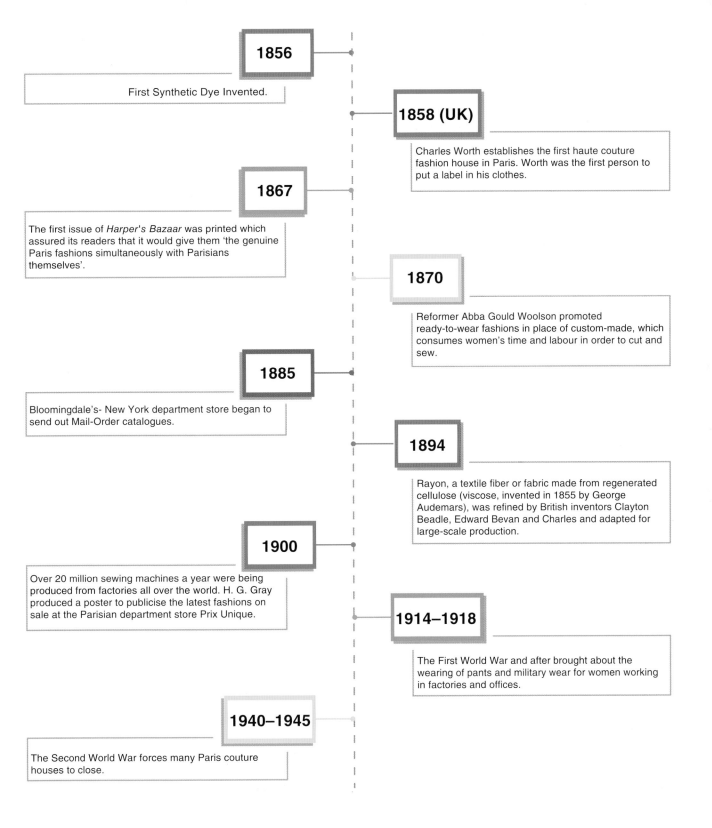

1856

First Synthetic Dye Invented.

1858 (UK)

Charles Worth establishes the first haute couture fashion house in Paris. Worth was the first person to put a label in his clothes.

1867

The first issue of *Harper's Bazaar* was printed which assured its readers that it would give them 'the genuine Paris fashions simultaneously with Parisians themselves'.

1870

Reformer Abba Gould Woolson promoted ready-to-wear fashions in place of custom-made, which consumes women's time and labour in order to cut and sew.

1885

Bloomingdale's- New York department store began to send out Mail-Order catalogues.

1894

Rayon, a textile fiber or fabric made from regenerated cellulose (viscose, invented in 1855 by George Audemars), was refined by British inventors Clayton Beadle, Edward Bevan and Charles and adapted for large-scale production.

1900

Over 20 million sewing machines a year were being produced from factories all over the world. H. G. Gray produced a poster to publicise the latest fashions on sale at the Parisian department store Prix Unique.

1914–1918

The First World War and after brought about the wearing of pants and military wear for women working in factories and offices.

1940–1945

The Second World War forces many Paris couture houses to close.

1955

Mary Quant opened up her first boutique in King's Road; in the Chelsea neighbourhood of London she becomes one of the most influential in the youth movement. She invented the miniskirt and her hot pants launched the model Twiggy as what we now know as a supermodel.

1960s

Young people's income was at its highest since the end of the Second World War. Designer Pierre Cardin becomes first to license his name for various products.

1961

John F. Kennedy took office as president, bringing with him a beautiful, young and fashion-inspiring wife as First Lady. Jackie Kennedy's innate sense of style and dress soon made her 'Queen' of American fashion.

1964

The first Biba store was opened in Abingdon Road in Kensington, London. The store's marketing strategy made it stand out. Biba was the first to set a standard for brand marketing and the first high street store to create a look.

1970s

Women emerged in the workplace tenfold and young people defined themselves as anti-fashion and developed an anti-establishment group who cut up and refashioned clothing and outfits, the movement was labelled Punk.

1974

Lauren Hutton, an actress and supermodel signed a Revlon cosmetics deal. Sonia Rykiel, French designer, dominated the 1970s' American market, she popularized knitted garments and designed her first pullover with reversed seams.

1975

High street stores became very popular and took over from the 1960s boutique. The market leader on the high street was Van Allan.

1976

Fashion communication started to change with Videofashion News, a video version of a fashion magazine being created.

1978

Kenzo Takada grew to success, drawing inspiration from many different cultures, and had an excellent understanding of what young consumers wanted. His catwalks were theatrical and innovative for the time.

1979

Saw Margret Thatcher elected as British Prime Minister influencing the future decade's power dressing for women internationally.

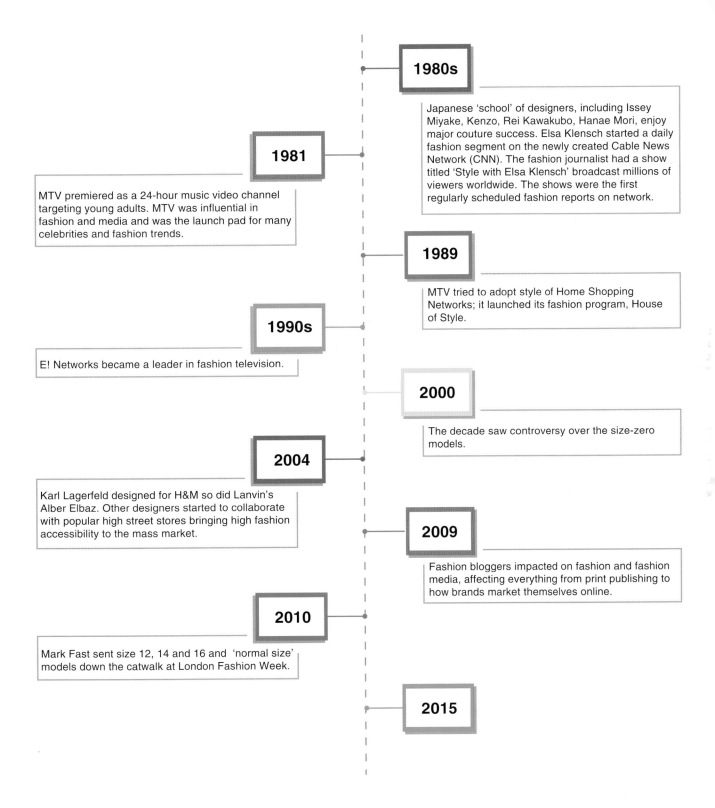

1980s

Japanese 'school' of designers, including Issey Miyake, Kenzo, Rei Kawakubo, Hanae Mori, enjoy major couture success. Elsa Klensch started a daily fashion segment on the newly created Cable News Network (CNN). The fashion journalist had a show titled 'Style with Elsa Klensch' broadcast millions of viewers worldwide. The shows were the first regularly scheduled fashion reports on network.

1981

MTV premiered as a 24-hour music video channel targeting young adults. MTV was influential in fashion and media and was the launch pad for many celebrities and fashion trends.

1989

MTV tried to adopt style of Home Shopping Networks; it launched its fashion program, House of Style.

1990s

E! Networks became a leader in fashion television.

2000

The decade saw controversy over the size-zero models.

2004

Karl Lagerfeld designed for H&M so did Lanvin's Alber Elbaz. Other designers started to collaborate with popular high street stores bringing high fashion accessibility to the mass market.

2009

Fashion bloggers impacted on fashion and fashion media, affecting everything from print publishing to how brands market themselves online.

2010

Mark Fast sent size 12, 14 and 16 and 'normal size' models down the catwalk at London Fashion Week.

2015

Hannah Marriot states that the sales of Chanel's collection – spring/summer 2014 – rose by 20 per cent, and the average age of Dior's couture customer has fallen, from mid forties to early thirties. A change Dior's chief executive attributes to the rise of rich, tech-savvy and growing markets in countries such as China, Russia and the Middle East. However, while couture is not obtainable for most, it paves the way for more accessible fashion ideas and trends, and we have to recognise that Paris still holds the position of global fashion capital. We are seeing changes in the distribution of global wealth and creativity, and with this, new centres of excellence for fashion's most distinctive art form.

'Haute couture consists of secrets whispered from generation to generation . . . if, in ready-to-wear, a garment is manufactured according to standard sizes, the haute couture garment adapts to any imperfection in order to eliminate it.'

Yves Saint Laurent

1.3
Chanel Runway, Paris Fashion Week, Haute Couture Fall/ Winter 2014– 2015. The fashion house of Chanel is a grand couturier and is a member of the French *Chambre syndicale de la haute couture,* the Paris-based governing body.
© Pascal Le Segretain via Getty Images.

Supply chain

A supply chain is a system of organisations, people, technology, activities, information and resources involved in moving a product or service from supplier to customer. Supply chain activities transform natural resources, raw materials and components into a finished product that is delivered to the end customer.

Ready to wear

adj. Of or relating to clothing, especially designer clothing, that is marketed in a finished condition in standard sizes.

n. Clothing marketed in a finished condition in standard sizes: *saves money by buying ready-to-wear.*

Designs in the ready-to-wear (RTW) market sector are high quality in terms of fabric, cut and finish and, although not custom-made, many RTW collections are exclusive, often limited edition and therefore still expensive but more affordable than a couture garment. RTW collections are more directional and trend-led than haute couture, often containing concept pieces that make a statement to garner press attention on the international runways.

Many fashion designers still work to traditional construction and design concepts following the tradition set by Parisian couture houses in the early twenty-first century, showing collections six to eight months prior to shipment. However, today some still show spring/summer collections on the catwalk in September and October, which are delivered to stores between January and March, and the autumn/winter collections debut in February and March and are delivered between July and September. We are also seeing new models evolve; for example, in-between seasons known as resort and pre-fall are designed to come to shops in midwinter and

The phrase 'ready to wear' is a translation from the French term '*prêt-à-porter*'; it is also referred to as 'off-the-peg' or 'off-the-rack'. The two things that make a clothing item ready-to-wear are that the garment that is finished can be worn and the garment can be worn without significant alteration, as it is made to standard sizes that fit most people.

The Industrial Revolution was the start of the innovation and technology advances in materials and the construction of garments. As technology improved in the use of sewing machines, prices came down and quality improved. Further development in making clothing led to closing of the gaps in price and quality between handmade and machine-made clothing, making it more attractive for customers to buy their garments rather than make them due to time saved.

Today, designers produce ready-to-wear clothing using standard patterns, factory equipment, and faster construction techniques to keep costs low.

1.4
Jen Kao SS12. American RTW designer Jen Kao is known for her innovative tailoring, intricately seamed leather pieces and experimental knits.
© Mike Coppola via Getty Images

1.5
Vivienne Westwood SS10. Vivienne Westwood has been designing RTW for over thirty years and has come to be known as one of the most influential British designers of the twentieth century.
© Patrick Kovarik via Getty Images

midsummer, respectively, with other interim collections being shown, too.

RTW collections are far less expensive than couture and are manufactured in standard sizes, which make them more suitable for large-scale production. However, the costs of staging fashion shows, advertising, high-quality design, fabrics, pattern-cutting and manufacture are high. Taking these factors into consideration can affect and reduce cost effectiveness in production, contributing to the higher price bracket.

Mass production

Mass production is the cheapest and most highly industrialised level of manufacture, with techniques invented at the end of the nineteenth century. Historic technological innovations, such as the development of the sewing machine, the zipper and synthetic fibers, influenced how garments were made, how they look and how they perform. However, it was not until after the war years that mass production really took over from haute couture. Today's mass-produced designs can be just as good as high fashion, especially with the likes of guest designers producing high-street collections. (More than a decade after Karl Lagerfeld's collection debuted at

1.6
The Inditex Group. The Inditex Group, which owns Zara, Pull & Bear, Massimo Dutti, Bershka, Stradivarius, Oysho, Zara Home and Uterqüe, is made up of more than 100 companies operating in textile design, manufacturing and distribution. The group's success is thanks to its unique business model and efficient supply chain, which enables a rapid turnaround to adjust to changing market demands.
© Bloomberg via Getty Images

Fast fashion

'Fast fashion' is a term that refers to affordable basics and disposable trends. It is also used to describe the production of clothing collections based on the most recent fashion trends.

Vertical integration

The degree to which a company owns, or has control over, its suppliers and distributors is referred to as vertical integration.

H&M, high–low partnerships are still a formidable marketing strategy for fashion designers and retailers.) Fabrics are usually cheaper though, and construction techniques are modified to keep the prices of such garments low.

Fashion designers working in this market sector produce designs based on popular trends and take influences from RTW collections ensuring the quick sale of garments, also known as **fast fashion**. 'Fast fashion' became a buzzword in clothing retail between 1997 and 1998 – a period during which fashion on the high street became dull and did not resonate with consumers. The same period saw the UK debut of the **vertically integrated** Spanish retail chains Mango and Zara, with great flexibility and speed in turnaround from design to product to shop floor. Today, these companies and others, such as Primark, produce millions of garments in an extremely short period of time.

'Technology is the fashion of the '90s. It affects everyone, and everyone is interested in it – either from fear of being left behind or because they have a real need to use technology.'

Jay Chiat, advertising designer

The impact of technology

A lot has changed in the fashion world in the last few decades. Technology has turned the entire fashion industry upside down – making all types of fashion more accessible to a large spectrum of consumers, but also making it more of a challenge for designers and retailers. Global economies are seeing a shift towards knowledge and a rise in the economic importance of ideas, images and information, which has increased the speed of innovation within business. The fashion industry has had to become more flexible to be able to respond quickly to new opportunities and to develop new ideas, and technology has been a major factor in improvements and changes, including fabric technology, computer-aided design (CAD), enhanced garment construction techniques and, of course, the internet.

The internet

The internet, now over twenty years old, has had a great influence on the way we communicate and interact with fashion and fashion brands. In the mid 1800s, fashion brands were sought through retail catalogues – allowing access from even the most remote locations. Fast-forward 100 years and the most effective ways in which to reach the consumer included magazines and television commercials. In the last twenty years, fashion consumers have been using computers and the internet as a way of developing a connection with the brands and designers.

Today, fashion consumers are able to search their favourite designer, brand or retailer online or through their phone and order whatever they desire in a matter of minutes. Accessibility to favourite fashion labels or brands has broadened through the use of mobile technology, social media and more.

Like real-world marketing, the fashion industry was the first to adopt social media marketing tools. It inculcated its businesses with social media platforms and provided itself with a fresh new perspective and a wider platform to showcase brands. This not only helped to grow business online but also helped develop trust and a better understanding among its clientele. There are very few fashion brands not present on social platforms; almost every fashion label is now socially active.

Fashion blogs

Fashion blogs have grown significantly since the early 2000s when they first appeared, and recent media reports state that some fashion blogs have become extremely profitable and the influence within the industry is growing. We see social media almost everywhere, with social media platforms a large part of our everyday lives. People start each day by checking their Facebook, Twitter, Instagram, Pinterest and Tumblr accounts and finish the day religiously on all these platforms.

Social media

Social media is the use of web-based and mobile technologies to turn communication into interactive dialogue. It includes blogs and websites or apps such as Facebook, Twitter and YouTube.

Blog

Derived from the term 'web log', which is a type of website. A fashion blog is solely or primarily dedicated to the coverage of fashion and trends.

An example of a blogger success is Danielle Bernstein, the US fashion blogger behind the **We Wore What** personal style-diary website. She makes a lot of money from Instagram.

Bernstein was interviewed in 2015 by *Harpers* US and at that time she had 992,000 Instagram followers. This meant her 'rate card' for an individual piece of sponsored content (e.g. one Instagram post) ranged from 5,000 to 15,000 USD (which equates to approximately £3,000 to £9,500), depending on the terms of the deal. Since the interview, she hit 1 million followers, meaning she can charge 'a good amount more'. Fashion blogging has developed from a hobby to a viable business prospect, with mainstream media acceptance and fashion bloggers becoming a part of the conventional fashion press.

With such attention and legitimacy, it is natural that the online market start considering these platforms as marketing tools. With online businesses growing, marketers are busy inventing new marketing strategies to capture this market. In order to expand and be in the good books of their customers, fashion business owners are now thinking of new ways to increase their social media presences, as it is essential today for any online business owners to have a sound and effective social media marketing strategy.

Connecting with the consumer

The communication between designers and bloggers has opened up the connection between consumers and brands. Before the advent of the internet, fashion shows were televised and transfigured into media-saturated spectaculars, but there was a relatively long delay between the runway show and the delivery of information to consumers. Today brands understand that their customers are consuming fashion at a faster pace than before and that social media plays a large part in this. Reports are immediate and designers are increasingly streaming shows live on the internet. In 2010, London Fashion Week (LFW) was the first in the world to grant access to the masses by live streaming the runways; what had previously been exclusive and elite then became accessible to everyone.

In 2015, Burberry partnered with Twitter to offer users of the social media site the chance to capture pictures of its LFW womenswear show live from the runway. By tweeting #Tweetcam to the @Burberry Twitter account, users triggered a camera to take a photograph from the best vantage point within the show space as the models walked down the runway. Each picture was then personalised with the user's Twitter handle, a time stamp of the moment the image was taken and then tweeted back to them.

The luxury fashion house, known for its forward-thinking digital and social activity around its LFW shows, had previously worked with Twitter on a number of initiatives. In 2012, Twitter provided an in-tweet live stream of Burberry's spring/summer show, and in September 2014 the fashion brand sold its products through Twitter Buy Now functionality.

The fashion app

One of the key changes in the way we communicate fashion over the last decade is the way we use the power of mobile technology. Since the debut of the smartphone the way brands follow you as you go about your work day, run errands and even when you are queuing for a coffee have changed the way we connect to the fashion. Fashion and shopping habits are changing and evolving in parallel with the way the internet is developing, and it is crucial that fashion ecommerce connects and embraces mobile devices as smartphone users have grown to a massive 37.8 million in the United States alone.

In 2014, it was difficult to avoid the buzz around messaging apps in the tech press; you would have thought that with the acquisition of WhatsApp by Facebook and when Snapchat was adopted by over 200 million users that messaging apps would have seen the largest growth. However, the conversations were around Snapchat, Instagram and WeChat shopping apps that dominated the market. Shopping apps are the fastest-growing area of the mobile app market, and time spent shopping on a mobile app increased in 2015 by a massive 174 per cent up from 77 per cent in 2014.

With shoppers savvier than ever, moving between channels, both online and offline, brands have to keep up with the pace to meet the challenge of providing consumers with exactly what they want. Gone are the days when speed was of the essence; customer service is important for the less forgiving customer, and a bad experience results in lost sales as the customer has multiple social media platforms at his or her disposal to communicate any frustrations immediately. Today's apps appeal to the time-poor multitasker wanting to make purchases on the go. These apps offer a quick and accessible way to access brands and shopping based on previous purchases, making it easy for the shopper and helping to build brand loyalty, simultaneously making the process easy and enjoyable.

'These days, to have one finger on the fashion pulse, you need to have the other one on your computer mouse, reading (or writing) the latest blogs.'

Karen Kay, fashion journalist

So what next? Apps for fashion shopping are set to impact on all areas of fashion, even luxury brands that are notoriously reluctant in online retaining. Brands like Fendi are making a 360-degree about turn to the customer experience by launching ecommerce platforms.

High-tech fashion

High-tech fashion uses advances in science and technology to design and produce fashion products. Methods used in high-tech fashion borrow from technologies developed in the fields of chemistry, computer science, aerospace engineering, automotive engineering, architecture, industrial textiles and competitive athletic wear. Fashion projects an image of rapid changes and forward thinking, which is a good environment for use of the latest technologies in production methods and materials. As technology becomes more integrated with one's everyday life, its influence on the fashion one wears continues to increase.

1.7
The fashion app.
One of the key changes in the way we communicate fashion over the last decade is the use of the fashion app, which is constantly evolving. At the Design Museum, London, Farfetch U.K. Ltd. demonstrates its new app in April 2017, which enables customers to have Gucci delivered to their doors within 90 minutes.
© Bloomberg/ Contributor via Getty Images

Techno materials

Techno materials include fibers, textiles, and textile finishes engineered for a specific function or appearance. The UK designer Sophia Lewis believes that 'the greatest potential for the future lies in experimental fashion using advanced synthetics to promote new aesthetics and methods of garment construction' (Braddock and O'Mahony, 1999, p. 80). While most synthetics of the twentieth century were developed to mimic natural fibers, the new synthetics are engineered to be strong and durable even when lightweight, transparent or elastic. Blending natural fibers with synthetics in new ways to produce 'techno-naturals' is adding to the aesthetic and performance advantages of textiles.

CAD (computer-aided design)

The introduction of CAD software in the 1980s, such as Photoshop and Illustrator, revolutionised all design industries, including fashion. Computer-aided design cannot replace pure talent, but it can help expand fashion creativity and increase productivity. CAD programs have been introduced into all areas of the fashion industry including design, merchandising and promotion.

We are now seeing the development of 3D printing and 3D-printed garments have become a common sight on the haute couture catwalks of designers like Dutch fashion designer Iris van Herpen. Collaborations are taking place such as Austrian architect Julia Körner, who after working with van Herpen on digitally fabricated garments, is now working on the creation of elaborate garments into everyday clothing production as part of what she calls an 'exciting moment in fashion design'.

Körner believes that developments in the properties of materials that can be fabricated on a 3D printer, including greater flexibility and density variation, are enabling more practical clothing to be produced – taking digital manufacturing out of the world of haute couture and making it more accessible. She also thinks technology adds an incredible advantage to fashion design, especially in ready-to-wear, as it is now possible to custom fabricate a garment that fits perfectly without refitting.

1.8
Iris van Herpen.
From Iris van Herpen fall/winter 2017 shown at Paris Fashion Week. The collection had many pieces that were the products of complicated laser cutting and heat bonding.
© Victor VIRGILE/ Gamma-Rapho via Getty Images

Body scanning and 3D-modelling techniques allow designing towards a perfect fit, and through minimal changes in the code she can create variations of adaptations in the design. This automated process is a revolution in customised fashion pieces within ready-to-wear.

Globalisation, ethical fashion and sustainability

The world is becoming increasingly exposed to global cultural influences and lifestyles. Westernised fashion, for example, has seeped into other cultures, Western designers and clothing lines are being copied and mass-produced in countries such as China and Vietnam; and the clothes can be exported anywhere in the world.

This global marketplace offers consumers a wider range of goods, and there are an increased number of options for the manufacturers, too. Competition keeps the prices of fashion garments low. The increased flow of communication between countries has helped to improve the cultural exchange, enabling us to learn more about cultural and fashion preferences. On the flipside, globalisation has highlighted the social and environmental impacts of the fashion industry; it has, for example, contributed to the decline of fashion manufacture in Europe, as fashion manufacturing is outsourced to countries in Asia due to the cost of labour being low and therefore the workforce can be exploited.

Today's mainstream fashion industry relies on globalised mass production where garments are transformed from the design stage to the retail floor in only a few weeks. With retailers selling the latest fashion trends at very low prices, consumers are easily swayed to purchase more than they need. However, overconsumption comes with a hidden price tag on the environment and workers in the supply chain.

Designers and retailers today are slowly beginning to take a more responsible role in the production of fashion products by considering their impact on the world's resources. Ethical fashion, which takes into account workers' rights and environmental concerns, is becoming increasingly important.

We are seeing the emergence of an alternative production model. **Slow fashion**, as the name suggests, seeks to slow down the pace of production and consumption by changing practices and attitudes all along the supply chain from farmers to designers, manufacturers and consumers. The term 'slow fashion' was given the name by Kate Fletcher in 2007. It is a sustainable fashion movement; slow fashion briefly described is a sustainable fashion movement that is gaining momentum. It attempts to slow the rate of change down to a more sustainable pace. Simply put, slow fashion promotes high quality versus fast production, durability versus design for obsolescence, and mindful consumption versus overconsumption.

'Slow fashion is more than just a slowing of the fashion process', says professor Dilys Williams, director of the Centre for Sustainable Fashion in London. 'It's an honouring of what fashion is really about, which is representing a time, a place and an identity in connection with others.'

In all areas of the fashion industry, we have seen fashion and technology merge and improve for suppliers and consumer alike. Sales, trend research and inventory management work can be done from almost anywhere, and decision makers can see what works and what doesn't in real time. Technology has changed and is changing the fashion industry in an ongoing basis.

'Slow fashion is more than just a slowing of the fashion process. It's an honouring of what fashion is really about, which is representing a time, a place and an identity in connection with others.'

Dilys Williams, director of the Centre for Sustainable Fashion in London

Influential designers and global fashion brands

The twentieth century has seen a great many inspirational designers and brands with huge imaginations, enterprising attitudes and unquestionable flair. In no particular order, here are some of the most influential fashion designers of the last hundred years.

Influencers of the early twentieth century include Coco Chanel, whose name conveys prestige, impeccable quality, unique taste and unmistakable style; Bill Blass, who will always be associated with modern, practical, tailored clothing; and Christian Dior, who created the New Look, presented at a fashion show in 1947.

The best of the luxury haute couture clothing brands around the world influence the rest of the fashion industry. They are the real trendsetters, stars and magicians in the world of fashion and can effortlessly make the grotesque look alluring. What these brands create for their clientele are not just clothes or shoes or bags, they create art. The love and respect people have for the legends behind brands such as Karl Lagerfeld, Marc Jacobs, Donatella Versace, Frida Giannini, Yves Saint Laurent, Oscar De La Renta and many more make it extremely difficult to select one over another, taking into consideration their commitment for perfection and excellence. So let's have a look at which designers/luxury brands have influenced the very fascinating fashion industry.

Designers

One of the most celebrated designers of the twentieth century, Yves Saint Laurent, is credited for introducing prêt-à-porter (ready-to-wear) in the 1960s. Giorgio Armani is one of the most successful Italian designers of all time, specifically for revolutionising menswear. Ralph Lauren is arguably the most widely recognised label in American fashion. Much of his original collection included classic tweed suits for men and feminine tailoring for women. American designer Donna Karan is known to support the needs of modern women with her clothing. In 1985 she founded her Essentials line, offering seven easy pieces every woman should have. Italian designer Miuccia Prada took over the family owned luxury goods manufacturer in 1978, turning it into a fashion powerhouse. Vivienne Westwood is responsible for bringing us punk fashion in the 1970s, and she continues to design rebellious, cutting-edge designs for women and men. A list of influential designers would be incomplete without mentioning

1.9
Karl Lagerfeld.
Lagerfeld is a German designer and is the creative director of Chanel, a position he has held since 1983. He also has his own label and is designer for the Italian house Fendi.

© Andrew H. Walker via Getty Images

Alexander McQueen, who was known for his iconic fashion and extravagant design and is credited with popularising low-slung jeans in the mid-1990s.

Conceptual design has had a huge influence on modern fashion. Japanese design first made a real impression on the fashion world back in 1982, when some twelve designers, including Issey Miyake, Kenzo, Yohji Yamamoto and Comme des Garçons, showed their collections at the Paris shows. *Mode Japonaise* had a big impact on contemporary fashion with its inventive shapes and monochrome tones.

The Antwerp Six were a group of influential avant-garde fashion designers who graduated from Antwerp's Royal Academy of Fine Arts in the early 1980s. This fashion collective presented a distinct, radical vision for fashion during the 1980s that established Antwerp as a centre for conceptual fashion design.

The most influential designers have made a statement, challenged the norms and created an individual style. Their designs were avant-garde and have withstood the test of time, while paving the way for the designers of the future.

Luxury designer fashion brands – Top five

5. **Armani:** Founded in 1975 by Giorgio Armani and Sergio Galeotti, the international Italian fashion house covers a wide range of products, from haute couture to ready-to-wear clothing items and jewellery to home interiors. It is their many sub labels that have established them as a brand with a distinct market share in various product markets.

4. **Chanel:** The brand is recognised and coveted by women and men all over the world. The brand has inspired a million counterfeit goods and fake products are all over the marketplace. From actress Marilyn Monroe's

1.10
Miuccia Prada.
Prada was founded as a leather goods company in 1913 by Mario Prada. His granddaughter Miuccia Prada, pictured here in 2016, inherited the company in 1978 and launched its first women's RTW collection in 1989.
© Mike Coppola via Getty Images

perfume to Paris Hilton's sunglasses, the Chanel brand has played a massive role in the designer fashion industry for many years.

3. **Louis Vuitton:** This French fashion house was founded in 1854. The company specialises in luxury trunks and leather goods monogrammed with the famous LV logo in addition to producing ready-to-wear, shoes, watches, jewellery, accessories and sunglasses. Operating through small boutiques in high-end department stores worldwide, Louis Vuitton is one of the world's leading international fashion houses in today's fashion industry.

2. **Dior:** Founded in 1946, French luxury goods company, Dior, was the house of the eponymous designer Christian Dior. Today the company designs and sells ready-to-wear, leather goods, jewellery, footwear, fashion accessories, watches, perfume, make-up, and skincare products while also maintaining its tradition as a maker of recognisable haute couture garments. While the Christian Dior label remains largely for women's products, the company also controls the Dior Homme section for men and the Baby Dior label for childrenswear.

1. **Burberry:** Burberry is a British luxury fashion house known for designing and distributing clothing, fashion accessories and licensing fragrances. Burberry is most famous for its trench coat, designed by founder Thomas Burberry in 1912. The company's distinctive tartan pattern has become one of its most widely copied trademarks.

Global retailers – Top five

Cheil Industries: Founded in 1954, Cheil Industries originated as a textile company and moved into fashion in 1989. The 1980s saw the South Korea-based fast fashion company diversify into chemicals and then to electronics materials in the 1990s. Despite diversifying into unrelated product lines, Cheil's fashion is currently among one of the world's leading fashion companies. Cheil Industries pioneered the adoption of the just-in-time [JIT] accounting system, which considerably reduces the time involved in the production process of clothing today. At present, the company manages a number of fashion brands across Asia, including Bean Pole International, 8seconds and 10 Corso Como.

In 2015, Cheil Industries completed a merger with Samsung allowing leverage by utilising Samsung's global brand name, international presence and business and technology. As of May 2016, the company had as many as 3,700 employees and revenues of $11.9 billion.

The Gap: Doris and Donald Fisher of Ocean Avenue, San Francisco, founded the Gap in 1969. The original investment of $63,000 recorded an amazing $2 million in sales only two years later. The Gap soon began to forcefully pursue expansion in the domestic market, building a company of twenty-five outlets by 1973. The following decades saw the company expand under the Fisher family leadership into international markets establishing the Gap as the powerhouse it is today. The Gap now controls five international brands – Gap, Banana Republic, Athleta, Old Navy, and Intermix. It manages more than 3,300 stores in ninety countries, and 400 franchise stores. The Fisher families maintain a 43 per cent stake but are no longer active in the day-to-day running of the company.

Fast Retailing Co.: The Japanese-based fashion retailing company Fast Retailing Co. can trace its origins to 1949 and is known for its leading subsidiary Uniqlo. Tailor Hitoshi Yania founded a menswear shop called Ogori Shoji, and in 1972, Tadashi Yanai, his son, joined the business after a career selling kitchenware and men's clothing in a supermarket. The company was listed in 1991 on the Japanese Stock Exchange and was identified as the fastest growing retailer in Japan. Today the company has revenues of $17.31 billion and is ranked by *Forbes* (American Business Magazine) as the forty-first most innovative company in the world.

H&M: The second largest fashion retailing company globally is H&M. H&M (originally called Hennes) was founded in Västerås, Sweden, in 1947 by Erling Persson. It originally retailed women's clothing and later added men's clothing when the company acquired menswear brand, Mauritz Widforss. The name changed to Hennes & Mauritz after this acquisition and then later to H&M, as this was easier to pronounce, particularly relevant at the time as the company expanded into international markets. Today H&M controls many global brands such as H&M, COS, Cheap Monday, Monki and Weekday. Operating more than 4,300 stores in over sixty-four countries, the Persson family actively manages the company with Erling Persson's son Stefan leading as chairman of the board and Stefan's son Karl-Johan is president and CEO.

Inditex: This company is best known as the owners of the fashion brand ZARA. It is the biggest fashion group in the world, with a turnover of $23.27 billion. The family owned company has its origins in Spain where, in 1975, Ortega Amancio started the company with his wife Rosalia Mera as a small retail fashion store called Zorba. The store was forced to change its name to ZARA after another business went by Zorba. Progression came in the 1980s when the company managed to significantly reduce time between design, production and delivery by utilising new methods in each of the processes. From then on, ZARA has been at the front of the fast fashion revolution, operating a highly efficient supply chain. The company also manages a significant number of other brands including Zara Home, Bershka, Massimo Dutti Oysho, Pull and Bear, Uterqüe and Stradivarius, with a total of 7,000 stores across ninety-one countries globally.

Case study: Burberry

Social media and digital technology

Burberry is a luxury fashion brand from the UK, and it is famous for its original trench coat and tartan lining, designed by the original founder of the company Thomas Burberry. Burberry celebrates 160 years of trading in the clothing industry, and today the company is well-known not only for its famous trench coat but also for its fashion accessories including bags, shoes, watches and its popular perfume. The brand also has a reputation for being the most technologically-savvy company through its approach to use of technology and digital media and how it connects with its customers.

'This is how customers live, they wake up with a device in their hand and life begins.'

Under the direction of Angela Ahrendts (CEO of Burberry between 2006 and 2014) and Christopher Bailey, Burberry's creative director until late 2017, the brand earned a reputation as a digital pioneer, breaking new ground through creativity and its experimentation with and integration of technology within its business.

Consistency is adopted across all of their accounts. At the forefront of this is the remarkably technologically and digitally savvy way they connect with their customers. They have been at the helm of developing ways to communicate with their 'fashion fans' by pioneering the incorporation of technology in the fashion industry, leading the way by creating a social media experience for their 'fans', by introducing live stream for shows, and social media purchasing that allows customers to buy directly from the catwalk. They even have their own social media site of the 'art of the trench'. Burberry has fully embraced social media as a means of reaching their customers and fans with as much as 60 per cent of their marketing budget now being spent on digital.

1.11
The Trench.
Burberry is one of the best-selling, technology-savvy brands today. Its distinctive tartan pattern has been one of the most copied trade-marks. It is famous for its trench coat designed by Thomas Burberry in 1912
© Henry Guttmann/ Stringer via Getty Images

> **dialect**
>
> noun: **dialect**; plural noun: **dialects**.
> A particular form of a language which is peculiar to a specific region or social group.

The strategy

Burberry can be described as one of the most innovative luxury fashion brands on the market today.

In 2009 Bailey joined Facebook as one of the first luxury brands to do so. By 2016, Burberry has amassed more than 18 million fans on Facebook, and its page shares catwalk, campaign and fashion content. Engagement from the fans is at its highest on Facebook with an average post gaining between 2,000 and 50,000 'likes'. The campaign and photo shoot that saw the most attention was with Brooklyn Beckham, receiving over 100,000 likes and 1,300 shares. Though Facebook constitutes its largest audience, the brand also uses Twitter, Google+, Instagram and Pinterest to engage with its customers. Its online digital flagship store, www.burberry. com, delivers to over forty different countries and is available in five languages. Customers have the option to click-to-chat and click-to-call with customer service assistants in fourteen different dialects.

Burberry has adopted a consistent theme across all of its platforms, and although the content is similar across the different sites, Burberry's brand managers are well informed about what content works best on how to manage this to their advantage – for example, using Facebook for streaming live shows, Instagram for more sophisticated visuals and Twitter to encourage interaction and user engagement.

Twitter

Burberry is most active on Twitter (@Burberry) around the time of the London Fashion Week when they increase their presence on the site from an average of five times a day. It is the

1.12
Social Media.
Burberry is most active on Twitter (@Burberry) around the time of the London Fashion Week when photos of the show are tweeted along with tweet of Christopher Bailey with celebrities such as actress and model Cara Delevingne.
© Stuart C. Wilson via Getty Images

platform that they have probably had the biggest impact on with their campaigns, which are often launched on the site, guaranteeing that the image of the brand will stand out from the crowd on social media. In 2015, Burberry partnered with Twitter to offer fans the chance to capture pictures of their London Fashion Week womenswear show live from the runway, by tweeting #Tweetcam, @Burberry Twitter account. The most popular posts, however, are usually the new collections that generally receive around 100–200 favourites and 5,000 retweets. Also successful were tweets of Christopher Bailey at London Fashion Week welcoming celebrities such as Cara Delevingne (model), Naomi Campbell (model) and Sam Smith (singer), all receiving more than 1,300 favourites and over 500 retweets.

'You can't start live-streaming a show and carry on doing everything else exactly the same as before.'

Facebook

A big part of the brand's social media success can be attributed to the personal approach of its creative director Christopher Bailey. Burberry decided from the start that Bailey would become the face (of Burberry) on the company's Facebook site. At the countdown to the shows, fans can see Bailey talking to fans from the design studio and backstage at the show. He will talk directly to fans on Facebook, and when the brand reaches a milestone on Facebook, for example when they hit 15 million likes, Bailey will be the one to personally thank the fans on the platform. Handwritten notes by the chief creative director are regularly seen on Facebook, Twitter or Instagram.

Often the campaigns that are the most effective are the ones that offer rewards to fans like exclusive content. For example, IKEA, the Swedish furniture giant, developed a campaign that offered customers a sleepover in the UK store; a hundred Facebook fans took up the offer to sleep in a bed of their choice, with cocoa and a movie for company. The idea was a clever way of getting busy fans to focus on what IKEA had to offer. Burberry adopted a similar strategy by posting special invites for Facebook fans through personally handwritten invites from the designer.

The social team then follow-up to live streams from different shows and collections with behind-the-scenes images. This is a clever way of making sure that the brand has maximum impact of exposure from its events.

'Whether it's Tumblr or Instagram or Twitter or Facebook or burberry.com, it's a question of how we can make sure that's one world.'
Christopher Bailey

The results

Burberry's continual focus on digital has helped them to become one of the most popular and admired brands in the world, with an exceptional rise in sales, almost 14 per cent higher than the rest of the luxury fashion market, consistent outperformance of competitors, and an incredible rise in stock value.

Chapter summary

During the course of the book, you will learn about various areas within the fashion industry. This chapter explored the history and evolution of the fashion industry with a case study on Burberry, one of the most influential global fashion brands that has a heritage and is also utilising new technology to manage and communicate with its consumers. Understanding the importance and relevance of technology in the future of fashion is a key component of developing knowledge as a fashion management professional. The following will test your understanding of the case study and a general application of the knowledge gained through reading the chapter.

Chapter 1 introduced the evolution of fashion and contextualised the development of the industry, placing fashion into a market and discussing some of the key influences and influencers that have made the fashion industry as big and as important as it is today.

The different levels of the industry continue to be prevalent, with the different market levels offering fashion products made and manufactured for their customers' affordability and needs. The speed of technology that has provided us with fashion on tap continues to attract people into the industry and offer the consumer what he/she wants, but we are now seeing this being challenged with the emergence of slow fashion practices and the development of new models of the fashion business.

The fashion industry has and continues to develop at a fast pace. Over the last few years, we have seen brands adopt new technology in how they design, make, sell and communicate fashion. Whether designers simply enjoy it or have cottoned onto its importance, building a world around the brand is tantamount. Fans follow news and interact on a level that previously didn't exist,

and brands learn about their audience. But it's not just about posting the coolest images; obviously the product has to speak for itself, too.

We have seen the development of social media strategies and recognise that a personal approach and personalities are as important as the products. Social media in the right hands ensures that every carefully considered tweet, Facebook post and Instagram shot is part of a brand-building exercise – and whether you're positioning yourself as a cult up-and-comer or are already one of the biggest luxury brands such as Burberry, it is a key component to the success of the brand.

If we face facts, we have to accept that social media is predominantly visual, so it follows that there's perhaps no other industry where its power is more relevant or poignantly felt than luxury fashion.

The previous case study outlined the social media and digital technology activities adopted by Burberry: as a way of evidencing what you have learned from the chapter and case study, answer the following questions by writing a short paragraph on each.

Case study and chapter reflection

Q. How has Burberry utilised technology in its development of a digital strategy to connect with their consumers, particularly?

Q. How do designer brands maintain and build their profiles and popularity online?

Q. What is key to telling a brand's story?

Q. As audiences are flooded with information from all channels, what is required to be a forward-thinking luxury brand and stand out from the rest?

CHECKLIST

1. The *Oxford English Dictionary* first recorded 'dressmaker' in 1803. What is the difference between a tailor and a dressmaker?

2. The fashion industry consists of four levels. What are they?

3. The fashion industry is divided into three main categories of manufacture. Name them and outline the differences.

4. Technology has turned the entire fashion industry upside down. What has the major influence been?

5. How has the internet opened up the connection between consumers and brands?

6. High-tech fashion uses advances in science and technology to design and produce fashion products. What has this enabled producers and retailers to do?

7. What keeps the prices of fashion garments low?

8. Name the alternative business model that we see emerging, and explain the changing practices that its name suggests.

9. The twentieth century has seen a great many inspirational designers and brands. Name five.

10. Which influential British brand is technology-savvy and uses digital media at the forefront of how they connect with their consumers?

EXERCISE

Fashion blogging

If you are interested in developing a fashion career and you don't want to be a designer, a fashion blog will not only prove to a potential employer you are serious about fashion, it could earn you money at the same time. Many students have their own blogs and that can be the first step on the fashion ladder to build a career in the business. It can also be a valuable tool for developing ideas and connection to projects you will undertake at fashion school. So why not share your love of fashion through a blog? Anyone can do it, but you will have to be smart and different to make it work – it will be your passion that makes it special. Remember that the most important thing in launching a blog is to have fun, so that people will have fun reading it. Don't let writer's block keep you from posting your first blog entry – just write from the heart and give it a go.

Step 1: Get a great domain name and your own host

By signing up with a hosting service, all your blog content is housed on that host's server. If you want to truly grow a brand and make a business out of your fashion blog, you want your own domain name and blog hosting in order to start a WordPress blog. Most of the best sites do it this way. Many hosts are free, and they have simple templates you can use to set up your blog in minutes. When you sign up, you'll also get to name your blog.

Step 2: Choose your niche

You really need to know why you are different. There are millions of fashion blogs out there, and unless you do something differently, you are going to get lost in all the noise. You don't want that, so consider focusing on a specific area of fashion that you enjoy the most. It could be that you are an expert on shoes, recycling or advice for your fellow students: choosing a niche is likely to increase your chances of being read.

Step 3: Be an information sponge

Read everything: newspapers, fashion magazines, other fashion blogs, social media posts, websites of established and up-and-coming fashion designers, shopping sites and reviews of collections. Save anything that catches your eye in an inspiration file that you can refer to later. You'll never know what may inspire a blog entry.

Step 4: Get out there

There's more to fashion blogging than sitting at your laptop. Blogging is hard work. Sometimes it can take two or three days to write one blog post. You have to make your brain work really hard. Attend fashion events, from runway shows to sample sales, and print business cards that identify you as a blogger and hand them out. Pretty soon, people in the industry will be inviting you to their events in the hope that you will blog about them.

Step 5: Network, network, network

Make friends, lots of them. Make friends with your readers and make friends with other bloggers that are already more established than you are and might be able to give you a helping hand. This means growing a mailing list, and it means being active on places like Google+.

Interview:
Jamie Huckbody

European Editor, *Harper's BAZAAR* Australia

Q: Where did you study and what was your major?

A: I studied at Central Saint Martin's College of Art & Design in London (1993–1997). I majored in fashion with communication & promotion.

Q: How did you first get into the fashion magazine industry?

A: The four-year BA (Hons.) degree included a year-out in industry. My first placement was at the Vivienne Westwood press office (where I spent my first day cleaning the staff toilets and kitchen). My second and third placements were both at *newspapers* – the *Evening Standard* and *The Independent*, respectively – working in their fashion departments. It was there, in the engine rooms of daily fashion journalism, that I really learnt my craft. It wasn't until I had graduated that I had my first taste of the fashion *magazine* industry. My first job was as editorial coordinator at *Vogue Australia*'s London office, and then I was made fashion & fashion features editor at *i-D* magazine.

Q: How has fashion changed since you graduated from university?

A: Since graduating in 1997, the fashion industry has changed almost beyond recognition . . . and, in my opinion, not for the better. Some factors which have created this dramatic change include the emergence of new consumer markets (Russia, the Middle East, China); the rise of the luxury goods conglomerate (LVMH, Kering, etc.); and the internet. Since the birth of the 'Information Superhighway' (as it was called when it first appeared on my radar as a student), the way we read, consume and interact with fashion has been revolutionised. The overall effect of all of these influences means that fashion has regressed in terms of design but has progressed in terms of 'democracy': everybody, no matter where they are in the world or on the financial scale, has access to fashion.

Q: How has the internet changed your job in the last ten years?

A: When I first started working as a fashion journalist, reporting from the international collections for the *Evening Standard* and *The Independent*, you read your 'copy' over the telephone to a 'copy taker' who would then send it via fax to the newspaper sub-editors for checking. The photographs that would accompany the words had to be physically collected as reels of negative film from the photographer and then rushed to the newspaper's lab for developing. (This involved early-morning flights, lots of cabs and endless amounts of running.) Every news report – sometimes there were three a day for one day's newspaper as the pages were constantly updated – involved a lot of manual labour and financial costs. Compare that with the way I file fashion news stories today: I type copy straight into my smartphone, upload the accompanying photos/video, and then send via an email to my editor or upload into a blog/Instagram/tweet format. The whole process takes a few minutes and is instantly accessed by an infinite number of fashion readers. Job done. The adverse effect of this is that 'anybody' can be a fashion critic – there is a lot of uninformed opinion out there clogging-up an already saturated 'mediaplace'.

Q: What trends do you think will never die, no matter what era?

A: There will always be a desire for clothes that have what I call 'common-sense luxury': well-tailored suits, chic Little Black Dresses, tactile knitwear; clothes that allow the wearer to get on with their lives while looking/feeling good. On the other side of the coin, there are those trends fueled by EGO and FANTASY which play a big part in fashion. So there will always be clothes that fit into trends labelled 'romantic', highly 'sexual', over-the-top 'glamorous'; or those which take inspiration from the historical-past or exotic cultures, whether they be geographical or sociological.

Q: Who are your most inspirational designers and brands?

A: Gabrielle Chanel, Elsa Schiaparelli, Yves Saint Laurent, Rei Kawakubo, Vivienne Westwood, John Galliano, and Alexander McQueen. These are proper 'designers' who have re-designed the blueprint of how women dress, and therefore how women function in the world. They also engaged with the arts/contemporary culture to create a design product with an element of artistry that helps their work transcend the norm.

Q: Burberry is classed as one of the most technology- and digital media-savvy brands. How do you think that other brands will use technology in the future?

A: To access the consumer directly – consumer data is the most valuable commodity today.

Q: What advice would you give to a student thinking of going into the fashion industry today?

A: The same as I always give: 'Know Your Onions'! Fashion does not exist in a vacuum, so students need to be engaged with the wider world and the things influencing fashion - the global economy, the arts, world politics, technology, and what is called 'the zeitgeist'.

Fashion trend prediction

With product lead times so long, reacting to current trends isn't enough. 'Professional trend forecasters' aid designers in looking ahead to future developments in order to maximise the success and profitability of their products.

The chapter will help you:

- Develop an understanding of how fashion professionals, including designers and buyers, use fashion forecasting and trend prediction to help them produce and buy what is predicted to be popular in a forthcoming season.

- Gain knowledge of how businesses today take advantage of the wealth of trend information and distil it into a meaningful future strategy.

- Learn how trend predictors use their curiosity and interest in a wide array of subjects, ranging from art and design, to science, technology and socio-economics, to determine the next trend.

- Introduce you to academically accepted theories that can explain the dynamics of fashion adoption and that continue to influence commercial designers and retailers.

- Develop an understanding of the use of trend prediction and how trend information is used by the fashion industry in relation to developing fashion products.

2.1
Trends. Fashion forecasting is key intelligence for the industry and involves research into lifestyle and culture.
© Mads Perch via Getty Images

Understanding fashion forecasting and trend prediction

Fashion trend prediction

Fashion professionals, including designers and buyers, use fashion forecasting and trend prediction to help them produce and buy what is predicted to be popular in a forthcoming season. Forecasting is used to determine how customers will behave and what they will want to buy in the future. Fashion forecasting is a complex, long-term process. It is not simply guesswork but involves in-depth research, observation and application. When done correctly, it can prove invaluable to business success and numerous companies have made it their business to predict the consumer trends of the future and filter this information back to those that produce consumer goods. The combination and sources of trend information used for inspiration is varied and will depend on the prediction strategy of the company and its target market.

Did you know that the terms 'trendsetter' and 'trendy' were not coined until 1960 and 1962 respectively?

The fashion forecasting industry is relatively new; its first significant emergence can only be traced as far back as the nineteenth century.

> The term [trend] was adopted more generally in the nineteenth century and tended to refer to the way anything changed. The textile industry, for instance, began to use the term to refer to changes in design styles, but it's use was still typically limited to the scientific and commercial world until the 1960, and it was at this point the media and public alike began to use the term.
>
> William Higham, *The Next Big Thing* (2009)

Higham states that the first ever fashion trend consultancy, Tobe Associates, was launched in 1927. In 1928, a number of different fashion designers got together to form the Fashion Group. The group began issuing fashion trend reports on a regular basis, providing advice to several different fashion houses at the same time and allowing many designers to use the same trend at the same time. Fashion houses saw that using such trends increased sales, resulting in a growth in the use of fashion trend reports, eventually developing into trade fairs and industry exhibitions, with global forecasting companies such as Infomat and Promostyl being launched.

In the 1990s, trend forecasting companies and the development of trend information into report became very popular and before long the practices had spread into media and marketing companies. The first type of trend spotting was based on the use of intuitive methods and the recognition of short-term trends (AKA fads). In the decades that followed, longer-term trends were recognised and additional methods were developed to identify these.

Trend forecasting, a practice that now spans many different industries and disciplines, is well established in the fashion industry, with companies having to prepare for a new season well in advance. The process starts up to two years ahead. The importance of the forecaster and analysis of the trends allow companies to be well planned in developing their products with the fashion intelligence available. The projection in terms of colour, design and fabrics allows fashion retailers to 'get it right'. Getting it wrong would cost the companies many thousands of pounds in unsold garments, which would then have to be sold as discounted goods, and as such the forecaster's role is invaluable to fashion companies today.

In trend forecasting it is essential for professionals to have a good understanding of the present – such as politics and global economies – and the effects this has on the consumer. They must have a good handle on news, current affairs, economics, cultural and creative happenings and socio-economic trends. In addition, they will use information sources such as design, colour, video services, newspapers, books, magazines and websites. Experienced fashion analysts evaluate consumer buying patterns, customer profiles and their lifestyle choices, all of which are used to aid the prediction of the trends to their clients.

> **Trickle-down**
>
> The trickle-down theory states that when the lowest social class, or simply a perceived lower social class, adopts the fashion, it is no longer desirable to the leaders in the highest social class. Applied to fashion, when a trend becomes popular with the general public, the trendsetters feel they need something new and start a cascade to fade out the old trend.

'We've always been much more fascinated with the trickle-up theory – high fashion inspired by those who can't afford to buy their "looks" so they create them. The streets can sometimes be a crystal ball.'

Minya Quirk, fashion director

The trend cycle

The fashion industry as a whole is a constantly evolving cycle, of which trend forecasting forms an important part. Trends (short-term drivers of one to three years) should inspire and inform a company's future vision from the board, brand and marketing to innovation strategies for developing products, services and experiences that will meet the needs and desires of tomorrow's consumers. As we are now living in the knowledge age, we can often be overwhelmed by the amount of information available to us, and the biggest challenge for fashion businesses today is understanding how to take advantage of all this information and distil it into a meaningful future strategy.

Trend forecasting is not the sole domain of specialised fashion companies and is used in other businesses to enhance the product for the customer. We have seen in recent years trend forecasting become somewhat of a trend in itself, as a large number of 'cool hunters' and 'trend hunters' are emerging onto the scene to work with many company and product types. While most successful companies do tend to collaborate with international trend agencies, the volume of information that can sometimes be involved means that some companies have now opted to set up their own internal trend forecasting teams, and the cycle is a key part of making the process work.

In a very simple breakdown of the trend cycle, the first stage involves the forecasting of design trends through a process known as trend tracking, which is an integral research tool that can help give companies that all-important insight

2.2
The trend cycle.
It is useful to
look at trend
forecasting as a
continuous cycle,
reflecting the
cyclical nature
of the fashion
industry as a
whole.

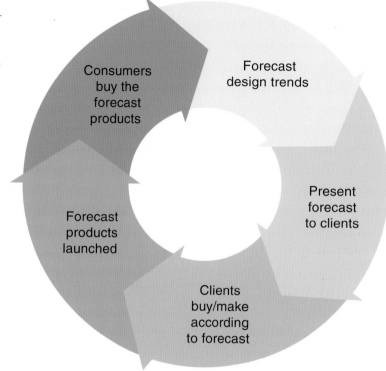

'Tracking trends
is a crucial way to
be informed about
society and under-
stand people, their
behaviour, needs
and mindset, and
how that could
impact the future.'

Anne Lise Kjaer, Future Vision

into the demands and needs of their consumers. It is a process that is undertaken by designers as well as forecasting professionals and all trend forecasters' predictions should be very similar; if not, they've got it wrong! The next stage is the presentation of information to the client, who will buy or produce products according to the forecast selected. The forecasted products are then launched and promoted by the client, the fashion consumers will buy the forecast products, and the whole cycle begins again.

Trend forecasting, however, is a tricky process and presents numerous challenges. One of these challenges is how to determine whether what you are witnessing is a trend or a fad. The difference between a trend and a fad is that a trend is

usually deep-seated and is the coming together of a number of factors including demographical, economic, political, social psychological and environmental influences. It is something more long lasting and substantial than a **fad**.

Fad
A fad is a fashion that is taken up with great enthusiasm for a brief period of time; a craze.

Origin of **fad**. Possibly from *fidfad*, fussy person, fussy, from *fiddle-faddle*.

The forecaster's role

The role of a forecaster is to analyse the movement of the market, look for patterns in consumer behaviour to find the 'thread' that unifies a collection of sometimes seemingly disparate ideas that will form the basis of the 'next big thing'. A forecaster's job is to spot upcoming trends and products that will be big next spring, next fall or even a few seasons beyond. In order to pinpoint a trend, a forecaster must absorb and pull together as much relevant information from as many sources as possible and collate it into a coherent, viable story.

Trend predictors feed their instincts by saturating themselves 24/7 with cues from the world at large, which requires a lot of curiosity and interest in a wide range of subjects varying from art and design, to science, technology, socio-economics, and travel to name a few. This means lots of travel, competitive shopping and media consumption, as the job involves presenting analysis to clients and activities such as reporting, writing and public speaking are a day-to-day part of the forecaster's role. Key for any trendspotter are the gathering of facts, taking an interest in all aspects of culture from the creative arts and media to subculture movements, travel experiences and developments in science and technology. Put this together with market research and the observation of socio-economic shifts and that will provide an insight into what the next emerging trend might be demonstrates the direction and potential reaction of consumer culture. At the core of this is personal intuition and having an eye for 'what's next', as none of this can be taught or necessarily explained, but constantly collecting ideas and images, building an archive over many years of designing and researching it allows the forecaster to pick up on an emerging trend through the recognition of one particular thread running through a spate of images. Although, sometimes, a solitary image can be so powerful that to some it can trigger an instant certainty in the trend.

In an interview on designboom.com Lidewij Edelkoort (Trend Union) says, 'trend forecasting is much like archeology, but to the future'. This idea of trend forecasting as archaeology is an interesting concept as what she is referring to is the importance of examining, uncovering and recording information that leads to the identification of an emerging trend. It is important for trend forecasters to have a very good knowledge of what was designed ten years, forty years or over a hundred years ago, as every trend has its ancestry somewhere in history. So, while you are looking forward, you are also taking into account historical references.

We have seen the trend industry grow massively, with everyone following trends on the internet and designing their own self-image. For trend experts and forecasters, it is an exciting challenge. Many are inspired by bloggers, street shots and the viral phenomena available online. However, professional forecasters need to have a unique take on trends, and the key to the future of the forecasting profession is for forecasters to take an alternative point of view, one that's adventurous and exciting, and to always think as influencers, not followers.

In an era of the internet, hyper-connectivity and the use of social media, trend forecasting is becoming increasingly important for the fashion business community as it develops a big and highly competitive business. The pace of fashion has increased, the speed of the trend cycle has also accelerated and the demand for trend information has risen. With the accessibility of information gained by the streaming live of catwalk shows, the ability for consumers to 'shop the look' before the models have left the catwalk and retail sector's obsession with reducing turn around times has created a necessity to constantly supply fresh trend direction. This has not only led to changes, it has led to major growth in the forecasting industry in a very short space of time. With advances in technology, we have seen the industry graduate from an industry producing niche print trend reports a few of times a year to online services with the ability to publish and update new material extremely fast. The practical appeal of information that can be accessed from any location, day or night, has developed the forecasting industry into a large area of the fashion business. As of 2011, the forecasting industry was valued at $36 billion and continues to grow, generating an ever-increasing number of agencies catering to a global audience.

Cool hunting

Cool hunting started in the 1990s as an attempt to understand a generation of young consumers. It involves researching and is synonymous with seeking inspiration for emerging trends in fashion, design, music, media, technology and youth culture. This information is then packaged and sold to market research companies and used to drive the development of new products. In short, cool hunting is used as a tool to forecast what consumers will need. Using cool hunting as part of its research strategy puts a company ahead of the competition. In the fashion industry, it is the practice of observing street fashion in cities such as New York, London and Tokyo to capture what is emerging from those people considered to be 'innovative consumers'. Its success lies in the ability to recognise the next big thing from what is not yet popular; it is when something becomes mainstream that it loses its novelty and appeal: 'the underlying concept is that cool represents what mainstream seeks to have' (Trendhunter.com).

Today you can find much of this content online, and many companies have developed apps to enable users to follow them on sites such as YouTube, Twitter and Facebook. Blogging is also a useful tool in the identification of the next big thing. Photographer Scott Schuman pioneered the street style blog phenomenon when he began posting his street fashion images online in 2005 (www.thesartorialist.com).

Cool hunting has opened up a whole new option for the job hunters: it can be done via the internet or face-to-face with the consumer. This career path can offer a creative fashion graduate the chance to travel extensively and experience different cultures to gather information. If you enjoy visual research, cool hunting is an exciting career option to consider.

2.3
Cool hunting.
Cool hunting is synonymous with seeking inspiration. It is important that you are able to think on your feet when working within the creative industries; being aware of what is going on around you within design practice and society as a whole. Cool hunters are able to unearth, record and translate what is happening on the street and develop this into the 'next big thing'.
Image courtesy of Trendstop

'I thought I could shoot people on the street the way designers looked at people, and get and give inspiration to lots of people in the process. My only strategy when I began *The Sartorialist* was to try and shoot style in a way that I knew most designers hunted for inspiration.'

Scott Schuman

Product development, lifecycle and trends

Forecasting has become a key part in the innovation and development of new products and as such forecasters need to consider both the direction of change and the speed of change in how trends develop in order to predict future needs and desires of consumers. Retail designers and trend specialists observe and analyse the changes in addition to using their **intuition** and experience to identify obvious patterns and meanings when sensing shifts and the repetition of ideas, which will then be determined as a trend.

However, due to the complicated nature of tracking fashion movement today, forecasters need to understand multiple theories of how fashion movement has occurred in the past to determine and develop new ways to predict in the future. To track the movement of fashion, knowledge of

fashion cycles, fashion adoption theory and the pendulum swings of fashion diffusion curves and the cause of movements in fashion are important areas of study for the forecaster.

Fashion can flow, curve, cycle, swing and repeat.

Fashion theories

There are three academically accepted theories that that can explain the dynamics of fashion adoption and continue to influence commercial designers and retailers creating the distribution of fashion. Each theory demonstrates the way that trends are likely to travel in order to aid in the most precise prediction of the future of fashion. A flow, or trickle from one element of society to another is the trickle-down, trickle-across, or trickle-up theory. Each theory acts as a guide to the process, and although it has been disputed and sometimes considered outdated, they are based on changing social environments, consumer preferences and market conditions.

Explained simply, the trickle-down effect or downward flow theory is considered the oldest theory of fashion adoption and distribution, described by Veblen in 1899, to function, the trickle-down movement depends upon a

> **Intuition**
>
> Intuition is the ability to understand something instinctively, without the need for conscious reasoning.

hierarchical society and the determination of the various social levels for upward mobility. Its downward movement could be considered the engine or force that moves fashion. In this model, a style is first offered and adopted by people at the top level of society and gradually becomes accepted by those lower in the levels. At the top of the pyramid, we have people with wealth and prominence who will adopt a style, and gradually that style spreads down into the lower classes. For example, a few seasons ago we saw Simone Rocha show little pearl collars on her dresses; these would have sold for hundreds of pounds. However, within a few weeks we saw pearl collars on the high street for a fraction of the price.

It is once the lower classes duplicate a look, those on the top move on to new styles to maintain their social positions and power. This theoretical model takes for granted a social hierarchy in which identifying with the affluent is what people are looking for and those at the top search for both difference and, eventually, distance from those socially below them.

Fashion is a vehicle of obvious consumption and upward mobility for those wanting to mimic styles of dress. Once those adopt the fashion below, the affluent reject that look for another. The converse is also true – street style and sub-cultures, such as punk, for example, referenced by fashion designers and known as the trickle-up or bubble-up pattern. In this theory, the innovation is initiated from the street, so to speak, and taken from those lower income groups. The innovation will then flow up to upper-income groups; thus, the movement is from the bottom.

The trickle across theory or horizontal flow theory – this is, the third theory – considers and discusses the horizontal flow of fashion. This theory assumes that fashion is across groups who are similar in social levels rather than down from high-level or to low-level. This theory acknowledges that mass production, mass communication and an emerging middle class contribute to a new dynamic that began after the Second World War. In the trickle-across model, there is very little lag time between the adoptions

2.4
Product develop-ment forecasting.
Product develop-ment forecasting is a key part in the innovation and development of new products directing the change and speed of change to predict future needs and desires of consumers
© Ed Reeve via Getty Images

Trickle down

Trickle up

Trickle across

Trickle down or downward flow. Depends on hierarchical society and the determination of various social levels. No upward mobility.

Trickle up or bubble up – innovation is initiated in the street, taken from lower-income groups to flow up to upper-income groups.

Trickle across or horizontal flow theory – considers the horizontal flow of fashion

2.5
Fashion theory up, down and across. Understanding the theories of fashion movement and how trends travel is important to aid the most precise prediction of the future of fashion.

of a trend from one group to another. Evidence for this theory occurs when designers show a look concurrently at prices ranging from the high-end to lower-end ready-to-wear. Some reasons for this pattern of distribution can be attributed to advances in rapid mass communications, promotional efforts of manufacturers and retailers, and the communication of that 'look' to all fashion leaders.

Today we have different markets and niche markets that have requirements for products that are not solely dictated to by the upper classes. Lifestyle, income level, education and age are all important factors in determining product acceptance.

It is a matter of informed opinion that all the theories will carry on being valid because the flow will continue to move in many directions and will challenge forecasters to identify what works best for the time. Moving between theories or using a combination based on the social, economic and political climate is key to keeping tabs on ever-changing fashion trends.

'Styles, which start life on the street corner, have a way of ending up on the backs of top models on the world's most prestigious fashion catwalks. This shouldn't surprise us because the authenticity which streetstyle is deemed to represent is a precious commodity. Everyone wants a piece of it.'
Ted Polhemus, 2010

In earlier sections we have looked at the fashion cycle and the trend cycle; in this section we will examine how this relates to new product development and the product cycle. This next part outlines the utilisation and application of trend forecasting in the context of fashion product development.

The product development process

In the fashion industry, new product development is a fast process, the process is completed at least one time for each of the seasons, with twelve months for the leather industry and fifteen months for the garment industry.

The process involves several interactions with designers and product developers making revisions where appropriate. Sometimes a department such as marketing and styling will become involved if necessary and the number of revisions and modifications will vary and take place even when the product has gone into store, making alignments in accordance with the demands from the customer, for example colour changes for a style in the garment sector.

Example: The ASOS collection and the development stage begin before the product is introduced:

At ASOS.com the buying team selects the materials, style and colours to produce the style. The products are produced by the appropriate supplier, and then they are distributed to the ASOS.com UK warehouse and ready for introduction into the market. As customers demand the latest fashion trend seen in magazines, catwalk or on the internet, the ASOS team introduces new products on a regular basis to meet the need of their customers. The cost incurred in introducing a new product is considerable; see below:

- The purchasing of new stock

- Managing the risk of poor sales

- The promotion of the product through the ASOS magazine, website and newsletter

- Updating the website with new images of the fashion items

- Updating the ordering system

The term 'fashion trend' refers to aspects of the appearance and construction of fashion products that relate to a particular season. Such trends are obvious in the look of fashion products, which are designed and manufactured prior to being delivered in the season. With product lead times so long, reacting to current trends isn't enough. Professional trend forecasters aid designers in looking ahead to future developments to help in the development of profitable and successful products. As we know, fashion trend forecasting provides insights into the style and colour directions that future fashion products will take in their final form and for designers, research and development (R&D) teams whose job it is to come up with innovative new products, that means working with internal and external trend professionals to identify the new and emerging trends appropriate for their customers.

For most of the larger companies, there are many options for selecting trend forecasting companies that offer their services. Many of the larger and more successful companies collaborate with international trend agencies. However, the quantity of information that is involved today can mean some companies have selected to develop and set up trend departments in house.

Online sites such as WGSN offer constant updates on their website and much information is provided almost immediately to keep customers informed about emerging trend development. The benefits these companies offer their customers are that they can reduce travel and expenditure, and the companies have access to information that can inform their product development in many ways.

Under insight and analysis, for example, WGSN's service is tailored to different phases in the product development cycle: news, think tank, creative direction, collections, materials, design and production development, product development in addition; buying, sourcing, branding, packaging, marketing, tradeshows, catwalks; what's in store, retail, visual merchandising, branding and packaging, trade fairs, business and strategy, all city by city. The think tank, for example, encompasses macro trends several years ahead while what's in store reports from retailers around the world, offering close to season information. On the other hand, the book publishing French trend forecasting agencies such as Promostyl offer long historical legacies, their exclusive fashion knowledge and the anthropological interpretive frameworks that are used to understand the long-term development of trends with tactile information conveyed through the fabric material samples. With such a large number of web resources, trend tracking done in a structured and diligent way becomes even more important so that the information gathered is translated into profitable product innovations.

The fashion product lifecycle

The following section briefly discusses the product lifecycle in relation to fashion products and the use of trend prediction.

Apparel and other consumer products can be classified by the length of their lifecycles. Basic products such as T-shirts and blue jeans are sold for years with few style changes and businesses selling basic products can count on a long product lifecycle with the same customers buying multiple units of the same product at once or over time.

Because trends and tastes change regularly in the fashion industry, products of fashion, by definition, have a shorter lifecycle, and therefore they have a much shorter time in which to reap their reward. At the start of the fashion lifecycle, costs for a new product will be high while revenues are low. However, during the growth period, revenues start to outstrip costs and contribute to the business's profitability. The lifecycle in fashion can be a matter of days. For example: Limited 100, an ASOS collection created in collaboration with students at London College of Fashion, sold out in five hours.

The transmission process of fashion is often illustrated as a fashion-diffusion process or a fashion product lifecycle (PLC). The concept of the product lifecycle is based on the idea that products have a measurable lifecycle that can be charted over a given period. The PLC consists of five different stages:

1. **Product development.** The phase when a company or brand starts to develop new fashion products. New fashion products do not have to be 'out-of-the-blue'; they may be purely additions to existing fashion lines.

2. **Introduction.** The product's costs rise sharply as the heavy expense of advertising and marketing any new fashion product begins to take its toll.

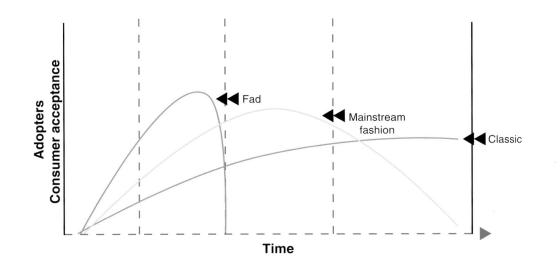

2.6
Product lifecycle. By definition, fashion is a style of the time; a large number of people will adopt a style at a particular time and when people no longer adopt it, a fashion product lifecycle ends. Fashion products have a steep decline once they reach their highest sales.

3.   **Growth.** As the fashion product begins to be accepted by the market, the company starts to recoup the costs of the first two phases.

4.   **Maturity.** By now the fashion product is widely accepted and growth slows down. Before long, however, a successful product in this phase will come under pressure from competitors. The brand will have to start spending again in order to defend the product's market position.

5.   **Decline.** A brand/company will no longer be able to fend off the competition or a change in consumer tastes or lifestyle will render the product redundant. At this point, the company has to decide how to bring the product's life to an end – what is the best end game that it can play?

The fad has the shortest lifecycle and is typically a style adopted by a particular sub-culture or younger demographic group for a very short period of time.

The overall sales of basic products are the highest of the three types of products, and their lifecycles are generally the longest, but these are not particularly trend-led products. Most apparel products have a fashion trend dimension, even if it is just colour, and as fashion trend features increase in a product, the lifecycle will decrease. Therefore, if you are designing a trend-led fashion product, you will want to have multiple products in line for introduction as each fashion product's cycle runs its course.

Some companies build their lines to include basic, fashion and fad products in order to maximise sales. For example, with a sweater line, a business may have four styles that have classic styling and colours and are always in the line. Four additional styles may be modified every two years to include silhouette, length and collar changes based on the current trend. One or two short-cycle fashion or fad styles based on breaking trends may be introduced once or twice a year. Styles worn by popular celebrities or sports heroes can be classed as examples of fashion and fad styles.

Finally, we look at how trends evolve and expire; Everett Rogers Diffusion of innovations theory; and how, why and at what rate new ideas are adopted.

There are five types of consumers that emerge at each of the lifecycle stages.

Fashion adoption consumer types:

*   Fashion innovators adopt a new product first. They are interested in innovative and unique features. Marketing and promotion should emphasise the newness and distinctive features of the product.

*   Fashion opinion leaders (celebrities, magazines and early adopters) are the next most

2.7 Rogers innovation curve. The theory of diffusion of innovations is useful in understanding how new ideas spread through populations.

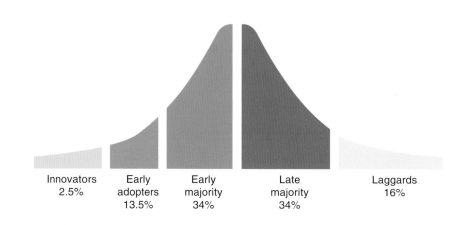

| Innovators 2.5% | Early adopters 13.5% | Early majority 34% | Late majority 34% | Laggards 16% |

likely adopters of a fashion product. They copy the fashion innovators and change the product into a popular style. The product is produced by more companies and is sold at more retail outlets.

- At the peak of its popularity, a fashion product is adopted by the masses. Marketing is through mass merchandisers and advertising to broad audiences.

- As its popularity fades, the fashion product is often marked for clearance, to invite the bargain hunters and consumers, the late adopters and laggards, who are slow to recognise and adopt a fashionable style.

The theory of diffusion of innovations is often useful in understanding how new technologies spread through populations. Rogers (1971) describes how an idea, innovation or product development passes from the fringes of our culture into late majority mainstream. If we think of trends in fashion this way when we consider a specific trend-led fashion item, we can simply identify which stage of diffusion an item is in at present or we can illustrate the entire process up to the current stage.

To illustrate the ideas described here, let's first consider a fashion trend that reached saturation in 2006, and then we'll consider it as a new trend that has yet to tip downwards.

Example: In 2006 the cowboy boot as a trend hit saturation. The start of the trend seemed to appear in 2005 when we saw the early adopters and the early majority snap them up. It wasn't until late summer 2005 when department stores such as Nordstrom and Bloomingdales started to offer a large selection of cowboy boots that they reached tipping point. This was months after they were seen on celebrities such as Lindsey Lohan, Mischa Barton and Nicole Richie who were photographed in cowboy boots as early as spring 2005. Celebrities are key drivers in the demand for a fashion product, generating interest and persuading large retailer to supply them to the majority of mainstream customers. The trend continued to spread as the large retailers really pushed the boots for the holiday season 2005 and continued into 2006. The boots made their way to the laggards as they were sold in smaller numbers until 2006 on sites such as Victoria's Secret and in department stores.

The forecasting process

Forecasters do not just focus on fashion, of course. Among other things, there are forecasters that specialise in electronics, interior design, homeware, etc. Some forecasting specialists foresee colour, fabric and even fiber direction.

This section examines the process used by the fashion industry when utilising trend information. It begins by looking at the colour, inspiration, fabric and mood board presentation techniques used in the fashion prediction process.

Colour

The first step in developing a colour forecast is research – from both a scientific approach and an artistic approach. One needs to look into the past, identify the current times and then predict the future. There are two colour systems that sell chips or swatches of colour standards, SCODIC and Pantone. At Pantone, Inc. the most widely used and recognised colour standard system in the world, colour forecasts are developed. In fact, Pantone has a hand in the colour of roughly half of all garments sold in the United States, according to NPD, a market research group. Colour is a critical element to every season and is the first development in determining the trend; it helps to consolidate trends on the high street and throughout fashion retail stores. Colour is also used as a global referencing tool, with many key software packages using it in their colour libraries.

A colour palette, known as a 'story', is a selected group of shades that are put together to form part of a particular colour trend. Creating a colour story digitally can be done by selecting colours from internet sites or by downloading colour images. Evaluation of the colours and the meanings that they evoke takes place. As the colour stories develop, the mood of the colours helps to further support the theme. Colour stories are often expressed using samples, such as fabric, yarn and ribbon swatches. It is important that flat swatches are used so that there is no ambiguity for yarn dyers. Many companies use clear identification systems like Pantone; colour numbers are often assigned to correspond with colour selections.

Developing a colour palette is the first thing that forecasters do when putting together a trend. The colour story evolves from the inspiration gained through research and the collection of unusual and historical imagery, such as photos and found images, which are developed into the palette. Each story will be given a name; naming the colours can be suggestive and communicate the theme, so choose the colour's name carefully. Many forecasting companies supply libraries of colours that provide a place to collect stories. Once selected, shapes can be filled with colour for the board to indicate the colour selections that represent the colour story.

Fabrics

As in the development of colour forecasting, the process for developing the fabric and materials forecast begins with research. By understanding the basics of textiles, the terminology and the details about fabrication, the forecaster can look to newness to add to his or her information. Many fashion forecasting companies send representatives to major fabric and yarn trade fairs. Première Vision (PV) is probably the best-known fabric trade show in the world; it exhibits in Paris in September for the autumn/winter season and February for spring/summer. Première Vision also holds shows in New York, Moscow, Shanghai and Tokyo. Colours and fabrics are displayed eighteen months in advance of the season. Throughout the duration of each show, PV produces daily trend reports and interviews in addition to a central trend area where predicted trends are displayed alongside examples of relevant fabrics. Many forecasting companies get there early to exchange ideas about significant trends for the forthcoming season; this includes colour and fiber trends.

There are a great many professional textile resources, most of which are available online. Three key players in the textile industry are Lycra, the Woolmark Company and Cotton Inc., all of which provide colour and trend services to promote their products in a competitive marketplace.

Forecast is also considered for trims, embellishments and materials for the forecast. Fibre producers' textile manufactures and trade associations present the latest in fabric and textile development at trade shows and fabric fairs. Fashion professionals attend the fabric fair's first viewing of collections of fabrics and textile designs for a variety fashion markets. Designers and manufacturers can also discover new suppliers, source materials, colours, new developments and all the samples.

Inspiration

A key element to any new season is its inspiration, which comes from a huge range of sources, including exhibitions, galleries, art shows, magazines, interior design and architecture. Fashion requires fresh ideas to inspire designs and offer something new to the customer. It is important that the intelligence collector carry a camera at all times, allowing them to take photographs to then edit and add their own effects. In addition to collecting new images, found images can also contribute to the collation of research material. Fashion store windows are also a regular supply of rich and decorative ideas. Many forecasters travel to major fashion cities for inspiration. Collected imagery can be organised into themes, with regard to shapes, feelings and colour, then a trend may well develop and be considered a 'direction'.

Compiling a trend board

The various looks for a season are shown on trend boards, which usually take the form of a professionally presented collage. The boards will contain colour, fabric and inspiration that are appropriate for each theme with the intention of communicating a visual statement. Experienced fashion designers are able to analyse a visual statement and explore their own interpretation, applying it to their designs.

The layout of the boards needs to be considered simultaneously with the content, and it is important to experiment with the location of the images to ensure that there is a focal point. Fabric swatches, which are relevant to the theme, may be included on the trend boards. If fabric is included, it is important to consider the position and the layout either as a section containing fabrics only or swatches across the board. It is important to present the fabrics neatly and professionally or they will not sit well with the rest of the trend information. Finally, a title for each theme should be added to the board so that they can be referred to easily.

Trend prediction as a tool for fashion brands

The interpretation of trends into key looks must be adapted for the target market: designers, buyers and colourists all need to analyse the 'tone' of the trend predicted and apply it to their designs or products.

The information produced and collated in the predictions is really only the first stage in the process; it is the ability of the buyer or designer to make use of the findings in the evaluation of style trends, designer collections, reviewing store windows, planning and store layouts. This is a skill that can be developed through various methods of visual analysis. Using fashion trend prediction as a tool also provides retailers, designers and manufacturers with an understanding of consumer needs, in terms of product and price, and a projection of return on investment. Intelligent anticipation of customers' desires should result in financial and creative success.

Trend prediction, particularly working with trend forecasting and prediction agencies, can help make sense of and distil the right seasonal messages to engage the brand's target audience, get to must-have items quickly and communicate the most relevant concepts effectively. It helps to save time for the brand and its designers by using their focused methods and helps them gain confidence that they are backing the right trends using proven market analysis. Fundamentally, working with trend forecasting professionals helps a brand understand the target consumers intimately, allowing the brand to connect with them better, and as a result increase sales.

By using statistical and analytical methods that have their history in the birth of social media and online shopping, some of the key agencies allow a brand to get a firm handle on their target consumer. Trendstop, for example, offers flexible custom trend solutions to get the results needed. Their experts are available for collaboration, to put trends into work with the client in a way that works for the brand and consumer, when and where they need effective solutions. Their forward-looking analysis helps reduce time and cost, increase accuracy of key product decisions and increase profit margins. And WGSN's global experts report and predict the long- and near-term trends in consumer behaviour, retail, marketing and business strategy, and across fourteen fashion product categories. They state on their website that over 93 per cent of fashion executives say that this intelligence has strongly influenced their sales while also helping them to streamline resources. But of course, designers are capable of doing their own research, spying the trends, predicting popular colours and sketching the silhouettes. But what trend prediction agencies offer is affirmation. If a brand's management team isn't convinced that boy-fit tanks are the next big thing, it's valuable that a group of self-appointed experts are confirming the designers' instincts. Indeed, that anticipated value is why WGSN is today's leading trend forecaster.

How trends are used

Brands, retailers and designers use trend information to create original desirable products that represent the values of the brand and, in addition, allow them to focus their products on their target consumers. Fashion trend forecasting resources help predict trends in the fashion industry where companies and designers work with them to help find the market and consumers by age, geography or income. They help in looking into how and what they buy, based on their culture, mood, beliefs, the occasion and geographic location. Each season, design and merchandising departments worldwide are waiting for what's in trend for coming seasons as they rely heavily on creating new product lines using this valuable data and information collected by professional agencies. Manufacturers include trends, colours, shapes and details in their line or collection planning, leading brands and retailers to refine range planning and provide a competitive edge using trend intelligence.

Visual analysis of trend prediction boards

The following is a basic three-step guide on how to analyse trend prediction boards and apply them to the design process.

Presentation analysis

The first thing to do when visually analysing is to consider how the board influences you; what are the key features of the images? Where would I see these images? What are the contrasting features? Are the colours and fonts sympathetic to the imagery? Do they clash? Taking time to really look at the images on the board will raise more questions that will need answering in time.

Extrapolation of ideas

Shapes can be organic or geometric. It is important to identify the line quality, shape and scale of the shapes, and of the relationships of each – both on the page and in the environment. Elements such as cultural and historical references, symbolism, visual messages, line movement and speed can all be investigated visually to provide a direction. Once the direction is formed, a mind map

2.8
Fashion trend forecast calculates as following.

Season ➤ Target market ➤ Consumer ➤ Fabrics ➤ Silhouette ➤ Texture ➤ Usage

NEW LOOK
70'S SUMMER

-ETRO-

Customizing, dyeing, cutting,
braiding, embellishing. Light tex-
tures, dense embroideries, and a
sense of bohemian ease.

-DRIES VAN NOTEN-

Inspired by John Everett
Millais' Ophelia, the Pre-Raph-
aelite image that launched a
million hippie fantasies.

-PRADA-

Clothes that might have been
rich in a former life were now
beautiful fragments.

-CHLOE-

Pretty yet precise, elegant but
not excessive, practical rather
than pouty. 'Folkloric' textiles.

-VALENTINO-

Chiuri and Piccioli touched on
many of Italy's patrimonies,
from its antiquities all the way
down to its kitsch. Centu-
ries-old interiors, colourful
dresses printed with vivid
flowers and arabesque forms

-CATWALK REPORT SS15-

S/S
15

- COLOUR STORY -

darling indulgence
AW15
asos
discover fashion online

2.9
Trend prediction boards. Trend boards can include magazine pages, colour chips, fabric swatches, packaging, photos and artwork. It is useful to break down the visual elements of a trend board in order to analyse the information.

Images courtesy of Crystal Padmore

can be developed, using words, images, colour and material, all of which can be applied to design ideas and interpreted into fashion products.

Presenting trend information

Fashion forecasting information (sometimes known as fashion intelligence) is produced and presented in a number of ways, such as hard copy publications and magazines, and increasingly online. The internet has revolutionised the forecasting industry, changing the way in which designers can access trend information. However, while the internet can provide trend information at speed, the traditional trend publication still remains popular; its tactile nature, with swatches, yarn samples and trims, ensures that it retains its place in the market.

Hard copy packages

Hard copy packages are normally printed and bound publications containing visual content for garments, key shapes and details, trend details, colours, fabrics and yarns. These packages are published up to eighteen months ahead of the season, which makes them extremely valuable. They are often split into various publications, with specialisms such as lingerie, womenswear or knitwear. The packages are usually published every six months and available by subscription, either from the company or through an agent. This is an expensive option, although prices vary depending on how many sections of the fashion packages are required. Some forecasting companies offer presentations and updates to key customers when new packages are introduced.

Magazines

A cheaper option for obtaining fashion forecasting information is to purchase specialist magazines such as *Textile View*. These publications focus mainly on fabric and colour, but can also include styling information. The magazines tend to be published closer to the season. They are far less detailed than fashion forecasting packages,

but they do offer some trend information in suitable timescales for most fashion professionals. Some fashion trade magazines, such as UK magazine *Drapers*, also contain fashion forecasting information, which is often in the form of reports from trade fairs. Some examples of international trend publications include the following:

Bloom

A lifestyle trend magazine that interprets flowers and plants for their design possibilities, with colours, forms and moods of the images used to provide inspiration for fashion print and design.

Collezioni

This international magazine comes in different specialist areas, each available biannually, with images of shows and details of emerging trends.

2.10
Bloom magazine is published by Li Edelkoort. The magazine was created in 1998 in response to lifestyles inspired by trends in flowers, plants and gardening.
Courtesy of Trend Union

Fashion Trend Forecast

Offers trend and analysis of the important international designer collections, best-selling product groups, detail solutions, colour, directions and fabric development.

Sportswear International

Worldwide industry magazine for denim, jeans and street fashion. This is produced six times a year, in addition to an annual 'Who's Who' guide.

Textile Report

Comprehensive trends and information for the entire textile and fashion market: womenswear reports, street fashion, designer shows, styling and colour trends, as well as fabric and print ideas and trade fair reports. Every issue has an update and forecast of seasonal trends.

View on Colour

The development and interaction of colour trends is offered in this publication. It communicates innovation in fashion, textiles, industrial design, graphic arts, packaging and cosmetics.

Technology and forecasting

The internet is becoming increasingly important for the distribution of fashion forecasting information. With its immediacy in offering information to customers, the web has an advantage over printed publications, which take longer to publish. Worth Global Style Network (WGSN) was the first to launch its subscription-only website, which paved the way for other websites catering for the fashion professional (see page 51 for more on WGSN). Fashion bloggers and online forecasting companies now provide extensive coverage of designer collections, which go online within days and, increasingly, hours, of the runway shows. The internet has changed the way fashion forecasting and trends are used and, indeed, the ways in which trend predictors work.

Retailers now demand trend information at a moment's notice. As technology continually evolves, it has an increasing impact upon the fashion, apparel and retail industries with forecasters open to new technology and fully embracing new tools for tracking and monitoring the consumer. Tracking fashion trends used to mean travelling abroad five times a year to review runway, retail and street fashion where it would take two weeks for a team to research and another two weeks for a team of ten to pull the complete report together. The report would then be published and sent to clients for review, direction and inspiration. The total process would take over a month. Today, many forecasting companies have reporters around the world that send up-to-the-minute footage of what is being worn on the streets and what retailers are showcasing. As many as 10,000 to 15,000 images a month can be sent from Tokyo to agencies in Milan, for example, which may then be categorised for clients.

'The thing to remember is that the person who discovers trends, the person who is cool, is interested in discovering trends precisely because they're hidden. They want to be the one who is distinctive and unusual.'

Malcolm Gladwell

2.11
The trendtracker.
The trendtracker is a phone and iPad app that offers subscribers daily fashion feeds from around the globe, including street fashion and instant coverage from the runways during Fashion Week.

Image courtesy of Trendstop

Social media and trends

Social media has created a platform for forecasters to take the information provided by reporters and to use it to track trends. For example, walking the streets of Antwerp only gives you half of the story of why a trend is popular; it is important to have a full understanding of how and why that trend came into existence. Now, some forecasters are using social media and online communities to pinpoint where the trend originated and where it is heading. The days of sauntering down the fashionable hangouts of each city have gone, and the focus has been redirected to visiting local blogs or social-media communities.

The job of many has now been replaced by the job of few, who have several platforms of information flowing in at any one time. No longer are there launch dates for trend analysis reports; they are more immediate and produced on a daily basis. Digital sketches can be drawn with new software programs, enabling them to be downloadable for clients to use immediately in production or online trend presentations. Technology has given trend forecasters tools that are subject to almost daily change. The research process of determining the next big trend remains exciting and valuable, as do new methods for tracking future trends.

Forecasting and trend prediction companies

Fashion forecasting agencies observe emerging lifestyle movements and cultural currents, working up to eighteen months ahead of the season. The combination of the information gained on colour, yarn and fabric shows, together with socio-economic and cultural analysis, provides clients with an early interpretation of a fashion trend. Research into trends in lifestyle, attitudes and culture – in particular, music, sports, cinema and TV – is all used to predict changes in customer demand.

Forecasters at such agencies keep ahead of the curve by translating the latest and most relevant lifestyle and fashion trends, interpreting design movements and product progress, giving due consideration to the latest in marketing trends and planning tools. This inspires creativity and innovation, which is useful not only for designers but also for merchandisers, manufacturers, wholesalers, importers, buying offices, retailers and trade show organisers.

Over the years, we have seen a great many trend agencies develop online and hard copy trend intelligence. In recent years, some specialise in either macro or micro trend prediction; only one is a focus for the particular company. The key players today can provide us with the key information needed. The following offers you the chance to catch up with the companies that have been around for a while – others are the new additions but all offer valuable insight into the future.

Promostyl

French agency Promostyl was founded in 1966 and is widely acknowledged as being the first fashion forecasting agency. The founder of the company, Françoise Vincent-Ricard, was working as a consultant in the industry and recognised need and potential for a 'intermediary' who interpreted and communicated to textile manufacturers what the designers would need the following year and what the customers would want to wear the year after that. With that she put together a small team to work with their clients, and a number of textile manufactures and Promostyl and the concept of the trend forecasting agency was born.

Today it is a global trend forecasting agency with headquarters in Paris and a network of agents worldwide. Centring on lifestyle trends, Promostyl provides adaptations for all markets with colour and silhouette direction and a balance between creativity and commercial viability.

Trendstop

Trendstop is a leading online forecasting service, renowned for the quality and accuracy of its trend analysis and forecasts. Its website is available in eight different languages and offers an extensive variety of trend resources to the fashion professional, with access to vast image galleries, focused key trend reports, emerging trends and major theme updates. The trend agency creates success for its clients by focusing on the quality of analysis and trend forecasts.

Trendstop's client area for womenswear offers the following:

- Forecast themes: key atmospheric moods for the season, eighteen months ahead of retail.

- Consumer analysis: themes are informed by in-depth social trend and consumer trend analysis.

- Trend confirmation: accurate trend information and backup data to confirm own thoughts on trend.

- In-depth analysis: detailed and specific trend analysis on colour, materials, surface design, key shapes, detailing, accessories, beauty and styling.

- Continuous trend feeds: updates of new looks and latest developments.

- Trend downloads: placement graphics, garment sketches, print repeats and visually inspiring trend boards.

Trendzoom

Trendzoom is a fashion and trend forecasting agency that delivers clear trend analysis and information to their clients in a calm, creative space. Their reports aim to grow uniqueness and

provide fashion companies with the ability to future-proof their businesses with confidence.

Many of the clients at trendzoom are long-term subscribers with new ones joining every day; their list includes high street multiples, department stores, fashion education and media.

Trendtablet

Trendtablet.com is a social media platform designed and curated by Lidewij Edelkoort. The tool is accessed for free and explains how trends grow and evolve. As a trend forecaster, curator, publisher and educator, Li lives in the future and her focus is the study of the connection between fashion, art, design and consumer culture. Trend forecasters recognise her as a leading figure in trend forecasting as a profession. Her magazines (*View on Colour*, *InView* and *Bloom*) have been highly influential in the creative industries since their launch in 1992. Trendtablet is an online tool

2.12
Trendstop.
This board from Trendstop displays in-depth trend analysis on colour, materials, surface design, shapes, detailing, accessories and styling.
Images courtesy of Trendstop

BORROWED FROM THE BOYS

explaining how trends grow, evolve and flow providing an understanding of how they interact with daily life.

WGSN

WGSN (Worth Global Style Network) was launched in 1998 and soon established itself as a leading online trend analysis service, providing creative and business intelligence for the fashion and design industries. WGSN is part of the Top Right Group, which also owns Drapers. It bought Stylesight in 2013 and became one of the largest online trend companies. WGSN's subscription offer includes market-leading trend forecasting for the fashion and creative industries, design-validation crowd-sourcing and big data retail analytics. WGSN have a solution whether your area of need is designing, marketing, merchandising or planning. Originally based in the UK, WGSN now has regional offices throughout Europe, Asia, South America and the United States.

WGSN is a subscriber service, with over 38,000 users, including Giorgio Armani, Walmart, Abercrombie & Fitch, Calvin Klein and Dolce & Gabbana, as well as colleges and universities worldwide. In 2005, the media group Emap bought WGSN from its British founders, brothers Julian and Marc Worth.

WGSN's editorial and design staff continually travel around the globe to deliver insight and creative inspiration, real-time retail coverage, seasonal trend analysis, consumer research and business information. This is the only trend service designed exclusively for the consumer lifestyle industries with expert insight on areas including automotive, home, hospitality and travel, food and drink and wellness, complemented by a worldwide network of expert freelance analysts, researchers and journalists.

LS:N Global

LS:N Global is a London-based insights platform that works on a subscription basis and documents key industry trends and consumer behaviour insights, providing business professionals with the confidence to make decisions about the future in an informed way.

The network

The network is a daily service updated by a global team of researchers, analysts, correspondents, forecasters and visualisers. Future proofing is the aim of LS:N Global, inspiring new brand innovations, products and services, providing the tools to enter the hearts, minds and pockets of their consumers.

The Future Laboratory

LS:N Global is a division of The Future Laboratory; it operates from offices in London, Melbourne and New York giving business professionals the confidence to make decisions to create economic, environmental, technological and social growth tomorrow. Their clients are helped to harness market trends and adapt to emerging consumer needs, placing their businesses in positions for success and keeping them ahead of the competition.

Products and services

The Future Laboratory offers a range of services designed to prepare businesses for what is next. These include:

> In-house presentations
>
> Futures workshops
>
> Innovation strategy and planning
>
> Activation and amplification
>
> Industry reports
>
> Events

Case study: Trendstop

Trendstop is a trend agency specialising and combining an online trend platform with hands-on custom trend support and offers global fashion and lifestyle trend analysis. The company offers a global online trend research platform and a cutting-edge design studio and consultancy service. As a leading fashion trend forecasting agency, much of their work regularly some of the leading fashion events in the world and regularly produce webinars on trend forecasts.

'Great products start from a great idea, and become a commercial success through a great execution. At Trendstop, we help our clients perfect both.'

Jaana Jätyri

Trendstop was set up in 2002 and is headed up by Finnish-born Jaana Jätyri. Jaana Jätyri is a creative visionary who has worked in the trend forecasting industry for almost two decades. Jaana Jätyri grew up in Finland and has lived in London for over twenty years, after moving to the UK when she was nineteen years old. She started a digital fashion design consultancy in 1999 after graduating from Central St. Martin's College of Art & Design and started Trendstop in 2002. Jaana's first business was a design consultancy helping designers in the late 1990s get computerised. Her business pioneered fashion CAD libraries for a notable client base including Marks & Spencer and River Island. The clients began asking for design ideas for next season.

The company specialises in understanding the consumer product trend cycle and using forward trend planning to successfully deliver product ranges and campaigns, working with companies on the development of their products. They are regularly asked to comment on leading trends in the press, and they have consulted for the biggest names in the industry including *Vogue*, *Wallpaper*, *Elle*, *Marie Claire*, *The Times*, *The New York Times* and *The Independent*.

Trendstop works with leading brands and retailers such as Versace, Diesel, ASOS, H&M, Target, L'Oreal, GHD, Chrysler, Porsche Designs and Miele to create successful products and campaigns. Success for their clients is their focus, meaning they concentrate on the quality of their analysis and trend forecasts to provide the most up-to-date and accurate analysis of emerging trends.

The internet and digital method of communicating trends has been a focus of the company from the start, and as such Trendstop pioneered trend forecasting on mobile and tablet platforms, through the innovative TrendTracker app with over 1,000,000 downloads to date. The Trendstop TrendTracker app is free, and it offers information on what's going to be hot before it's even lukewarm! This app provides professional fashion trend forecasts, photo galleries, videos and a daily dose of fashion news.

With time to market a critical factor in today's world of fast fashion and flash trends accelerated by global social media, Trendstop helps companies identify the trends they need to focus on, communicate the fully current trends and provide a picture of a trend that is easy to

ART HOUSE RETRO

2.12
Trendstop.
Trendstop Boards display trend analysis on colour, materials, surface pattern, detailing, accessories and styling.

Images courtesy of Trendstop (SD)

understand at all stages of the product development and retail cycle.

The company provides not just high-level trend overviews but practical and commercially viable product development direction on concepts to support company decision making and seasonal trend themes.

Trendstop.com offers a wealth of trend information for companies looking for hands-on assistance, including a range of trend information,

concept, design and product technical services that help direct the selection and translation of trends in line with the company's commercial objectives. Their expertise is in translating trend concepts into commercially viable, contemporary successful products, ensuring all products and campaigns are on trend and relevant to their target consumer.

Sources: Trendstop.com, Linkedin, Future Fashion Now by Trendstop, www.twitter.com/trendstop.

Chapter summary

Chapter 2 provides an in-depth look at what influences a trend and how trend prediction and fashion forecasting are important for developing fashion products and aiding designers in the process of maximising the success and profitability of their products.

Fashion trends are used to determine how customers will behave and what they will want to buy in the future, and as such are a complex and time-consuming activity. Companies need to either invest in their teams to enable them to undertake trend research activities or employ external influencers in the form of trend prediction companies.

While the fashion forecasting industry is relatively new, the first ever fashion trend consultancy was launched in 1927. Companies now have access to many different forms of fashion trend intelligence, with today's trend-watching practice spanning across many industries and disciplines. Trend prediction is well established in the fashion industry, and the industry prepares for the new season well in advance, starting with fiber and textile producers' new developments almost two years ahead. Without the forecasters' well-planned projections of designs, colours and fabrics, retailers are likely to lose a lot of money in unsold garments if they 'get it wrong'.

It's the role of the forecaster to read the signals to pinpoint the trend, and as such they saturate themselves 24/7 in cues from all over the world, by travelling, reading, reporting, writing and gathering facts that they analyse and interpret to provide insight into the next emerging trend.

The trend industry and demands for trend information have risen. Everyone is following trends and curating their own self-image; however, for professional forecasters this provides an exciting challenge as influencers not followers. With the internet and increased accessibility of information, the pace of fashion has accelerated. Live catwalk streaming and new material published daily has made this once closely guarded world of trend information more accessible to all levels of the market and the consumers themselves. With the emergence of fashion blogging, bloggers themselves are a great source of inspiration for trend forecasters and are sometimes employed as consultants as they have their finger on the pulse.

One of the critical aspects of trend forecasting is understanding the theories attached to the adoption of a trend; having a handle on the way a trend may trickle up or down is a large part of being able to 'predict' what's next. The fashion industry is a constantly evolving cycle, of which trend forecasting forms an important part; however, forecasting trends is a difficult process with many challenges. Determining whether you are witnessing a trend or a fad is one of the challenges that face the trend professional. Understanding the theory behind the trend is an important factor for the forecaster considering the needs and desires of the consumer.

As trends and tastes change regularly in the fashion industry, products of fashion, by definition, have a shorter lifecycle, and thus have a much shorter time in which to reap their reward. For the fashion designer/product developer, understanding the product lifecycle and how the trend will be adopted influences the speed at which a trend will be picked up. The fad has the shortest lifecycle – typically it's a style adopted by a particular sub-culture or younger demographic group for a very short period of time with some companies building into their lines the inclusion of basic, fashion and fad products in order to maximise sales.

There are many product developers in addition to fashion apparel whose companies subscribe to trend prediction services, including the lifestyle industry, cars, beauty, interiors, and so on. There is a wealth of trend information available in hard copy packages from companies such as Promostyl, a trend agency founded in 1966 and one of the longest-standing subscription services to offer trend forecasting. There is also information available online, such as Trendstop, Trend Tablet and WGSN, which was launched in 1998 and soon established itself as a leading online trend analysis service, providing creative and business intelligence for the fashion and design industries.

Finally, we have to accept that while trend forecasting is still a relative newcomer it has fast become one of the most important weapons in a retailer's competitive armory. In a fast-moving and crowded marketplace, identifying 'what's hot and what's not' is crucial to staying one step ahead of the competition.

Case study and chapter reflection

Q. Trendstop is specialist trend agency that combines a leading online trend platform with other areas of trend development. Explain what they do better than other trend services and why this is.

Q. Explain the importance of understanding the consumer product trend cycle and how this fits into the trend cycle.

Q. Trendstop provides up-to-date and accurate analysis of emerging trends. Explain how a trend forecaster could gain such precise information.

Q. Explain the stages of the product development and retail cycle.

CHECKLIST

1. Who uses fashion forecasting and trend prediction to help them produce and buy what is predicted to be popular in a forthcoming season?

2. When done correctly, trend prediction can prove invaluable to business success. Explain what this process would involve.

3. Trend forecasters have to have a good handle on a variety of areas to inform their analysis. What are those areas?

4. Name the theories of fashion adoption and explain what they mean.

5. Who said, 'Trend forecasting is much like archeology but to the future'?

6. How has the internet changed the trend forecasting business?

7. What type of organisation is NPD and what do they say about Pantone?

8. Explain in brief the ASOS product development model.

9. The product lifecycle (PLC) consists of five different stages. What are they?

10. Trends evolve and expire: Rogers's theory of the diffusion of innovation can explain this. Draw a diagram of this curve, and name all fashion adoption consumer types.

EXERCISE

Cool hunting

The emergence of cool hunting has opened up many job opportunities for creative graduates. A cool hunter, also known as a trend spotter, is paid to find out what's cool! They spend their time:

- Studying current trends

- Spotting new trends while they're still beginning to flourish

- Predicting new trends

- Presenting their findings and predictions to employers and brands

To become a cool hunter, you will require good visual research skills. It is all about looking for forward-thinking individuals who are leaders in their own groups. The following exercise is designed to help you explore the activities of the cool hunter, to develop your eye and enhance your translation skills in the developments of a cool hunting visual presentation.

Step 1: Research

Visit a city or a town close to you and look around, taking inspiration from the places you find yourself in; record what you see using a camera and by taking notes. Visit malls and shopping centres, lifestyle and concept fashion stores. Include some street photography, recording what people are wearing: your research should take into account current market influences and reflect contemporary culture.

Other suggestions for sources of inspiration are art galleries, advertising images, interior design, illustration, photography, graphic design, print and pattern, textiles, sculpture, film, sports and music.

Step 2: Compilation

When you have taken photos and written up your notes, put them together on a board. Include a variety of research methods, visual images, written information, drawings, photographs, samples and notes.

Once you have compiled your research, it can be developed into a trend board, an online forecast or a cool hunting blog.

Step 3: Analysis

Filter out the predominant themes that emerge from the trend research. When you are working on your forecast, it is important that you are ahead of the current trends within the fashion stores. Remember that what everyone is wearing right now is likely to be going out of fashion very soon, so try making a connection between influencers and consumers.

Interview:
Jaana Jätyri

Fashion forecaster, CEO Trendstop

Q: Trendstop has been operating for over fifteen years. What inspired you to set up the company?

A: My first business was a design consultancy selling CAD tools and fashion design libraries to make it easier for designers to get computerised back in the late 90s'. My first clients were Marks & Spencer and River Island. The clients began asking for design ideas for next season based on runway looks, and in 2002 Trendstop was launched as a dedicated online trend forecasting service.

Q: How do you think technology coupled with the influence of social media have impacted on the way trends evolve today?

A: It has revolutionised everything about trends; how they are expressed, bought and sold. The consumer is now in the driving seat compared to retailers dictating trends fifteen to twenty years ago.

Q: How does the trend forecasting process work; what does it involve for you personally?

A: I have dedicated my past twenty years in the industry to identifying the process of how to understand the consumer mindset, and offer them the right product at the right time. I have managed to distil that knowledge into a unique trend forecasting methodology that has been proven to increase the number of best-selling items in any commercial fashion collection, time and time again. This methodology is the Trendstop Accurate Trend Prediction Formula.

Q: Why is trend forecasting important to fashion businesses?

A: As the consumer ultimately decides what gets bought in the market, it is important to be able to predict their needs and wants ahead of time. [However, traditional opinion-based trend forecasting doesn't typically start from this perspective, and this type of trend forecasting is becoming less relevant as it is not fast enough for the speed of social media conversations and fast fashion.]

Q: What is inspiring for you right now?

A: New thinking, new ways of looking at things, expressions of that thinking.

Q: What advice would you give to students who are interested in trend prediction/forecasting as a career?

A: Be curious, be interested in everything. A good trend forecaster is a good researcher. Trend forecasting is a glamorous topic, but not to be a good trend forecaster takes a lot of work; just like not everyone who wants to be a footballer gets to play in the Premier League. Trend forecasting is not just about being able to create a pretty mood board. A lot of knowledge goes into a trend forecast that is truly valuable.

Getting a product to market

This chapter discusses the role of the manager in its different forms within the organisation and what responsibilities, characteristics and qualities the manager will have to exhibit to make a successful brand work, in addition to the activities and value of the operations that are in place to change raw inputs into fashion products for the end user. Information on introductory marketing management theories and framework used within fashion organisations as well as a case study is used to demonstrate the above in practice. In this chapter, we will look at the different activities, areas and operations that take place in the typical fashion organisations using examples from both brand and mainstream businesses.

The chapter will help you:

- Understand the context of different organisations, products and services that make up the fashion industry.

- Develop an understanding of the different roles that contribute to various fashion organisations and the hierarchy of fashion company structures.

- Learn about the basic theories and models that contribute to strategic marketing management in the fashion industry.

- Understand how creativity crosses boundaries and is used in the management practices of a fashion organisation.

- Appreciate the methods used in the fashion industry to get a fashion product to market.

3.1
Shiatzy Chen, FW 2016/17, ready-to-wear collection. The principles of fashion management include the marketing, promotion and the sale of fashion products.
© MARTIN BUREAU/ AFP/Getty Images

The fashion organisation

The basic management activities for the fashion manager include the marketing, promotion and sale of fashion products and involve the tasks necessary to deliver the request for garments to meet the needs of potential customers and designers. Some of the responsibilities involved are developing campaigns, managing projects such as advertising concepts, visual merchandising displays, managing the manufacturing process and marketing activities including sales strategies.

Marketing and management play very important roles in the fashion industry. With billions of pounds at stake, the management of projects is critical for its growth and success by establishing brand awareness and discovering the next trends that contribute to the profits generated by the fashion industry and the fashion manager plays a key role in this.

The core functions of selling products and managing the supply chain are the key purposes of the organisations involved at the various levels of the industry, and those involved are challenged with the unique task of utilising both their creative and business acumen in order to generate sales. It is the remit of both fashion managers to generate and execute meticulous strategies aimed at ensuring the retailers they support are positioned in a more stylish and prominent place than their competitors.

3.2
The activities and the value of the operations that are in place to change raw inputs into fashion products for the end use.
© Kim Steele via Getty Images

Having a grasp on how a fashion company operates is critical for the person thinking of entering the industry at management level at some point in their future. Understanding the fashion industry and its contribution to the global economy is the starting point for many.

The fashion industry comprises of design, manufacturing, distribution, marketing, retailing, advertising and promotion of many types of fashion garments, including women's, men's and children's fashion, and involves products from expensive couture fashion to mass-produced high street products. In broader terms, fashion is labelled the 'fashion industries' which is used to describe the myriad of industries and services employing millions of people internationally. Incorporated inside the fashion industries are many companies and organisations making the fashion industry work. Each area has its own place in the industry and individually has a variety of responsibilities and actions that contribute to a particular part of the industry, concentrating on the goal of satisfying consumer demand for fashion, making sure that all participants contribute to operating at a profit.

This book discusses technology and how this has impacted the industry and how things are changing. However, the basic structure of the industry changes little, as the need to source fabrics and trims, design and make garments, sell, promote and market these garments involves typical processes and is the mainstay of the fashion and manufacturing industry today.

The following section breaks down in a simple form some of the core areas and provides brief descriptions of some of the key organisations and fashion businesses that make up the industry. Also covered are some of the different models and business structures to give you some understanding of the types of organisations involved in fashion today and their place in the fashion industry.

Textile design and production companies

Let's start with textiles and production companies. For a long time, India has played a key role in the production of textiles. However, things have changed over the past few years, and with political changes and shifts in modern communication, we have seen the production and manufacture of textiles move to countries such as China and throughout southeast Asia, expanding the availability of textiles within the industry. The structure and operation of textile companies vary with the interaction between the designer and the manufacturer. The small designer sources the fabric through textile agents. Larger companies/ brands have their own mills or work closely with the mill that produces fabrics/textiles to their own specifications. The main costs incurred in the production of the fabric is the labour involved, which has resulted in most manufacturing of textiles being moved out of places like the US and UK to overseas. Recently, however, there has been a small increase in the manufacture of fabric in places such as the US, but the majority of textiles come from India, China, Southeast Asia and Mexico, and we also see places such as Eastern Europe providing garment manufacturing and textile facilities.

Fashion design and manufacturing

The production of fashion garments takes place after the textiles have been purchased from the mills where it is then passed on to the sewing manufacturers. Designs have been submitted and patterns are made, cut in quantity and assembled. There are some cases where the garments and patterns have been cut at a specialist shop and then passed to the sewing factory. The industry is mainly made up of the small manufacturers (Indian, Asian and Mexican) who specialise in patterns, cutting, trims and so on. However, some of the larger brands do have consolidated manufacturing.

Distribution

There are many layers to the distribution and the supply of fashion products to the next level before they get to the stores. The more generic the garment, the more things that have to be done before the product will appear in the shops. Large brands distribute directly from their offshore manufacturing units to retail, while many independent designers will take their garments directly from the manufacturers and distribute themselves. They may use a sales representative who represents a number of designers and sells directly to the retailer, but common items such as T-shirts will be produced in bulk and sold to distributors of promotional fashion products who print them afterwards and sell on.

Fashion retailing, marketing and merchandising

The retail market is made up number of established larger brand retail companies. However, there are many smaller more niche retailers in the fashion marketplace. The larger retailers have an advantage over the small- and medium-size enterprises (SMEs) due to the fact that they can get a much better price, as the quantities they buy are larger, and the outcome of this is the larger profit margin made, allowing better retail prices to their customers. The way smaller retailers may operate is to narrow down the range and to concentrate on specific types of fashion products rather than trying to compete with larger retailers.

In the retail industry today, however, we see more companies selling products in other ways. For example, the internet has opened up opportunities for retailers to connect with their customers by offering their products for sale online. (Also see Chapter 7 on new micro brand business models and entrepreneurship.) Increasingly, people want to shop through the use of mobile apps on their phones or in the comfort of their own homes rather than the traditional brick and mortar stores. Emerging technologies have changed the way retailers are doing business, and there are indications through research that customers who shop online spend more than eight times than the traditional shopper. There are many trends emerging in the use of technology that are having an impact on way fashion retailers and brands interact with customers. In Chapter 4, there are more details regarding this and multichannel retailing.

> **SMEs**
> SMEs are small- and medium-sized enterprises or small and medium-sized businesses.

The role of the fashion manager

The role of the manager in the fashion organisation takes on many different aspects, as the complex nature of the business involves a myriad of skills, knowledge and experience. In this section, the role of the fashion manager will be looked at within a variety of areas and levels within the organisation. A review of the responsibilities, characteristics and qualities of the manager will be covered, and we will look at what needs to be done to make a successful brand work.

The fashion industry, as you will now have discovered, is very large and multifaceted. It is an industry that employs many people in various roles. The contemporary fashion industry is a creation of the modern age and is ever-changing, offering something for everyone. From the big brand designer names to the lower-level high street fashion brands, the fashion industry needs all of them to function properly behind the scenes of the companies that bring fashion products to us. Some of the companies have a massive hierarchical structure within which they operate, and the following section will review a number of different roles at varying levels of the fashion company hierarchy. After the list of roles, I will pick out few from each category to cover in some detail.

3.3
Christian Dior retail display.
The retail market is made up of a number of established larger brand retail companies. However, there are many smaller more niche retailers in the fashion market place.
© Tom Sibley via Getty Images

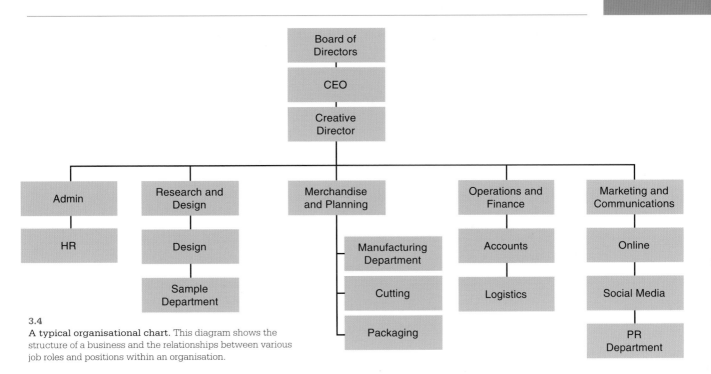

3.4
A typical organisational chart. This diagram shows the structure of a business and the relationships between various job roles and positions within an organisation.

Senior fashion company roles

The professionals in a fashion company are the best known in the fashion world. They know so much about the fashion industry and are considered masters of their field. These people work with their companies to ensure the smooth flowing of operations and guarantee that the industry flows without hindrance. They have administrative authority and can make strategic decisions required for the smooth functioning of the work involved. The various job profiles at this level of fashion organisation hierarchy can include the following roles:

Fashion creative director
Marketing and/or promotions manager
Marketing director
PR manager
Sales director
Head of fashion designers team
Senior fashion designer
Advertising director
Advertising manager
Buying & merchandising director
Branch manager

The following section will cover three of the roles in detail, starting with the creative director.

The fashion creative director

The fashion creative director uses skills in exercising creativity in developing concepts, leadership, communication ideas and working with industry-related technology. The form a fashion creative director can take could be anything from a creative director of fashion apparel to an art director of a fashion magazine. The key skills needed by the creative director are communication, creativity, leadership and a strong understanding of contemporary technology.

Communication

The key to translating ideas to the team is through strong, clear communication skills. It is important for the creative director to be able to communicate cutting-edge ideas and have their vision be understood by the rest of the team to carry out through to final products. The execution of their ideas for a new product line depends on the skill of the director to express his or her concepts in the forms of sketches, the right wording and presentation to the team to carry out the project and bring the ideas to life. On the flip side, the creative director must have the appropriate listening skills to allow the other team members the opportunity of having their voices heard and integrating their creative input into the selected vision. Another critical skill for the creative director is to have good skills in networking with potential collaborators within the fashion industry.

Creativity

When formulating a fashion concept, creativity is the most essential skill for the creative director to have. Whether it is working in a store, fashion magazine or creating a new product line for a fashion brand, being able to form a creative vision is crucial. The ability to generate fresh new ideas that appeal to the brand's target customer is key as is the creative vision, which must match that of the rest of the brand's message.

Leadership

The creative director's leadership skills enable all the loose ends to be tied up and to pull the fashion project together. Many decisions must be made and the creative director will make the final decision on how the project's vision will be presented. They will have a strong ability to take control of the project and make the final creative decisions on important details such as colour, shapes, fabrics and graphic design. The ability to pull all of them together requires skills in organisation, time management and the ability to lead and inspire each member of the team throughout the overall production process.

Tech

Finally, the creative director will have a selection of technical and artistic skills, such as CAD or photography, to help them investigate ideas that can be visually communicated to other designers inside and outside the team in a practical form. Drawing skills and photography allow jotting down of ideas to help in the brainstorming of ideas quickly. Being artistic and utilising technical capabilities allows creative directors to create, share and communicate fashion prototypes that would be difficult if only verbal or written methods were the only methods available.

The marketing manager

The fashion marketing manager is at the forefront of the fashion garment and product industry. The role of the marketing manager is to ensure their brand's fashion products reach their customers. It is the responsibility of the marketing manager to target the money spent by the fashion customer each year.

Duties

The duties of the fashion marketer are handling the brand image through the successful delivery of brand campaigns. They are expected to increase sales and market share of the brand by reaching out to the target audience of the brand in question.

They are required to manage the flow of the product from the concept to the product presentation to the consumer. Areas such as quality control, ensuring the best-quality product reach the shop floor, may also be a part of the role of the marketing manager.

Once product concepts have been developed, it will be part of the role of the marketing manager to devise a marketing plan that will include the design of promotional material, approval and the creation of new fashion products including the market research of new lines. Once the conception of the ideas has taken place, the marketing manager will be involved in designing events such as fashion shows or trade events, the development of online and offline marketing events and brochures or other live sampling events that target their audience. It is also the remit of the marketing manager to oversee things such as store openings and the communication of the brand image to all staff members, ensuring they fully understand the brand image and a clear and consistent message is sent out.

Industry

Fashion is fluid and changes regularly; with this, fashion companies need fashion marketers to get the message out. But, like all marketing managers, a fashion marketing manager must be able to identify emerging trends and convince their target customers to buy them.

Fashion PR manager

The fashion industry is a world reliant on creating trends that attract and keep the attention of the fashion-conscious public. It is the responsibility of the fashion PR manager to put the face of the brand into the public domain. They are the representative of the brand and are responsible for creating the buzz among the press, including influential fashion bloggers and journalists, in a creative way. You will need skills in advertising, fashion design, purchasing, retail, promotion and planning if you are thinking of becoming a PR professional.

Forging press relations

The number one goal of the fashion PR manager is to promote the fashion business. The majority of the time, it is the responsibility of the PR

manager to 'get the word out'. This involves working with editors and writing articles for leading fashion magazines about the company and their products. Necessary for this type of job is a business-oriented mind and a keen interest in fashion in order to create media-penetrable fashion material.

Brand building

For the PR manager, much of their time is spent planning and delivering shows and promotional events that build the brand name in the eyes of the public. One of the most important parts of the job involves clearly defining and maintaining the company's 'brand'. The best PR manager strives to keep the message clear and consistent, never sending out mixed messages; for example, the style of your event must mimic the style of the brand and is niche in that respect.

Communicating the message

The job of the fashion PR manager will involve a lot of time with members of the company, including designers, marketing executives as well as merchants and customers. It is the responsibility of the PR representative to encourage the buyers to promote their fashion products at events; therefore, excellent communication skills are essential.

Middle fashion company roles

The next section of fashion professionals is described as the middle fashion company roles; these people represent a vital group at the executive level. Their positions in the fashion company hierarchy mean they don't have decision-making authority, so they work on the direction orders of the senior-level management professionals. However, they play a vital role in the company and have important experience in the fashion field with a thorough knowledge of the industry. The various role titles and profiles at this level of the fashion company hierarchy include the following:

Production artists

Logistic manager

Studio management

Commercial director

Visual merchandiser

Client strategist

Target marketing strategist

Senior apparel designer

Fashion stylist

Senior photographer

Surface pattern designer

Studio production manager

Fashion designer

Logistic manager

The term 'logistics' means the planning, organising and managing of activities that provide goods or services. A logistics and distribution manager deals with shipping companies and runs the distribution facility, working with brokers to ensure the operations are running smoothly. Most logistics managers will have a qualification or degree in transportation; this allows them to plan the operations and ensure that the right goods leave the warehouse facility on time, go to the right place, in the right quantities by the most efficient means.

Duties

The logistics manager will have a workday that includes running a distribution centre, ensuring the incoming materials are properly stored and are in good condition, and that the outgoing goods are going out in good order and in the correct quantities. Daily activities will be to prepare documents, review invoices and customs documents and negotiate with transportation companies about services and costs.

They may also need to look at and resolve supplier, transportation and employee issues. They will be in charge of the review of distribution centre workload, planning schedules that will also be part of the work remit.

One of the duties will be looking at reducing costs; however, while this is taking place, consideration of the customers' needs will inform the best method to meet them. According to ONET Online, 74 per cent of logistics managers will have a degree, with 17 per cent having a master's degree. The logistics manager will gain several years of experience working in a distribution centre before being able to apply for the position of manager.

The use of complex computer software is a part of the manager's skill set; this software will be used for the purpose of managing the inventory and procurement of goods and services.

The role of logistics manager can be very stressful, as the work is particularly fast-paced. Managers must work fast to solve problems that arise and ensure operations are on schedule.

Fashion production manager

The process of producing fashion collections twice a year is a challenging job for even the best and most experienced fashion designer; without their most loyal staff behind them, it would be close to impossible. One of the most important roles in a fashion house is that of the production manager. This pivotal role calls for a person with an organised mind and a passion for detail. If you enjoy multitasking, then this may be the role for you. The job requires responsibility and a desire to making sure the designer's vision is achieved.

Production managers are prepared

It may come as a surprise, but a degree is not always necessary for gaining a role as production manager: look at the advertisements for these roles and you will find that the qualities most sought after are organisational skills and a willingness to work long hours. That doesn't mean that a degree will be lost; it's just that there may be a way of getting into the role through experience and skill developed elsewhere. In addition to the organisation and management skills, the ability to communicate to the team members and a second language are also valuable skills to have.

Production manager's responsibility

A production manager's key tasks are to oversee matters such as sampling garments and tasks relating to this in the factories and workshops overseas. Design changes in finishing the garments are fundamental to the success of the collection and are the responsibility of the production manager. Their role may include tracking the costs of the collections for the designer, to keep a close eye on how the collection is forming and to keep a running total of money matters as collections are developed. The liaison and communication between the designer and fabric and trim wholesalers will be a key focus for the manager, and an inventory of items used in the collection is kept under review near the deadlines and close to the delivery of garment booked after the shows.

Handling of events

Sometimes the production manager also assumes the role of the events manager. The role includes booking and overseeing models and hair stylists to convey the designer's styling directions. There may also be the responsibility of booking schedules to arrange the shows in different fashion locations. It is not unusual for a designer to show at multiple locations in the same season. The production manager's job may run to the coordination of the events, particularly those scheduled during 'fashion week'.

Coordination of public relations

While top-end designers may pay PR professionals to handle publicity needs, it is the role of the production manager to field media inquiries and gossip news stories. The production manager will be briefed on 'talking points' so that they are ready to communicate the position of the brand **verbatim**. The production manager may also communicate through writing press releases, position papers and other data for reporters and media.

Verbatim

adverb: **verbatim**; adjective: **verbatim**

1. in exactly the same words as were used originally.

Travel coordination

The production manager will hold important information relevant to the trips made. The manager will have insider knowledge on the best hotels, problematic airlines and other matters that may have an effect on the chances of a seamless trip. The manager will be on call 24/7 and will be looking after VIP lists, backstage and last-minute details, which will have an effect on the overall success of the fashion show.

The fashion designer

The role

The role of the fashion designer is to study fashion trends and interpret these through the sketching of an initial idea into a garment or accessory design. The nature of the role of designer may vary in different types of designer and market levels. Most designers will work for manufacturing companies and have regular working hours. However, some designers work on a freelance basis, working much longer and more stressful hours, or work for themselves as small enterprises (see Chapter 7).

The designer's role is to oversee the creative process from concept to the final product, and he or she may be involved in the whole process through to the sample fitting. The smaller the company, the more responsibilities the designer may have. For example, the designer may have greater duties that include pattern-making and sewing, while in much larger companies, this will be the responsibility of a specific team.

Design and production process

The market level determines the design and production process. Fast-fashion designers may specialise in a specific category of garment (i.e. coats or dresses), while other designers in a smaller company may be responsible for designing garments across a range of fashion products.

Designers today also need to be computer literate, as much of the design work is done on a computer using computer software. CAD is being increasingly used in the design of fashion products. Some start the process and sketch by hand, then the design may be put into a computer. This saves time and money as alternate colours and fabrications can be done quickly on the PC/Mac.

Key to gaining a role in a fashion company as a designer is a degree in fashion. This can equip you with pattern-cutting design skills in addition to a working knowledge of colour, fabric, textiles, trends and the history and context of fashion. This background will provide a potential designer with a better understanding of the garment production process, ability and skill to improve functionality, fit and aesthetics in their designs for specific clients in order to meet customer demand.

Travel and fashion shows

The role of the designer can involve extensive travel in order to communicate with clients globally.

Most designers will have an assistant, but in most cases, the designer is in full control of the fashion show and will be involved in selecting the models and venues and be responsible for the mood of the show.

Junior fashion company career level

The junior professionals in the company hierarchy are the secondary workers in the fashion company. These professionals work at the operational level of the fashion company and get their orders from middle-level professionals. The various job profiles at this level of the advertising company hierarchy include the following:

Communications coordinator

Assistant fashion designer

Senior accessory designer

Accessory designer

Garment designer

Art director, fashion

Colourist

Retail manager

Assistant photographer

Store manager

Trend forecaster

Textile designer

Event coordinator

Sample cutter

Sample room manager

Customer representative

Retail manager

The responsibility of the fashion retail manager is to oversee the sales staff or fashion store, depending on the size of the retail establishment. Responsibilities include the recruitment and ongoing training of members of staff that will sell on the shop floor, in addition to handling customer inquiries. The main job is the upkeep of the shop floor, where team management skills are imperative, as is the ability to communicate, lead and make decisions.

Handling customer complaints may also be a frequent task; therefore, considerate communication is a key skill of the retail manager. Also very important is extensive knowledge on how to display products for the greatest impact. A retail manager is expected to understand what their customers want and how best to sell it to them.

Sample room manager

The role of the sample room manager is to supervise sample makers. They may have many staff members making sample garments required for the latest collection. The sample room manager must be technically savvy, with strong pattern-cutting and construction skills in addition to the ability to manage people and work across departments. Other areas of expertise include creative production and fitting experience; strong organisational skills and problem-solving skills are critical too.

Event coordinator

If you are interested in the career of a fashion events coordinator, it is important that you understand the three main types of fashion events:

- The product launch

- The fashion show

- The fashion awards ceremony

Fashion industry events take place during fashion weeks; these are normally one week in duration. Fashion designers, brands and 'houses' show their current collections on the catwalk/runway to buyers and media professionals so they can look at the most up-to-date trends and so the industry will know what is 'in' and 'out' for the season in question. Spring/summer shows are in September, and the autumn/winter shows are in February. The key fashion weeks are held in the four fashion capitals: New York, London, Milan and Paris. But there are more fashion weeks around the world and the list is growing. There is more information on this in Chapter 6.

It is the event coordinator's responsibility to oversee every aspect of the event, from initial concept to the final presentation. It will depend on whom they are working for as to whether they have assistance and managers to aid them. If the venture is a small affair, the events coordinator may be the only one responsible for all the arrangements.

3.5
Junior managers.
Fashion retail managers, sample room managers and event coordination all come under the more junior responsibilities in the organisational hierarchy.

Top: © Bloomberg via Getty Images
Bottom: © markhanna via Getty Images

Managers working in the fashion industry are challenged with a variety of roles and responsibilities that are delivered at varying levels in the fashion company hierarchy. Whether it's for a large clothing company, a boutique or an outlet chain, the fashion manager will have an important role to play in the business. The remit will vary; however, the manager will be involved at some level in the planning, designing, developing, resourcing and delivery of goods or services for the fashion business.

The section following outlines some of the basic management theories and models appropriate to fashion business management and marketing. Further details on marketing can be found in Chapter 5. Some models are a fundamental part of the planning and the strategic nature of some of the roles mentioned in the last section, particularly the roles involving marketing and aspects of marketing management.

Basic management methods for fashion managers

Management theories are a collection of ideas on how to manage a business or organisation and are put in place to aid in the productivity and organisation of the service quality of a company. Most managers don't use a single method or theory when implementing strategies in the workplace; most use a combination of a few, depending on the type of industry or business. Management theories help a manager to relate to their business and its goals and guide them in

how to implement effective means to meet the goals and achieve the highest standards. The following section will outline some of the basic theories that will help in understanding what a brand would need to consider to maintain its success in the marketplace, with a particular emphasis on the marketing aspects of a brand.

General business analysis

Understanding a fashion business in depth is the goal of self-analysis and is based on detailed current information: the organisational structure, costs, profit, management, sales and other factors. When looking at something like a new marketing project, product line or store opening, the strategic plan to support these goals and activities involve a variety of different processes by analysing the business and its activities. Approaches include focus on marketing competencies and the resource-based outlook of the company, which is core to any thinking about self-analysis from a marketing perspective.

This next section sets out some of the core activities that would be expected of a manager to guarantee success within the realms of the project set.

Value chain

One model used frequently in businesses is known as the value chain analysis model. It examines the fundamentals on which competitive advantage can be based. The concept is known as Porter's value chain model, which focuses on systems and processes of how inputs are altered to outputs bought by the customer. Using this perspective, Porter illustrates a chain of everyday activities that are common to all businesses, which are then divided into primary and support activities.

The term 'value chain analysis' or VCA can be described as a tool used to analyse the internal activities of a brand or organisation (there are several visual examples online, search for 'Porter's value chain model'). The goal in its use is to identify which activities are the most valuable to the brand and which could be improved to provide the brand with a competitive advantage.

Porter introduced his value chain to the business world in 1985, and in the fashion context, it represents the internal activities a company does to produce fashion products and services. While primary processes add value directly, they are not always the most important. Today we see the competitive advantage derived from technological improvements in innovation and new business models, or processes adding value to activities like research and development. Conversely, primary activities are more often than not the source of cost advantage; this is where the costs can be managed properly after easy identification in the process.

Creativity

Creativity in business is an important issue and particularly in fashion businesses needing to keep up with the latest trends and stay ahead of the competition. Creativity and creative thinking – the dreaming up of new and unique ways of designing and doing things – are a critical part of that process. For any company to succeed, creative thinking is an essential part of its practices, more so in a creative fashion environment when things change so quickly. The forward-thinking manager will need to encourage creative thinking to prevent stagnation and to keep the business moving ahead. However, the concept of creative thinking to some managers is not always an easy concept to grasp, and some stimulus may be essential. There are techniques to help with the process, and getting as many workers onside to create exposure and develop a wide variety of ideas will in turn benefit the business.

Here are some of the most common strategies used to help in developing and stimulating ideas.

Mind mapping

Mind mapping allows the group to contribute ideas on a topic without regard to how practical they may be, encouraging them to think outside the box, to find a solution that might not happen otherwise. This method removes the practical constraints, allowing the idea to surface and the team can mold this into a workable solution.

Asking 'what-if' questions

Asking 'what if' questions can lead to new discoveries, resulting in growth and improvement. What if we did this type of clothing range? What if we branched out into accessories? What if we opened a second store just for accessories? What if we purchased our major competitor? and so on. 'What if' questions are quite often used as the source of big ideas.

Role-playing

This type of activity can provide a different perspective that can direct you to helpful ideas. For example, pretending to be your customer as a sales person will provide a clearer picture of the customer experience, which can then lead to developing a plan for you to overcome any problems you may identify.

Provocation techniques

Provocation is a process used to stimulate creative thought; in this process, you would consciously reject a truism to help create a different way of doing something. For example, you may propose to get rid of all the sewing machines in the studio; this will help you to think about how you would get your samples made and work out different ways of developing your garments. While this would on the surface not be a good strategy, it may help you come up with new and interesting methods in the manufacture and design process.

Fashion industry analysis

The industry is made up of a number of large retailers and brands, as they make up a large chunk of the market. However, many smaller businesses, boutique and niche stores are part of the market, too. The bigger suppliers have an advantage over the smaller ones as they get better pricing and access to suppliers, meaning the prices are better, but all retailers and suppliers need to be aware of the changes to be made to their products in order to service the industry. The industry lifecycle can go some way in explaining how the products and services offered may change over time.

Industry lifecycle

There are distinct changes in an industry lifecycle, put briefly these are introduction, growth, maturity and decline. The industry is constantly updating products and services and evolves over time.

For example, trend prediction started with hardcopy books seasonally communicating fashion trends to the designer. Now, with the internet, we are seeing online products and services and the accessibility of trends through mobile apps.

The stages are similar for all industries, except some will experience them in a different way. A company's strategic plan will be dependent on the stage the company finds itself in. For companies to extend their lifecycle, they need to either find new products or new uses for products. In a fashion company, it is imperative that new trends and designs for products are developed and communicated to the target consumer so the company continues to be viable. The mapping of sales to the phase of where the company is on the lifecycle model is how the company can judge where it sits on the lifecycle model.

For example, at the introduction stage, sales are typically slow. They then take off at the growth stage, and then level out at the maturity phase before sales gradually decline. However, generally a company can see an increase in profits as the product goes through the lifecycle. Using economies of scale and a company is often able to get a better unit price by reducing the costs over time.

Introduction stage is when the industry is in its infancy. This is when a new product range has been introduced to the market and new industry is born. At this stage, the company may be alone in the industry. The stage is the offering of a new product, and marketers sometimes call these 'question marks' as the product's success and its life in the industry are unknown and unproven.

Marketing tactics at this stage are focused on the people labelled 'early adopters' or 'innovators'. Market demand will increase from the introduction stage and the next stage it will enter is the growth stage.

Growth stage requires a significant amount of capital. This stage requires funds for marketing to be continued and investment in plant and machinery to make the product required by the consumer demand. Industry, however, at this stage can experience more standardisation of the product due to the economies of scale. Marketing departments may refer to these products at this stage as 'stars' because of the high growth and market share.

Maturity curve means the rate of sales has slowed. At this stage, there may be competition from late entrance to the market trying to steal market share from existing products. At this point, the marketing efforts must remain strong and stress the importance of differences in the product to encourage sales.

Decline happens if product innovation has failed to keep pace. In any industry, it is inevitable that a product will go into decline. If new technologies cause the industry to become obsolete, sales will suffer and the lifecycle will experience decline. At this stage, companies will remain to compete in the market and consideration will need to be paid to remain competitive or grow.

Market analysis

Understanding market dynamics and the prospects for the participants is the purpose of market analysis. The identification of emerging key success factors, threats, trends and opportunities allows the company to ask questions that can guide the process of information gathering and analysis. A critical factor in understanding a gap in the market, in order for the strategy to be aligned to that gap, is an understanding of how to measure the size of the market, the identification of trends and the ability to predict the way the market is going to develop. This is done by forecasting and is a commonly used method. There are long-, medium- and short-term methods for the purpose of planning.

Forecasting examples

Modern short-term forecasting

Fashion businesses today are able to access immediate information and trends through online means.

Short-term forecast process

Weekly information is required for many organisations. Updated forecasts are made available to the client about hot trends, particularly at the beginning of the season.

Long-term forecasting

An accurate analysis and reporting of longer-term trends are important to some companies rather that the regular speedy updating of trends on a weekly basis. This allows for planning, and the accuracy of information provides deep knowledge about the inner working of the industry, providing time to design new products or implement new strategies.

As mentioned in Chapter 2, the longer-term process for some involves forecasts eighteen months to two years in advance. The analysis of fabrics, trends, colours and so on provides long-term detailed versions of the trend forecasts.

Marketing management theories and frameworks

This section provides a basic outline to some marketing-specific activities a manager will need to consider in ensuring the success of a fashion business.

The fashion marketing environment

The 'marketing environment' is a term that refers to what a company needs to do to maintain good relationships with its customers. This consists of the macro- and microenvironment and factors of influence, including social, economic, political and legal, in addition to demographic and technological influences. The next section concentrates on the nature and purpose of strategy within a marketing context, how it is formulated in an organisation and the variety of activities relevant to maintain a competitive edge.

Strategic planning for the marketing manager

There are many models and methods used to analyse the company positions, products and services offered in order to develop plans and strategies to maintain or gain a competitive advantage. A fashion brand is the same as any other business in this situation and therefore business and management principles used throughout the business world are utilised and adapted for the fashion context. The fashion marketing manager will have a clear idea of the brand's core offer, activities, processes and how to use the appropriate models within their area of expertise to help in determining what they do next.

Strategy: Within a marketing context

Understanding what separates a successful fashion brand from the rest is how the brand's story resonates with their consumers. To build a following, planning the appropriate strategy is a key component to the success of the business.

Strategic planning is used to set priorities, focus resources, reinforce operations and ensure everyone is working towards a shared goal for the intended outcomes. It also allows for changes that would need to happen in order for a company to respond to a changing environment. It is a disciplined effort by the organisation to produce key decisions and actions that shape it, guide what it does and who it serves. The way it does this with a focus on its future. Strategic planning communicates not just where it is going but how it will get there and how it will know when it has been successful. In fashion marketing, this will mean a marketing plan is designed to enable the brand in becoming the market leader in its specific area of the fashion industry. Therefore, the fashion marketing strategy is the detailed planning involved in market research and developing a marketing mix appropriate for the brand.

The starting point for any strategy is the need to take into account the appropriate promotional mix. Every organisation needs to have very clear marketing objectives, and the key way of achieving organisational goals will rely on the strategy selected.

Developing a strategy involves creating clear aims and objectives around which a framework for the project can be established. The company can then organise the day-to-day tools, etc. to meet the objectives. Marketing therefore must be seen as the method of developing and putting into practice a strategy to plan and organising ways to recognise, anticipate and satisfy consumer demands, in such a way as to achieve profits. Therefore, it is the strategic planning process that lies at the centre of marketing. Many aspects will need to be considered as part of the process to achieve the best marketing plan. Following this section, further detail on how this can be achieved is outlined.

Business environment

Macro- and microenvironments can have a significant effect on the success of a fashion marketing campaign, and there are factors that need to be considered in depth during the decision-making process. It is the consideration of these factors that will improve the success of the brand's marketing campaign and reputation in the long term.

Fashion companies need to respond and adapt to changing environments to survive, and they can actually initiate changes in the environments to their own interests. This demands an understanding of the factors and forces that can bring about change in the environment. Ideally, companies need to respond to changes as they occur or even anticipate them way in advance of them happening; failure to do so could put the company in jeopardy and limit long-term survival. However, it is not simply a matter of adapting to change; companies can also exercise their own influence on the environment. Some of the ways this is achievable is to recognise the importance of technological changes in the business environment. Development and commercialisation of new technologies can then become a part of the business environment and in turn impact upon what other organisations do.

For example, new technologies help brand worlds become even more vivid and interactive, bringing more customers into the stores. These include interactive storefronts and photo booths like those in Diesel's Berlin and Barcelona stores, interactive outdoor advertising as used by Mango in Spain, and virtual changing rooms.

Internal and external environment

The environmental factors that are affecting marketing function can be classified as internal environment and external environment. These factors need to be considered, as they may have an effect on the marketing strategy of an organisation and the business environment, particularly the political, economic, social and technological issues also known as PEST.

PEST is described as a business analysis tool that can be used to understand market growth or decline and as such it allows us to look at a business position and potential direction. This and other such models, for examples SWOT analysis, can be used to review a strategy or a particular situation or idea the organisation/brand has to

consider. PEST is quick to use in developing ideas and is often used in team-building exercises for business planning and business reports. It uses the four key perspectives, the factors used are normally external, and therefore it is helpful if this exercise is completed prior to completing a SWOT, as the SWOT is usually made up of half-and-half factors. Matching a brand's products and services with opportunities and threats in the marketplace is the key objective.

A company can exercise considerable control over its internal environment, but a company cannot exert control in the same way or to the same extent over the external environment; it can only try to influence it.

The following case study discusses how the Prada fashion house has effectively positioned both Mui Mui and Prada brands and how through investing significantly in marketing and through an ambitious program of global expansion, the brands have progressed from an exclusively Italian operation into a worldwide one.

3.7
The political, economic, social and technological issues also known as (PEST).

Case study: Prada

Prada is an Italian fashion house founded in 1913 by Mario Prada. The Prada Group (Prada) is a leading player in the design, manufacture and the distribution of luxury goods including leatherwear (including handbags) apparel, footwear, eyewear, accessories and perfumes. The company owns and operates four fashion brands: Prada main line, Mui Mui, Cat shoes and Church's (Men's shoes). The brand sells its products from 345 directly-operated retail outlets, 30 franchise outlets and a number of concessions in high-end department stores such as Saks Fifth Avenue, NY, Harrods (London UK and KaDeWe [Berlin]). The company is now listed on the Hong Kong Stock Exchange under the ticker 1913, and it undertook an initial public offering (IPO) in June 2011.

> On June 24, 2011, Prada Spa (HKSE ticker 1913) listed 20 per cent of its shares on the Hong Kong Stock Exchange, where the company was valued at €9.2 bn.

Since Mario Prada, the founder of the brand, opened his small store in Galleria Vittorio Emanuele II Milan selling leather bags, beauty cases and leather accessories, Prada has become a brand synonymous with elegance and style. In fewer than 100 years, the family-run store transformed from a one-store operation to a global brand and one of the world's leading retailers and producers of haute couture and luxury products. The success of this has been achieved by a number of successful business strategies.

The company has often set the latest trends, and its success can be attributed to its continually evolving fashion lines. Prada has been strong in its product offer and has very successfully expanded its fashion lines to include not only the leather goods the brand was built on but also footwear, fragrances, eyewear and RTW clothing for women and men.

In addition, Prada has embarked on a successful and ambitious program of global expansion, turning it from an exclusively Italian operation into a worldwide one, with stores on three continents, thus providing the brand with a strong foothold in several markets.

The acquisition of existing brands has supplemented the Prada offer with product line expansion. The strength and presence in their own markets provided Prada with integrated products and brands to support the main Prada lines. The company has successfully integrated Church's, a British shoe brand, and Italian shoe manufacturer Car Shoe, and in 2014, Prada acquired the 80 per cent of Angelo Marchesi srl, the owners of a Milanese pastry shop founded in 1824 as part of the Prada Group.

The high-fashion brand Miu Miu, aimed at attracting younger customers, was established for the more avant-garde female clientele. The brand attracts celebrity models and spokespeople, such as Katie Holmes, Ginta Lapina and Lindsey Lohan, as a range of promoters of the brand.

The fashion house has effectively positioned both Mui Mui and Prada brands through investing significantly in marketing. These are much sought-after and prestigious brands that carry Koudos through this careful and creative promotion of their products. The result is that Prada's logo tab is now widely recognised and has come to denote style, sophistication and refinement.

3.8
Prada Group is one of the world's leading players in the design, production and distribution of luxury leather goods (including handbags), footwear, apparel, accessories, eyewear and fragrance.
© FG/Bauer-Griffin via Getty Images

Chapter summary

The chapter has outlined the basics of fashion management and marketing models, including the processes from the textile mills to the sale of fashion products. It has covered the various roles and tasks involved in the chain necessary to deliver the request for garments, meet the needs of potential customers and create a strong and robust strategy for the company or brand.

We have looked at the industry in its broadest term and the myriad of industries and services employing millions of people internationally, making the fashion industry work. Each area has its own place in the industry, and each has a variety of responsibilities and actions that all contribute to a particular part of the industry with the goal of satisfying consumer demand for fashion and making sure that all participants contribute to operating at a profit.

Many of the fashion management activities undertaken involve critical attention to strategies and methods to develop campaigns and manage marketing activities and strategies. Strategic plans are key to the success of a fashion business and play a critical role to achieve the goals set.

We have seen how the macro- and microenvironments can have a significant effect on the success of a fashion marketing campaign and the factors that would be needed during the decision-making process to improve the long-term success of the brand's marketing campaigns and reputation.

Fashion companies, like other companies, need to respond to changing environmental conditions through adaptation and the development of new products and services if they are to survive; if they are clever, they can even initiate changes

in the environment to their own interests. Understanding of the factors and forces that can bring about change in the environment is a critical skill for the manager, in this context.

And one of the most fundamental pieces of information needed is to understand the customer and the customer's needs. Through the analysis of customer behaviour i.e. individuals, groups, or businesses, understanding the processes they use to choose, buy, secure and use the products, experiences and services, allows marketers to make a distinction between the complex decision and understand when a customer might go through a complicated search and evaluation process prior to making a purchase. This helps a company or brand target this customer, develop a product that offers great appeal for that consumer, initiate sales and provide that competitive edge.

Case study and chapter reflection

Q. Describe the Prada operation and its current product offer.

Q. The success of Prada has been achieved by a number of successful business strategies. Explain one of them and say why this is the case.

Q. The acquisition of existing brands has supplemented the Prada offer. What are they and why this has been good for the brand.

Q. The company has effectively positioned both the Mui Mui and Prada brands through investing significantly in marketing. Discuss Prada's marketing methods.

CHECKLIST

1. List the key areas of the fashion industry business activities.

2. What has affected the change in where textiles are made and produced for the global fashion industry?

3. Explain the difference between online and bricks-and-mortar retail.

4. Describe the activities of three different managerial roles in an organisation.

5. Explain value chain analysis (VCA).

6. Outline and explain the four key stages in the industry lifecycle.

7. Forecasting is a commonly used method of analysis. Explain the three different methods.

8. Strategic planning is used to set priorities. Explain why it is important for the company.

9. Explain how a company can bring about change.

10. What is the difference between PEST and SWOT?

EXERCISE

How to brand your business

The idea of creativity in marketing was discussed earlier in the chapter, and the following questions are powerful in raising further questions for so many branding style exercises. Using the right side of your brain and the steps below to create a visual picture to help branding a business.

Step 1

IIllustrate a stick figure (pen portrait) communicating your perfect customer just before they want what you have to sell to them.

Step 2

Think about what problem you will be solving for your customer and illustrate this as a representation.

Step 3

Ask yourself: what is their perceived idea of how you have solved their problem? Add a thought bubble of what your customer will be thinking.

Step 4

What do you think others will say when you have solved the problem? Add a 'choir' of competitors and write what they will be saying.

Step 5

How do you think this problem has been solved? Show yourself as a CONQUEROR and direct them to the resolution.

The advantage of using images, illustrations and thought bubbles to help in the process of brainstorming your branding messages is that it accesses a completely different part of your brain. By simply illustrating your customer's situation, problems and possible solutions, you will think of new ideas and messages that you may not have considered without this method.

Interview:
Simon Johnson

Design manager, Gant AB Stockholm

Q: Where did you study and what was your degree?

A: BA fashion design (Liverpool John Moores) and BA Fashion Technology (Manchester Metropolitan).

Q: What is your specialism? Tell us about your previous experience in the industry.

A: All in menswear and predominantly in the UK. I have worked for large companies, medium-sized companies and small companies. Some were over 100 years old and some only 30 years old. I have worked on all areas of menswear throughout my career and started, like most graduated designers, as an assistant. I have worked primarily in the commercial sector, but some companies have been more progressive than others.

Q: How did you first get into the management side of fashion design?

A: In my experience, this happens as an industry default. I, like most designers who have worked in the industry for a set period of time and have worked their way through the ranks, had a holistic view on the inner workings of fashion industry mechanics. Working as a senior designer for example usually means there may be some management responsibilities in your job role. This is how it worked for me, and for many of my colleagues.

This is, as I see it is 'soft management', as you are responsible to support the design process, but there is little to no emphasis on the development of the designer/s in question. This is usually absorbed by the head of design, who coordinates salary queries, disciplinary actions and promotions.

Q Do you think your degree equipped you to become a manager?

A: No, not really. The first course I studied in Liverpool John Moores focused exclusively on refining and honing creativity. The second course I studied at Manchester Metropolitan was chosen because I wanted to understand the technical side of the industry better. It segmented different disciplines within fashion from costing to illustration and seemed like a better-suited course for my career needs. At Manchester, we touched on illustration, range building, costing, quality control, textiles, knitting, manufacturing, pattern-cutting, pattern-grading, CAD (design and pattern manipulation) and design development.

Q: There has been a huge growth globally in fashion-management-related courses in the last ten to fifteen years. . . could you let us know if you think it is important that the fashion industry is professionalised?

A: Yes, I do. Too many designers fall into management and are ill-equipped to do the job. They either flounder or pick up bad habits.

Q: As the fashion sector has become more sophisticated, and it needs people who can take the business on to the next level, specifically how do you think the internet changed the way fashion design managers operate today?

A: I think it provides them with the opportunity to learn and develop skills, but most of this can be learnt by just being open minded, altruistic and sincere. Listening to a TED talk on YouTube doesn't make you a good manager. It is important to have the grounding and basics that are important for the industry to continue.

Q: It is well documented that that the industry needs better-trained managers. What would you say was the most important thing to think about for a fashion graduates entering the complex world of twenty-first-century fashion?

A: To be adaptable. If you can adapt, then you stand a chance. The industry is full of negative people and negative energy breeds negative energy, so it's a downward spiral for everyone.

Q: Have you any advice for a potential student wanting to enter the fashion industry as a design manager?

A: This is a tough question to answer. My advice would begin with asking a potential student why they want to be a manager? What are their expectations of this job? And what is there drive to do this? The duties of a manager in the current fashion industry are extremely unpredictable and varied. Some companies see the manager as simply an experienced designer, whereas other companies expect a rudimentary understanding of buying and merchandising. Others also expect leadership skills too, and some professional training, but this is dependent on the company. A fashion manager's role is ambiguous and can vary dramatically depending if the company operates in a matrix or hierarchy system. Be clear of your direction and work hard to make your ideas come to fruition.

4

Fashion transition

Taking a fashion product from creation to store is a complex journey, and getting the right fashion products to the right sales channels can be a highly complex process. The path of a product from factory to store involves many people and processes, and arrival at the store marks the end of a garment's journey from concept to runway to factory to sales floor. This single moment is the fruition of months of design, development and production. This chapter discusses the transition of the fashion product, starting with the buyers' role and working backward through the fashion supply chain.

The chapter will help you:

- Understand the role and responsibilities of the buyer and what they do to gain maximum profitability for the company they buy for.
- Learn about the processes and events involved on the buying cycle and what influences the building of a range.
- Discover how a merchandiser operates within the buying team and understand their contribution to the overall buying process.
- Develop an understanding about the different online and offline retail platforms available to today's fashion buying customers.
- Learn about the evolution of the fashion marketplace.
- Understand the way technology and social media are helping companies connect with their customers.

4.1
Viktor & Rolf –
Runway – Paris
Fashion Week –
Fall/Winter 2015/
2016. Fashion
transition involves
all the stages in
the garment
supply chain from
the yarn supplier
through to the
consumer.
© Pascal Le Segretain
via Getty Images

Fashion buying

Buying is one of the most important roles in fashion retail; the buyer is responsible for buying the correct products at the right price and getting them in on time to meet the needs of their customers. Fashion retailing has over recent years enjoyed considerable growth in increasingly affluent global societies; thanks to faster international communication, there is now a global demand for fashion products. The ability of fashion retailers to quickly deliver on-trend looks to the shop floor is imperative.

The buyer's role

The role of the fashion buyer may differ from company to company, but fundamentally fashion buying requires solid financial and analytical skills. Duties will vary, but all fashion buyers are responsible for overseeing the development of a range of fashion products aimed at a specific fashion consumer and price bracket, and it is their responsibility for ensuring the profitability of the range by meeting certain financial plans set for each season. All merchandise must be appropriate for the customer and offered at a reasonable but profitable price. This requires knowledge of the full spectrum of current and forthcoming fashion

trends: high fashion from the runway through to mass-market trends.

As fashion and trends change with increasing speed and irregularity, the fashion buyer must be able to make quick decisions so they can keep and stay ahead of the market. The role does vary between large and small companies, and in the case of the latter, the job may sometimes extend into the creative and technical areas of design and quality control. The role is quite different if you are buying for a high street fashion chain rather than a small independent retailer, as these buyers will mostly buy ranges of branded merchandise without the opportunity or need to become involved with the design or development of the product. In addition, the buyer's role in America can include more administrative responsibilities, including financial input, which in the UK is often done as part of a merchandiser's job (discussed later in the chapter). As it is necessary to get a product from factory to store, a buyer may also file balance statements, purchase orders, price ticket information and marketing materials.

The selection process involves long days of tiring negotiation. The buyer is often expected to work all hours and therefore needs to be versatile, as the buying schedule may include sitting behind a desk one day and writing reports and communicating by conference call, email, phone and Skype the next. They also need to be analytical and computer savvy, as they have to understand and interpret data describing past and present trends in order to forecast the trends for the future.

The role nearly always includes some form of international travel and requires extensive preparation accompanied by busy meeting schedules. However, foreign business travel must not be confused with leisurely sightseeing trips. Attending fashion events and fashion shows while away can be glamorous, but foreign trips are more often

4.2
The buyer's role.
The buyer's role is to develop and buy a range of fashion merchandise that achieves profit margin and is consistent with the retailers' buying strategy.
© Andrew H. Walker via Getty Images

than not fast, furious, uncomfortable and exhausting. The buyer may only get a fleeting glance at a collection from which they have to assess trends and products relevant to their customers. The mass of information needed to be distilled to make it relevant to their market level will be done quickly and under immense pressure. Furthermore, the ever-increasing use of technology in retailing is forcing the buyer and merchandiser to become much more systematic than in the past. Fashion buying and merchandising across all types of fashion retailer has required and continues to require a more sophisticated understanding of information communication technology (ICT). Effective use of ICT within fashion retailing is one of the most important competitive weapons of the future because it can help identify trends more accurately and thereby reduce business risk.

To summarise: The role of the buyer is to develop a range of products appropriate for the retail market to which they are assigned. The buyer needs to liaise regularly with suppliers, home and abroad, in addition to other departments, merchandisers and quality control. While the role may not always mean attendance at the Paris catwalks, fashion buying is a critical role that can offer the opportunity to be at the forefront of delivering exciting, innovative, successful and profitable fashion and style to the marketplace.

If you want to get into fashion buying as a career, consider the following:

- Train on the job and gain work experience; it is the best way to learn about buying. It can be hard work in the initial stages, but it will be worth it. Once you've got the experience to show potential employers that you're serious, you've paved the way to a buying career.
- Forward-thinking and planning is essential. Working on the shop floor in a clothes shop will show that you have hands-on experience; work experience in a buyer's office

shows you've learnt about the business. A degree proves that you have discipline and an aptitude for learning.

- You need to have good ICT and administration skills.
- Be prepared to start at the bottom and work hard; if you do, you might be at the top one day.

The buying cycle

The buying cycle refers to key events and processes with which the fashion buyer is involved in order to buy a garment range for a retail store or mail order company. The fashion industry is traditionally split into two main seasons: spring/summer and autumn/winter (fall/ winter). Today, however, thanks to the competitive nature and constant development of the industry, fashion businesses require a more frequent introduction of merchandise, which results in most stores introducing new **ranges** at least every three months.

The length of the buying cycle varies between companies, however; generally it takes approximately one year between reviewing the current season's sales and delivering next year's range into stores. For example, in August, a buyer from NEXT (UK) will review the current year's spring/summer sales and begin **directional shopping** to inspire concepts for autumn/winter range for a year's time. Although the buying cycle for a whole season's range can take up to year, it is common practice to develop smaller ranges and individual garments more quickly, and most

Range

In fashion retail, a range is a collection of garments that is developed to sell to customers. Ranges may be organised in different ways according to the size and structure of the business.

**4.3
Fashion trade
fair.** Attending
fashion trade fairs
is a crucial stage
in the buying
cycle. Trade
shows offer buyers
the opportunity
to visit regular
suppliers and to
discover new
designers.
© Francis Dean via
Getty Images

buyers keep between 10 per cent and 25 per cent
of the season's budget available (referred to as the
open-to-buy) to respond to trends by purchasing
'hot' items. For those retailers aiming at
a younger, more fashion-conscious customer, the
buying cycle is even shorter, enabling the retailer
to respond to trends much more quickly. The pace
of such (fast fashion products) can sometimes
reduce the quality of the merchandise and the
speed of manufacture may take priority, but being
able to buy a current fashion item at a competitive price is usually more important to the target
customer than its quality. The time taken to make
bulk production orders can vary greatly, but as a
rough estimate, production of fabric can take
about six weeks; the manufacture of a single style
may take around four weeks. This is a simplistic
estimate as there are many other things that need
to be taken into consideration throughout the
process.

The buying process relies on a wide range of
information, which must be researched, analysed
and evaluated to achieve a focused merchandise
plan. The buyer's role at this stage, in addition to
attending the main fashion events in the buying
calendar, is to plan the garment offer for their

customers. The buyer has to constantly review
sales figures (available at least once a week) in
order to access how the range is performing. It is
usually the responsibility of the whole merchandising team to compile a historical report of the
season's figures and the performance of the range
so the best sellers and the poor performers can be
identified. The review (normally a presentation to
the merchandising/buying team and sometimes
the design team) along with garments from the
range to analyse would take place at the beginning of the buying calendar. Information from the
quality control (QC) team may also contribute to
the presentation; however, a separate quality
meeting would normally take place to analyse and
discuss any quality issues in the range.

Once the review has taken place and the buyer is
armed with the knowledge of the styles the customer likes and dislikes, a framework can be built
for the new season and a rough idea of the range
will be identified. Fashion intelligence acquired
from other buyers (e.g. the colour of fabric) can
also be taken into consideration at this stage. For
instance, if the colour of a new garment has performed poorly in another department, the product
can be viewed within the context of current
trends as to whether the product should be
included in the new range or completely dis-
missed. Careful consideration will be paid to a
good seller; however, if its success is considered a
'fad', then it might be discounted as a material
influence on the new range.

Key to the role is the setting of the budget; merchandisers would normally plan the budgets in

Directional shopping

Directional shopping is a term used for trips
to gain inspiration for design concepts for a
new season. Most buyers would visit cities
such as Paris, New York, London and Milan
depending on the company's travel budget.

> **Fad**
>
> A look that becomes popular is widely accepted, and then rapidly disappears. Fads often appear in the accessory market: for instance, oversized plastic watches followed the fad of extremely embellished ones.

conjunction with the buyer. This is based largely on the previous season's performance, but the buyer would have more information and knowledge about the products and the trends than the financial department or the merchandisers, and as such would need to utilise their expertise to influence the budget.

Well before the design concepts have been developed, it is possible to have an idea of the total value of a range through the defining of the number of styles and the quantities. It is the responsibility of the merchandise department to define the number of styles and the retail selling prices. The finance department will sometimes have some involvement in the financial planning of the range, although it is ultimately the responsibility of the buyer to decide what the range should include and what the retail selling prices should be.

Example: Ted Baker buying cycle

Ted Baker's fashion collections are developed to satisfy and meet the requirements of the predicted target customer. The predictions are based on past sales, input from designers, merchandisers and buyers. Fashion trends and other fashion-related industry trends such as music and entertainment influence the collections at Ted Baker, with the majority of the elements that determine the concept combined for the new season's collections. In addition to garment shapes, Ted Baker also develops its own textile materials and colours that have an effect on the development of the trims and other details that are added later to coordinate and complement the total look and design of the ranges. Then the final garments are put into groups that form the product lines that meet the production costs and delivery timescales. The time it takes to produce the bulk orders of garments can vary, but Ted Baker's rough estimate reveals that the production of fabric takes about six weeks. The manufacture of a single garment style would take around a further four weeks. Each style has to be planned in advance into the production schedule for the factory making the products. Furthermore, the integrated system used by Ted Baker across the business controls and aids the distribution of the stock to manage sales channels.

Fast fashion buying cycle

In recent years, the fashion cycle has steadily decreased as fast fashion retailers sell clothing that is expected to be disposed of after being worn only a few times which dramatically shortens the consumers' buying cycle. This quick changing of stock and the low price of fashion goods encourage consumers to visit the store and make purchases more frequently.

Slow fashion buying cycle

We have also started to see more on the slow fashion movement. 'Slow Fashion' is about designing, creating and buying garments for quality and longevity and encourages slower production schedules. By adding transparency in production processes, it is hoped that this will resonate with the consumers and begin to have an effect on the slowdown of some areas of the fashion industry, including the buying cycle.

Range planning and the selection process

All fashion ranges are made up of a multitude of styles, some may be part of a coordinated range of garments that work together and are sold as such, while the majority of fashion styles are sold as individual pieces. Range planning involves compiling a commercially acceptable collection of products within financial and design parameters prior to production and delivery. The initial plan will usually take the form of a list of appropriate products/garments to be purchased for the season to a set budget. Most stores will label their products as 'classic', 'core' or 'contemporary', and the buyer will research a number of things prior to the purchase as part of the range-planning process, including the following:

- Historical sales figures
- Fashion forecasting
- Directional shopping
- **Comparative shopping**

Fashion style trend reviews begin many months in advance of the season, but overall planning of the merchandise process is generally started between six months and twelve months ahead depending on the focus of the company and its target customer. For example, the more fashion-led the product, the shorter the planning process. A company specialising in a more classic-styled product normally has a planning cycle of around twelve months.

The process involves defining the detail of each range offer from fabric, details and styling through to manufacture. Price, however, will vary according to the type and size of company. For example, in companies that manufacture

original designs with in-house design teams, the process will involve sampling and developing the designs, but in a mainstream buying department, it will involve a working document that is presented at different stages of the process including pre-selection and final range selection meetings, which then becomes a definitive list of products offered to the customer for the season.

Fabric sourcing for the range comes under the remit of either the designer and/or the fabric technologist. It is, however, the responsibility of the buyer to make the fabric selection for the garments. Many buyers will, as part of the 'directional' or 'comp shopping' trips, make a visit to Premier Vision (a Paris Fabric fair that takes place twice a year) to gain an overview for the season in question. In a company where most of the garments will be purchased from garment manufacturers, the designers working for them will undertake the selection and sourcing of the fabrics.

When buying the range, the buyer will need to plan the following, some of which will involve guidance from the merchandise department:

- Number of products in the range
- Proportion of different types of garments/products (i.e. how many tops to bottoms)
- Specific styles to be included
- Cost prices
- Selling process
- Size to be offered across the rage
- Manufacturer
- Order quantity

Other considerations that need to be taken into account are:

- Seasons and phases
- Sales history
- Options and colourways
- Sizing and retail prices

Comparative shopping

Often referred to as 'comp shopping': this is part of the range planning process at the start of a season by the buying and design teams. Visits to competitor's stores to look at things such as fabrics, prices, styles, etc. This is compiled as a report and distributed throughout the team.

When the buyers have completed the planning stage, a pre-selection meeting takes place where presentation of the samples and proto-types for the range will be presented to the buy-ing team, merchandise and quality-control team. Departmental managers attend this pre-selection meeting to offer a critique on the range; new samples may be requested and the range plans rewritten to include any changes. At this point, critical discussion will take place including the overall strategy for the season; the supplier base may also be discussed at this stage. The meetings provide the opportunity for further evaluation of the range, and it is impor-tant to note that numerous amendments are very likely to be made to a range at

pre-selection as this is the first opportunity the whole team will have had to see it. The final range selection meeting is the chance to pres-ent the range in its entirety, with perfect sam-ples for each style.

In summary, range planning involves specifying the details and fundamentals of a range of fashion products for a particular season. The key details required are:

- Style, fabric and colourways
- Cost price and selling prices
- Manufacturers and suppliers
- Sizes
- Quantities to be bought

4.4
Fashion trade fair. Attending fashion trade fairs is a crucial stage in the buying cycle. Trade shows offer buyers the opportunity to visit regular suppliers and to discover new designers.
© Christian Marquardt via Getty Images

Fashion merchandising

Fashion merchandising can be described as the business side of the fashion world and involves finance, visual merchandising, data analysis, trend forecasting, marketing strategies, advertising principles, publicity, product development, buying and retail management. This part of the chapter provides an introduction to merchandising operations within a fashion retail business. It outlines the day-to-day activities of the merchandiser in fashion retail organisations and provides an insight into how closely buying and merchandising work together to ensure business success.

The merchandiser's role

The merchandiser plays a key role in working with the buyer to achieve the correct balance of the products within the season's range. As discussed in the section on range planning, the merchandiser will work with the buyer to establish the number of pieces in the range – the proportion of different types of garments/products, specific styles to be included and so on.

Fashion merchandise buyers (merchandisers) will interact with wholesalers and clothing manufacturers to purchase lines of clothing, shoes and fashion accessories to be featured and sold at retail stores. A fashion merchandising role is a demanding task that involves visiting clothing, shoe and accessory manufacturers; attending trade shows; making decisions on purchasing items for sale in retail stores; and determining prices and developing advertising and marketing to ensure that the clothing and accessories sell each and every season. It may also involve monitoring consumer trends, choosing store inventory, designating costs and ensuring that the store has the latest fashion styles in stock. Fashion merchandising requires research to stay abreast of consumer trends, which involves interviews, surveys and other types of studies, often performed by retailers, fashion marketers or market research firms.

A list of merchandising operations

- Customer profiling
- Creating range plans
- Mood boards
- Identifying trends
- Trend forecasting
- Supply chain
- Critical path
- Seasonal calendars
- Margin and mark-up
- Practical buying and merchandising exercises

The merchandiser's responsibilities are similar to those of the buyer; the merchandising team is responsible for maximising the profitability of the department and must buy products that will work with those of other buying teams, so that colours, fabrics, styling and silhouettes will work together on the shop floor. The merchandiser's role will vary according to the size of the company and its merchandising structure. The role of the merchandiser is normally integrated into the buying of a particular product type, such as jackets or coats, and each area will have a team responsible for both range planning and stock allocation.

Merchandise management is usually divided into two main areas: stock planning (to be delivered to the business) and moving delivered stock around the business, such as allocating to stores. Stock planning involves the analysis of sales patterns and trends in buying, following which the merchandiser will recommend quantities of fabric needed to fulfil orders going forward. The quantities of garments are calculated for the range, based on the research, and figures will be put forward to the buying managers. Moving stock involves monitoring and managing the delivery of new stock into the distribution centre, ensuring that overall stock levels and buying are in line with the company sales plan.

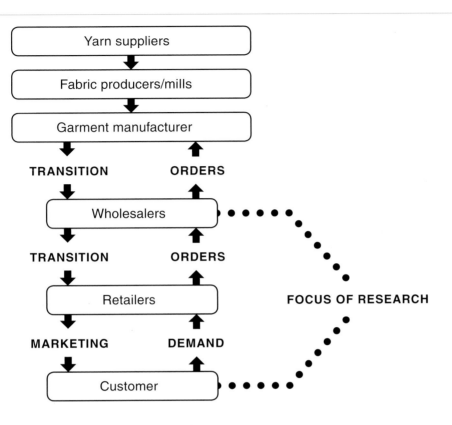

4.5
Merchandising structure.
Merchandisers are involved in supply chain management, as illustrated in this diagram of a generic merchandising structure.

Fashion merchandising as a career

Fashion merchandisers use their expertise within the field to integrate the needs of consumers and designers. Since fashion merchandisers have to make sure that the fashions appeal to diverse consumers, they're often required to attend fashion shows and communicate with various manufacturers, retailers and suppliers to predict future trends. Because of the need to stay current with trends and offer competitive pricing, the work is generally quick-paced and requires energy and tenacity. Many fashion merchandise buyers travel internationally on a regular basis to foreign manufacturing sites and fashion shows.

The above may sound attractive and glamorous, however, merchandise planning is a demanding task; it requires logic and intuition to ensure that the business carries the right product range at any point in time. It is critical that the merchandiser has highly-developed analytical, estimating and forecasting skills to identify the macro and the micro trends as they occur in the trading year. It is not about purely spotting trends, the merchandiser must also be able to react and make recommendations for change, which will need to be accurately and clearly implemented and acted upon.

A merchandiser may work for a fashion buyer, distributor, manufacturer or retailer, and they need to be business savvy and understand what goes into the advertising, distribution, marketing, manufacturing and preparation of products. But like fashion design, fashion merchandising is a highly competitive field and requires a degree in one of the following: fashion merchandising, business administration and marketing which are usually necessary to work in the field. Master's degrees in business are becoming increasingly important for those going for upper-level purchasing manager positions in large companies.

Global sourcing and the supply chain

The impact of global trade in the apparel and fashion industry has generated the concept of 'fast fashion' which is apparel produced very quickly and at a low cost. This 'cheap chic' look now dominates the fashion retail world, and as mass-produced fashion products and accessories are available at low prices for most consumers, it makes it easy to obtain fashion pieces and simple for anyone to look relatively stylish. Global sourcing is the main contributing factor in the changes to the fashion industry over the last few decades, for instance, the practice of **sourcing** products from the global market for goods and services across geopolitical boundaries. However, global apparel supply chains require collaboration from many sectors, including customers, retail firms, manufacturing firms and factories.

> ### Sourcing
>
> Sourcing is the buying of components of a product from an outside supplier, often one located abroad.

The iconic fashion designer for Gucci, Tom Ford, proposed the idea that fast fashion created democratic fashion with the idea was that fashion was no longer dictated by the elite, but was more accessible to the masses and became more affordable. Both Zara and H&M pioneered the concept in the 1990s with both brands opening stores in major cities around the world. At the first store opening of H&M in the US, customers were waiting around the block to get fashion styles that were cutting-edge and affordable. Fast fashion means that the traditional fashion cycle was reduced from the traditional six months from design to store availability to a cycle that could be less than four weeks. In addition, the traditional seasonal restocking of fashion pieces has changed to stores restocking with new items almost continually, increasing the motivation for customers to buy the product before it is gone for good.

Supply chain management and global sourcing

Many factors have made the supply chain and sourcing strategies for companies the focus of detailed creation. With rapid demand from customers for new products and services and with the availability of advanced planning, globalisation of the economy, improved communication tools for coordinating the industry will see the outsourcing and off shoring of services such as human resources, ICT, accounting and even research, which is predicted to grow massively in the next ten years.

Importing fashion goods

Fashion companies are producing more and more garments overseas, particularly those who design and source for major fashion chains. There are relatively few places on earth that are more than twelve to fourteen hours' flying time away. With international business travel becoming increasingly cheaper, fashion buyers and suppliers can work easily and conveniently in any country. This, in addition to increasing speed and ease of communication, enables an international fashion business to work effectively anywhere.

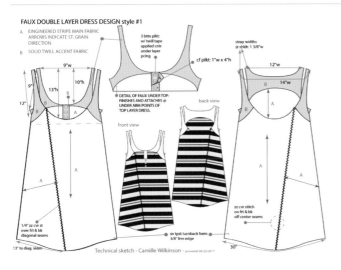

FAUX DOUBLE LAYER DRESS DESIGN style #1

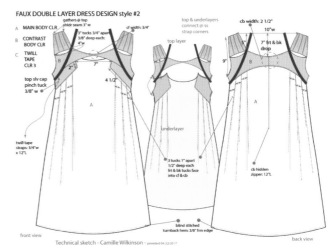

FAUX DOUBLE LAYER DRESS DESIGN style #2

4.6
Camille Wilkinson. In range development, designs are communicated through line drawings and technical specification sheets.

© Camille Wilkinson

Importing fashion products is more common now than ever before. The global market is expanding rapidly and many buyers purchase products from an importer, essentially the 'middle man', or directly from the supplier.

Role of the importer

Importers play an important role in the fashion industry. Long-distance sourcing requires a different set of skills from those of the buyer or designer; although some of the skills do overlap, particularly when it comes to conveying detailed technical requirements remotely.

Most companies have a variety of sourcing methods and will work with lots of suppliers. The most straightforward method of buying is the selection of garments from showrooms or trade fairs. Increasingly, however, more fashion businesses, particularly the larger companies, will buy direct from a manufacturer based overseas, such as in the Far East, or work with fashion importers. This is the main opportunity for the buyer to travel.

Sourcing trips involve spending time working with business associates and factory owners in order to build ranges for the following season. The trips are planned far enough in advance for the garments to be sampled, developed and finalised before the ranges are supplied to the stores.

Range development

Range development involves working with an importing agent or manufacturer to build the sample range. It includes making colour or fabric changes, all of which will be communicated by the designer through line drawings and technical specification sheets. The buyer will normally liaise with a sales representative of the manufacturer, although in many cases they will liaise directly with the designer and the garment technologist. Further development will involve the buyer detailing things such as proportion, fit or trim. This method is most used by mass-market retailers, making the development of the range a joint effort between the buyer and the manufacturer's design department.

Sample development

A key factor in achieving agreed delivery dates is a smooth sample development process, which begins by supplying the manufacturer with a specification sheet: a precise detailed drawing of the garment (also known as a spec sheet or line sheet). Samples are produced at different stages in the buying process; these require approval from the relevant buying departments at every stage before production can proceed. Working in this way enables the retailer to have tight control over the co-ordination of the range. Many retailers have in-house design teams and will provide the manufacturer with a fully detailed spec sheet including a working drawing (a precise technical drawing of a garment), fabric information and trim detail. The manufacturer will then make the garment pattern and sample. A length of fabric will often be provided by the retailer to make the sample garment, which will then be passed to the manufacturer who will focus solely on garment production. This process is known as **cut, make and trim**.

The first sample is usually made to the designer's specifications by a sample machinist; the designer must be aware of any production issues, such as the type of sewing machine in the factories, in order to design garments suitable for mass production. Designers are involved throughout the product development stage of the range and are often consulted during production; for example, to check if the bulk fabric and trims are correct. When the designer and the buyer have agreed the final designs, the buying team will make an official request for samples of all the products to be ordered. Samples can range from prototypes to photo samples, which are production garments sent to the press or used for marketing.

Retail

One of the key determinants of a retailer's success is its retail environment, the format it uses to present to its target customers. A retailer must choose a format based on the kind of store design they want to render, the locality they would like to establish, the various products and services they wish to provide and their pricing approach. The most important aspect of retail format is that it is tailored to the target demographic. The following table provides an overview of the key sectors within fashion retail.

The evolution of fashion retail

Fashion shopping has always been associated with the idea that customers visit shops or stores, make a selection and take the selected garment away with them. The advent of online shopping has changed the way the consumer purchases a garment; new digital technologies are challenging the concept of selling fashion and conventional retail shops are now under increasing pressure.

Prior to World War II, most people had few clothes, which were hand-made, either at home or by local seamstresses or tailors. The concept of factory-produced clothing only developed after the war, with increasing demand for less formal clothing and a cultural and fundamental shift towards casual wear. With this shift came the need for different ways to sell the new fashion products to the consumer.

> **Cut, make and trim**
>
> Cut, make and trim, or CMT, involves a manufacturer who cuts the fabric, makes and trims the garment using fabric bought, then checked and delivered by the retailer.

Key sectors within fashion retail

Type of outlet	Description
Independent boutique	These are normally privately owned and predominantly branded stores in exclusive locations. This may be a designer's own store, such as Prada or Versace, or independently owned, such as Colette in Paris.
Medium multiple independents	These stores are small- to medium-sized, with 10–20 outlets, offering privately owned brands and known brands. They generally offer more exclusive and upmarket fashion products. Whistles is one example.
Large national multiples	Public-owned high street giants, usually with anything from 50 to 500 outlets. Examples include Topshop, Gap and Forever 21.
Franchise shops	Franchises are owned by a parent company that allows private investors to set up a shop or group of shops. There have to be strong brand controls to ensure the shops are all alike. Benetton and French Connection are both franchises. Franchising is a quick way for a retailer to expand its shop chain.
National department	These are large-scale, public-owned fashion stores with multi-floor store layouts, such as Harvey Nichols and Selfridges in the UK; Galeries Lafayette and Printemps in France; and Neiman Marcus and Barneys in the USA.
Concessions	A brand or retailer will rent space to open a small specialist department within a larger store, normally based on a rental or commission basis. These concessions are often let within department stores to increase the range interest. It is also a cheaper way for brands to gain high street presence.

Things have changed since the high street fashion revolution of the 1960s and the growth of large fashion chains such as the Arcadia Group (the UK company that owns Topshop and Miss Selfridge, amongst others). Companies such as this are responsible, in part, for the decline of many smaller, independent clothing shops.

During the early part of the twentieth century, the department store was the main supplier of fashion to the wealthier classes. These retail outlets relied heavily on manufactured brands, and over time the stores predominantly catered for a slightly older clientele because there was very little demand for what is now termed as 'young fashion'. Thanks to the popularity of the high street, which catered to a younger consumer, many department stores throughout the 1960s and 1970s closed. Today, the ones that have survived have been developed into modern retail environments, introducing designer brands and collaborations to appeal to younger, more fashion-conscious customers.

4.7
Selfridges.
Selfridges is a UK department store with a multi-product and brand offering, from high street concessions through to high fashion labels.
© View Pictures via Getty Images

High street multiples

High street multiples, also known as fashion chain stores, are retailers with more than twenty stores. This sector has grown over the last fifteen to twenty years, as smaller store groups have merged into larger ones. In the UK, the high street multiple dominates the fashion retail sector and offers the largest proportion of fashion buying jobs. These companies with centralised management enjoy considerable **economies of scale**, but this also means they run the risk of becoming homogenised in terms of the product offer. Similarities from store to store can be seen across the high streets of the UK. Fashion multiples tend to be less predominant across Europe and the US, where there is more emphasis on independent fashion retailers selling branded merchandise.

Independent fashion retailers

Independent retailers or boutiques are not attached to major chains. This sector is currently experiencing competitive pressure from major fashion multiples and is the least likely group of retailers to utilise the internet to sell their goods. However, these independent fashion retailers offer the consumer an individual approach; they are able to deliver their product focus quickly and are very agile in buying terms.

An extension of the independent boutique is the pop-up shop, an initiative that appears unannounced, quickly draws in the crowds and then disappears or morphs into something else. Increasingly popular around the world, they add to retail the fresh feel, exclusivity and surprise that galleries and theatres have been demonstrating for years.

Online fashion retailers

Online selling is rapidly becoming a mainstream distribution channel for many product types, and fashion is no exception. It not only provides an excellent means for a fashion retailer to display their most up-to-date lines, but it has also enabled them to sell direct to their customers. Online fashion retailers generally fall into one of four categories: virtual e-tailers, such as ASOS and Net-a-porter; bricks-and-mortar retailers and catalogue companies that have expanded their operations to include online retailing; and multi-channel retailers who sell products in stores, through catalogues and online. By taking the notion of online retailing one step further and offering international delivery, the opportunities for global growth are huge.

Economies of scale

Reduced costs by increasing the number of items produced and sold.

4.8
Online fashion
retail. www.
eboutique
.maisonmartin
margiela.com;
http://'www
.vestiairecollective
.com/; www.henrik
vibskovboutique
.com.

Top: Courtesy of
Henrik Vibskov;
Bottom left: Courtesy
of Vestiairecollective
.com; Bottom right:
Courtesy of Maison
Margiela webpage

'We are the two things that are faring better at the moment: the Internet and younger fashion. We tick both the boxes.'

Nick Robertson, ASOS

The retail calendar

The retail calendar primarily relies on the sequence of events from concept to distribution; from yarn selection to the finished garments in store. Each product has to be researched, designed, sampled and shown to the potential customer, who may be a textile manufacturer, a garment designer, a retailer and, ultimately, the fashion consumer. Here we look at the fashion calendar, which covers trade fairs, timing and sample development.

Trade fairs

International trade fairs are an essential part of the retail calendar. Yarn fair Pitti Filati takes place in February and July in Italy; textiles fairs Première Vision and Moda-In take place in February and September. The designer collections are shown in the four main fashion capitals of New York, London, Milan and Paris, which take place consecutively in February/March for the following fall/winter season and in September/October for the following spring/summer. Buyers are invited to view the collections and appointments are made to visit fashion houses after the shows to order from the collection ready for the new season.

Timing

The calendar depends on the intervals of time in between each stage of the fashion/textile design process before the garments can be manufactured. This process involves the development, implementation, sale and distribution of the fashion products. Samples shown at yarn, textile and fashion fairs are exactly that: they are prototypes and, as such, still have to go into mass production. No retailer can afford to produce items **on spec** and all production is matched to orders. At trade fairs, orders are taken against samples; there is a significant time lag between placing an order at a trade fair and receiving the prototype, which is why the ready-to-wear designer trade shows are held well in advance to enable the retail buyer to place their orders for selling in the stores the following season.

On spec

On spec means 'on speculation'; the term is used to describe work that is done without a contract or job order.

4.9
Trade fairs.
Retailers and designers will place orders for yarn and fabric samples at trade fairs, such as Première Vision and Pitti Filati.
© AKAstudio-collective/Courtesy of Pitti Immagine

The two-year cycle

As with many manufacturing processes, the fashion industry cycle is a long one. The cycle begins with yarn development and fabric research. The yarns are developed and manufactured into fabric, which become fabric samples and will be presented to the fashion designers or garment manufacturers to make their fabric choices for the next season's collections. The designers will then show their prototype collections to the buyers, who will select the items they present to the public in the following season. Each process takes around six months, and the entire cycle from the spinner to the wearer is usually in excess of two years.

It is important to note that the couture cycle is shorter than for ready-to-wear and mass production because couture clothes are shown direct to the customer. In addition, some mass-production retailers, such as Zara and H&M, own their own retail outlets, which also contributes to a shorter cycle.

Fabric sourcing

International fairs are the main vehicles for yarn producers to show their products to the fabric manufacturers. Fabric collections can be huge; therefore, fabric is only offered in full lengths. The actual fabric does not go into production until every fabric style has received enough orders to make its manufacture viable, and many fabric samples never go into production. The selection stage in each part of the industry, from yarn to fabric to garment, is vital to the success of the fashion industry. Without enough projected orders, the yarn producers, cloth manufacturers and garment wholesalers would not be able to continue in business.

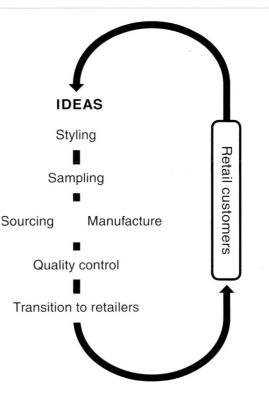

IDEAS

Styling

Sampling

Sourcing   Manufacture

Quality control

Transition to retailers

Retail customers

4.10
Sourcing process. The sourcing process is an ongoing cycle that traditionally takes two years. Fast fashion retailers follow a much shorter cycle, although the stages remain the same.

'We're going to have to become far more efficient in the ways we run our businesses in order to remain profitable. Those efficiencies are not going to come at the point of the sewing needle any longer. They're going to come through innovative business practices.'

Bob McKee

Distribution channels

The place element of the fashion marketing mix refers to where fashion products are made available to fashion consumers. This is also called distribution. Distribution channels are the means by which businesses get their products to their customers. Distribution usually involves intermediaries, such as retailers. There may be a series of links in a chain of distribution as products are sold between different businesses on route to the final consumer. There are three main types of distribution channel:

- Direct to the consumer
- To the retailer
- To the consumer via wholesalers and retailers

Fashion distribution refers to the wholesale global market of bulk clothing sales. This is where producers, wholesalers and sellers are all involved in a commercial, business-to-business process. There are a number of methods in the distribution of fashion products, and over the past decade, much has remained the same; however, significant changes have also been made due to the internet and the technological changes and their part played in the development and opening up of the global marketplace.

The evolution of traditional channels of distribution

Though ready-to-wear apparel has been available for a long time, the ability to walk into a store, pluck a garment off a rack or order it online is a relatively new concept. In the not too distant past, a garment would last for a very long time, therefore not requiring constant updating. The creation, production and distribution of clothing is the largest manufacturing business in the world and as such it is important for anyone thinking of entering this industry to appreciate the changes taking place and the magnitude of these changes in order to understand the dynamics involved and

be aware of how retail channels operate now and how they may well develop in the future.

Traditional channels of fashion retail distribution

The last decade witnessed enormous change to the old and traditional methods of reaching the market: taking clothes from the manufacturer to the consumer. The list below reflects the main forms of distribution (getting the clothing to the consumer) over the period 1700 to 2000:

1. **Pre-Industrial Revolution person-to-person trade.** In the eighteenth century, if you wanted to acquire clothes for yourself or as a gift, you would have to go to a skilled artisan and negotiate a price for him or her to make the garment for you. The transaction was person-to-person, the garments were unique to you and the trade was a bespoke. The richer you were, the more flamboyant you could be in the styling of your clothing, which was immediately recognised as a mark of your identity, personality and wealth.

2. **The early clothing markets.** In some areas, such as Petticoat Lane in London, traders would sell clothes and other items, usually cheap and second-hand. Things escalated up a level later in the seventeenth

Petticoat Lane

Don't expect to find Petticoat Lane market on Petticoat Lane, as the street name no longer exists. It was changed in the 1800s to Middlesex Street. It is said that this change was made to spare the blushes of Victorians who didn't like to have a street name that referred to underwear.

century and the area got a lot busier when clothing markets became an attraction for groups of people, often immigrants, to create what in today's terminology would be termed a cluster of skills and experience.

3. **Fashion retail shops, pre-organised distribution.** Around the same period as the Huguenot weavers were turning Petticoat Lane and Spitalfields into an apparel manufacturing and trading centre, clothing retail shops started to appear.

4. **Fashion retail shops, post-organised distribution.** In the late nineteenth century, the department store introduced the idea of consolidating large amounts of mass-produced goods for public consumption. Huge, beautifully constructed buildings offered restaurants and tearooms as well as consumer goods. These prestigious retailers started to sell 'off-the-peg' standard-sized garments in numbers as well as made to measure.

5. **Mail order catalogues.** During the Victorian period, acceptable formal dress for middle-class women included long dresses, corsets, petticoats and heeled shoes; dressing well and following fashion meant a great deal to many women. Mail order soon became big and helped to promote fashionable dress during the late nineteenth and twentieth centuries.

The above provides a brief outline of the main forms of distribution, which, until 2000, only changed slowly and under controlled conditions. In the next section, we look at how shopping on the internet has changed to way consumers buy fashion products online.

Distribution channel evolution post 2000

How it started

Online shopping predates the internet and started without the benefits of computers. The first online-shopping system, developed in the late 1970s, was probably just as fast as the first online systems, which were restricted by the speed of the dial-up modems widely used in the 1990s. It wasn't until 1990 that Tim Berners-Lee created the first world wide web server and browser, which opened for commercial use in 1991. It wasn't until 1995 that Amazon appeared online and followed by eBay in 1996.

Huguenot weavers

Huguenot weavers, stigmatised by oppressive laws, moved into Spitalfields to escape persecution in France. In 1681, Charles II of England offered sanctuary to the Huguenots, and from 1670 to 1710 between 40,000 and 50,000 Huguenots from all walks of life sought refuge in England. They tapped into the area's reputation for manufacturing and selling clothes and woven goods, and the market started to take the shape it still has to this day. Future generations of Jewish and East Asian immigrants have also made their mark on the market.

In 1979, Michael Aldrich, an English entrepreneur, pioneered online shopping through the development of a system invented by using a modified television via a telephone line to a processing computer.

The dot-com bubble

In the late 1990s, internet retailing grew exponentially with fashion retail companies expanding into the online sector of retailing. Companies like Boo .com, an online fashion retailer, spent $188 million in a very short time in their attempt to create a global online fashion store. The value of the companies on the stock market created inflated share prices and failed to make a profit, causing what is known as 'the dot-com bubble'. It was the enthusiasm for this new way of selling online that opened up new possibilities for fashion retailers including luxury fashion brands. In the aftermath of the dot-com crash, many retailers were reluctant to use the internet as a selling channel until more recently. LVMH (Louis Vuitton-Moët Hennessy), however, did make a foray into online retailing and set up its own web-shop. eLuxury (eluxury.com) sold products from LVMH with is core brands being offered for sale on the site (e.g. brands names like Louis Vuitton, Dior and Donna Karan were offered online). It started off in the US market and then spread to France and the UK. Other luxury brands such as Gucci and Armani started to invest in e-commerce. Even though the success of these web-shops is apparent, there is still an on-going debate about whether or not luxury brands should undertake the e-commerce route to sales. The major concern is the watering down of the exclusivity and prestige of the brands. In 2010, the eluxury.com site was closed and replaced by Nowness.com, which does not sell anything. Instead the new site at http://www.nowness.com is a media starting point that emphasises LVMH's expertise in all things luxury.

Dot-com bubble

The dot-com bubble was a historic speculative stock market bubble covering roughly 1997–2000.

Boo.com

The online fashion retailer Boo.com, after a number of highly publicised delays, launched online in 1999. The company sold branded fashion products on the internet. The company went into liquidation in 2000 after spending over $135 million of borrowed money that they were never going to make back in the eighteen months they operated.

New retail approaches and channels to market

Multichannel

We have seen a second phase of e-commerce after the collapse of the dot-com bubble in the early 2000s, with multichannel retailing growing and developing within every retail product category, including fashion apparel. Multichannel retailing is a strategy used in marketing to offer customers a wider choice and ways of purchasing products from a website or store, via telephone, mail order, catalogue or comparison-shopping site. It is the aim of the strategy to offer a multichannel retail option to the customer in order to maximise the income (revenue) and create customer loyalty through consistency of choice and convenience. With the customer's perception of the brand influenced by the experience of buying the fashion product, the successful multichannel strategy must offer the customer a consistent, quality experience. Fashion brands need to ensure a complete and consistent customer facing experience with all staff in the company including all retail outlets, the processing of the orders, website developers and customers services. All need to understand and comply with the company's customer services standards set. In addition, policies such as returns and delivery charges will also need to be consistent across the individual channels.

John Lewis's (UK) definition of omnichannel is a progressive one; it offers its customers flexibility such as returning anything anywhere.

Omnichannel

Omnichannel retailing is a multichannel approach to shopping online, whether customers buy from their mobile phones, use a desktop computer or make the traditional bricks-and-mortar store purchase. The concept of omnichannel retailing is about offering the customer the opportunity to interact with the brand/company in whatever way they want to at whatever stage of the buying process, from when they placed the order, to changing it at any stage along the way. According to data collected in the US by google.com in 2015, for many holiday season purchases, the online mobile shopping clicks exceeded those from desktop computers, identifying that for customers making their buying decisions 'on the go', the mobile device is key. Evidence also suggests that customers are no longer discriminating among their mobile devices when it comes to buying online. One of the key things about omnichannel retailing is that it also gets people into the store; then once at the doorway the buying doesn't stop. A large percentage of shoppers use their smartphones for researching their products and also use it as part of the shopping experience. They say it is an important part of their purchasing decision-making process, and it extends to being used in many cases as a personal shopping assistant once inside.

Multichannel retailers today are having to change the way they operate given the way digital continues to touch every part of the customer journey. Companies are looking at the way they think about omnichannel shoppers, for example, understanding what their shopping behaviours mean to their overall business. The retailers are realising the most valuable customers are those who buy from them online or in store and by understanding this; the more sophisticated retailers are ensuring their marketing strategies are geared up for this type of customer allowing them to convert to any channel. According to a study by IDC, multichannel shoppers have a 30 per cent higher lifetime shopper value than customers that only use one channel to purchase fashion products. Reaping the benefits is at the centre of omnichannel shopping; once the retailers know what attracts the shopper and how they can connect to such valuable consumers, they can structure their company to make the most of these insights. However, that is easier said than done.

Social media

Social media is a necessity in today's retail environment and can be used as a shopping platform in itself. Some of the most forward-thinking retailers are aligning their strategies to it and developing a space to nurture brand loyalty and fine-tune customer service. It is one of the most popular ways young people use their time, and many brands are using this as a way of targeting these customers as part of their retail strategy. At the time of writing, Instagram seems to be the platform of choice and is one of the most popular methods of communication through social media. Figures by digital marketing agency Greenlight show in the month leading up to London Fashion Week 2016, there were 5,602 posts on Instagram using #LFW2016. Data on Twitter showed that tweets with #LFW2016 were posted 1,178 times over the same timeframe, which was a huge decline on the previous year, when Twitter saw over 6,000 tweets mentioning #LFW2015.

Boohoo.com

In the 2016 High Street Fashion Awards: Boohoo.com won the best online retailer.

It seems to be particularly young brands that have adopted the use of social media, like Instagram, into their social strategy, and as a small fashion brand, this is a way of marketing at a lower cost, you can see other small business marketing methods used in Chapter 7 . Many of the high-end brands have embraced this with enthusiasm; Burberry, for example, has over six million followers on instagram and has used Brooklyn Beckham (David Beckham's son) as a photographer as he posts images on his instagram site live on the platform.

Driving sales through social media

To better understand how social media is impacting the e-commerce industry, Shopify analysed data from 37 million social media visits that led to 529,000 orders.

Here are some interesting data points they uncovered:

- Facebook dominates as a source of social traffic and sales. Nearly two-thirds of all social media visits to Shopify stores come from Facebook. Plus, an average of 85 per cent of all orders from social media come from Facebook.
- Orders from Reddit increased 152 per cent in 2013.

- Perhaps most interesting and surprising was community style site Polyvore, which is generating the highest average order value ahead of Facebook, Pinterest and Twitter. Also noteworthy in this category is Instagram, which is also generating higher average orders than those same sites. This is especially impressive considering the only clickable links in Instagram are those in profile biographies.
- Facebook has the highest conversion rate for all social media e-commerce traffic at 1.85 per cent.

Case study: Topshop app

Topshop is a UK fashion store and a leading name in high street fashion. The company specialises in fashion, shoes, make-up and accessories, has more than 440 shops in 37 countries and is controlled by Philip Green as part of the Arcadia group. This forward-thinking store recognised the potential in mobile channels and now has a significant amount of its revenue coming from sales online through the use of mobile devices.

The brand operates more like a luxury brand than a high street retailer, offering the opportunity to engage and interact with the store through the use of mobile apps. By inspiring their customers to interact, share and engage with them through their devices, Topshop connects with its customers. On their homepage, they have a section entitled

'Topshop on the go' which lures the shopper in to find out more with just one click!

Topshop worked closely with the company Red Ant, a technology company for retailers, to create a fully transactional multichannelled iPhone app, bringing together the full range of Topshop products. The app was created to make Topshop's complete product range easy to access on mobile, to mobile-savvy customers. In its first four weeks on the market, the app generated over 280,000 downloads and offered seamless product sharing, which generated customer interest and delivered a fully transactional shopping experience in addition to offering weekly updates. It published to draw attention to its 300+ new pieces driving impulse purchases.

Through a close working relationship, Red Ant and Topshop were able to develop the new channel for sale and engagement, with opportunities for significant mid- to long-term growth in addition to a very slick and market-leading interface and feature set.

Drawing together their various digital and social media channels (blog, videos, Facebook, Twitter, Tumblr and one-off campaigns like London Fashion Week) into one place, the app offers enhanced in-store and social engagement features, including scanning, sharing and favourites. It was also implemented exclusively via the existing e-commerce setup, requiring minimal work from the Topshop systems teams.

4.11
Topshop operates more like a luxury brand than a high street brand by offering customers the opportunity to engage and interact with the store through the use of mobile apps.
© Ben A. Bruchnie/ Stringer via Getty Images

Not only does Topshop provide an amazing user experience across their mobile devices, they also perfectly marry their in-store shopping experiences with their downloadable 'on the go' app. The app provides the user with a smooth shopping experience, with the ability to buy direct from the app, and an innovative barcode scanner, linking the user to any nearby Topshop store highlighting the stock available in each.

For a long time, Topshop has had the most up-to-date social channels sharing its trends and latest products, and in London Fashion Week in 2014, Topshop brought what has been reported by Social Bro as 'the world's first fashion show created by digital imagery' to life. Using user-generated content, the Topshop fashion show was created solely by customers, and encouraged Topshop lovers to post their looks using the #Topshop Window hashtag with the images featured on their digital fashion show in their flagship store window. The Instagram campaign highlighted Topshop as a social media innovator yet again, as the campaign gained a huge amount of attention from customers and the general public alike. In the fashion industry, it is important to stay current so that you innovate your brand; the channels and devices you use to market your products are critical to remain competitive. With the mobile market in particular, growing at such a rapid pace, it can be easy for your brand to get left behind.

Chapter summary

Chapter 4 has explored the journey that takes a fashion product from concept to the shop floor. As you now understand, it is a complex but exciting journey with lots of considerations to be taken by some very hard working and dedicated fashion professionals. Key to the process is the transition from an idea on paper to developing it into ranges of fashion garments for the fashion customer. The chapter also outlined the roles of buyer and merchandiser and explored the fashion calendar and the buying cycle and how this is changing. We have looked at the selection process and what needs to be taken into consideration, the different distribution channels and the dynamic changes taking place in online retail. The next part of the chapter will help you reflect, link the chapter content to the case study and, by answering some questions, allow you to assess what you have learnt from Chapter 4.

Understanding the profitability of a range by meeting certain financial plans set for each season is the prime responsibility of the buyer and he or she will be supported by the merchandiser to ensure that the customer is offered appropriate merchandise at a reasonable, but profitable, price. The role, however, can vary from country to country and can vary between large and small companies, high street fashion chains or small independent retailers, as some of the roles will include purchasing items from branded ranges. But over all, the buyer is a key member of the team that works on developing and delivering ranges into store for the customer.

To an extent, the buying calendar dictates buying activities and consists of the key events and processes the buyer and the teams are involved in to ensure the ranges will be developed, designed, sourced and delivered to stores within the appropriate seasons. Once the relevant research has been done and the framework for the new range has been developed, the range is then planned with many factors taken into consideration: the range will be planned around the number of

products, the cost, the manufacturer and much more before the ranges go to the pre-selection stage.

The merchandiser's role is a demanding role within the buying team; it is the merchandiser's job to ensure that there is a correct balance of products in the season's range. It is their job to interact with wholesalers, manufactures and other members of the team, and they are involved with consumer trends, interviews, surveys and other types of research. The merchandiser manages stock planning, which involves analysis of sales patterns.

The global supply chains may involve the importing of goods, and this is done via the fashion importer who plays an important role in the fashion industry. As explained, long-distance sourcing requires a different set of skills from those of the buyer or designer, although some of the skills do overlap. Most companies have a variety of sourcing methods and will work with lots of suppliers. However, some companies will buy direct from a manufacturer based overseas, such as in the Far East, or work with fashion importers. This is the main opportunity for the buyer to travel.

Obviously, the sole aim for buyers, designers and merchandise teams is to develop ranges of fashion products for customers and to sell them what they want. Fashion retail has come a long way since the markets of Petticoat Lane in the 1700s and a shopper has many options of where to buy their fashion items. Whether it is a luxury item from a beautiful store or a piece for a high street store, the retail calendar will have been adhered to.

Multichannel retailing is a marketing strategy that companies are developing to offer customers a choice of ways to buy products. The multichannel approach to sales that seeks to provide the customer with a seamless shopping experience, whether the customer is shopping online from a desktop or mobile device, by telephone or in a bricks-and-mortar store has been developed by the most forward-thinking retailers. This is reaping rewards for companies such as Topshop who have developed apps to connect with the customer and drive sales (see case study).

As a way of evidencing what you have learnt from the chapter and case study, answer the following questions by writing a short paragraph on each.

Case study and chapter reflection

Q. What is new in the distribution of fashion products and what is driving change at Topshop?

Q. 'Topshop operate as if they were a high-fashion brand, rather than a high street brand.' Explain why this might be said.

Q. How does Topshop do better than other online retailers? Why? What could Luxury brands learn from Topshop, if anything?

Q. Why is it important to be innovative with your brand and the channels and devices through which you market your products?

CHECKLIST

1. What does the buyer need to do to ensure profitability for the appropriate fashion product for the customer?

2. The buyer's role can vary; discuss the key differences of a buyer in the US and the UK.

3. Explain what directional shopping is and where it fits in the buying calendar.

4. The buying process relies on a wide range of information and the buyer will have to present to the team in order to develop a framework for the new season. Outline the things the buyer would have to take into account in order to present an accurate account of the current range and its success or failure.

5. The merchandiser is a key member of the fashion buying team, but the role differs and sometimes overlaps with the buyers. Explain the differences of the role of buyer and the role of merchandiser.

6. Investigate the supply chains for 'fast fashion' and 'slow fashion' and discuss the differences in relation to their appropriate supply chains.

7. List and outline the key sectors in fashion retail today.

8. Draw an operational diagram of the story of the dress: from the initial design idea to the buyer's review and arrival in store.

9. What is fashion distribution? Explain the various types of fashion distribution.

10. Who were the Huguenot weavers? What did they bring to London?

EXERCISE

Developing a range plan

A range plan or product mix is formulated well in advance of the buying season. Careful planning is essential and the previous year's sales are often referenced in the planning process. The following steps will help you understand the process undertaken in range planning.

Step 1: The brief

A range development brief contains information for the buying department. Focus on a category, such as dresses, to compile the brief. This should include the overall number of individual styles as well as the quantity of styles within each sub-category, such as short, long, print or party dresses, for example.

Step 2: Research

The next stage is to research trends, including styles, colours, stories or themes, in order to fulfil the brief. Analyse this along with fabric choices, taking into account the availability of the fabric. Identify your target market and provide a customer profile. Establish the intended purpose of the fashion range using the analysis of current styles and fashion trends.

At this stage, you will need to develop initial concepts to identify a range of possibilities in fabric, theme, stories and colours. Fashion range accessorising can also be planned at this stage, which is usually done in consultation with a designer or design team.

Step 3: Range development

Once you have identified the appropriate styles, trims and accessories for your target market, you need to research the feasibility of the production of these styles to confirm whether you will be able to make them. Now you can prepare artwork, drawings, specifications and samples in an appropriate format, including any additional documentation.

Step 4: Presentation

Present the range using a combination of flat sketches, fabric swatches and colour palettes. Evaluate the balance of the range and discuss to agree the mix.

Interview:
Michelle Vaughan

Fashion buyer, branded footwear buyer, ASOS.com

Q: What made you want to become a fashion buyer?

A: I was working as an allocator on the merchandising side but found what the buying team were doing was far more interesting than my own role. Luckily an opportunity arose to move across to buying side and I jumped at the chance.

Q: What does your job as a fashion buyer involve?

A: I'm responsible for sourcing and building a balanced, commercial and profitable footwear range in line with the department's strategy.

Q: What's the best thing about your job?

A: No two days are the same and there's never a dull moment; discovering and growing new brands; seeing brands/styles you've brought be successful; seeing all of the season's trends and brand new collections.

Q: What's the worst aspect of your job?

 A: Having to buy brands/styles that you don't think are right for your department because there is a larger conversation/politics within the business ('JFDI' – just f***ing do it!).

Q: Do you get to travel much? If so, what do you like or dislike about international travel?

A: Yes, I travel quite a bit. It is a part of the role I quite enjoy, particularly if there is the opportunity to go to new places. However, the reality is that the travelling often sounds far more glamorous than it actually is and that you spend all of your time inside at a trade fair and don't see anything of the country you are visiting!

Q: Do you need to be good at maths?

A: You do need to have some mathematical skills and an understanding of numbers (for buy plans, margins, etc.). Ultimately, as a buyer, you will be responsible for working closely with the merchandiser to deliver the sales and profit targets so you would probably struggle with this if your maths skills weren't great.

Q: Do you think your degree has helped at all?

A: No, I did a Psychology degree rather than a fashion-related degree and had quite an alternative route into buying (mind you it has helped with dealing with some team members!).

Q: Any advice for students thinking about buying as a career?

A: Competition for entry BA positions is fierce, so any experience interning/temping within a buying department would stand them in good stead to gain a position after graduating. Be prepared to work really hard and realise that they could spend a considerable amount of time doing admin and slogging away before they get to do the more interesting aspects of the role.

Fashion marketing and communication

Fashion marketing could be described as the face of the fashion industry, combining elements of promotion, advertising, design and business administration, and it is the fashion marketer's responsibility to ensure a new clothing line gains the attention it needs to be successful by communicating this to the line's target audience.

Today's fashion consumers are hungry for fashion content, and not just any content, they are looking for solutions to their buying problems and for those that will help them lead successful and exciting lives. The thing is, today's consumers are inundated by thousands of marketing messages, most of which they ignore. For the fashion brand, it is crucial for the success of the brand that they know how to get through to their target customer. It is more than just finding a way to sell more products; it is about the information the brand provides. Intelligent marketers know this and will create a strong brand relationship with their customers by providing good, clear and even leadership style content.

In this chapter, you will learn about various forms of marketing, communication and how a company engages with their consumer to provide a clear brand message that is understood by their target audience.

The chapter will help you:

- Appreciate what is involved in the marketing of fashion products.
- Understand how the marketing mix works.
- Grasp how the study of consumers helps fashion brands and businesses to improve their marketing strategies.
- Understand the basics of fashion communication and how brands get their message out.
- Appreciate the methods used in the fashion promotion and communication in the fashion industry.

5.1
Fashion communication is about the power of the brand and the logo.
© Robert Alexander via Getty Images

Understanding marketing

The key aspects of fashion marketing are how to focus on the target market the products will be aimed at, determining where the products will sell and how to attract the customers to generate profit. Other aspects of fashion marketing are the communication of the product, including how a collection should be displayed, which involves the creativity and resourcefulness of the marketer.

In addition, we look at why it is currently important that fashion marketers are well-read in aspects of marketing and business and how it helps to have an interest and flair in popular culture, as the activities of the marketer are continually shifting with advances in social media and technology. There is a need to plan, design and coordinate fashion advertisements that will reach the masses to entice them to purchase products or take the desired action, and there are both traditional and new approaches used in marketing that are important to the brand's growth and place in the market.

Why is marketing important? Before the 1970s, the focus of fashion marketing was primarily on women's fashion, and the media addressed this consumer group more than any other. Today, however, with greater consumer consciousness, new technology and a higher level of education, there is greater focus on product and media communication than ever before. In the fashion and luxury industries, selling a lifestyle and gaining access to the dreams and aspirations of the fashion consumer can be as significant an incentive to purchase as product innovation and quality. As a result, marketing has long been a basic cornerstone of any modern fashion brand or luxury business. Marketing efforts were historically concentrated on print media and independent communication by a brand, but today, brands seek to create a dialogue between the customer and their brand.

What is marketing?

Fashion marketing is a crucial part of the industry linking products of fashion designers and brands to the wholesale buyers and consumers. If executed well, the success of marketing and branding a line can be attributed to a good marketing strategy. In other words, an innovative and efficient marketing plan is almost as important as the design/collections themselves.

Much of fashion marketing happens behind the scenes and involves: keeping abreast of fashion trends and consumer buying habits; putting together advertising campaigns that target specific consumer groups and appeal to their tastes; and being aware of the latest style innovations and the fashion industry as a whole. Fashion marketers are responsible for identifying and creating fashion trends to sell products created by designers; they are the link between the designer and consumer. Fashion marketers not only identify the successful trends and the consumer groups that will be the most interested, but they also know how to market the clothes to these target groups.

Fashion as a concept is about the narrative behind the garment; marketing is the connection of the designer and the company, the brand, to the customer. This does more than increase sales; it encourages brand loyalty among its consumers, which in turn can drastically improve a company's image in the public domain.

> **Target market**
>
> The target market is the group or groups of customers for which the marketer will focus their attention. The group is clarified after rigorous analysis and segmentation of the market has been undertaken.

Before the internet, fashion brands were built using classic marketing strategies with traditional media, such as printed materials and television, to push the latest product campaign to the consumer. While we can assume that traditional methods will always be there, we can't ignore how today's internet-era consumers have much more power than before and interact with a brand they consider worthy of their time via a variety of channels. The rise of on-demand content and an abundance of digital and social media has prompted a growth of micro marketing techniques. People will continue to expect more and more products and services that speak directly to them and address their individual needs.

The concepts of marketing management

The following section outlines the marketing concepts that are the philosophy that drives a fashion company to focus on the needs of their customers. Fashion brands must analyse these needs and make decisions to meet them in a way

that their competitors can't. These concepts, which once dominated the marketing world, are still used and practiced in many fashion companies today.

The four marketing management concepts that most brands will use in their marketing objectives are outlined below. The focus and means may differ but the aim is to achieve profits.

1. **Product concept** – This management concept concentrates on the quality of the fashion product with a good price. This would mean the product would require very little marketing and generates the demand.
2. **Selling concept** – This management direction means that aggressive selling would need to be done, as consumers will not buy unless promoted to them.
3. **Marketing concept** – This management positioning recognises that the fashion consumer needs have to be identified and then the brand will adapt their offer to satisfy those needs more effectively and efficiently than

5.2
A fashion consumer can see a product and link through their phone – within seconds – to moving catwalk images of it on a model.
© MARTIN BUREAU/ AFP via Getty Images

their competition. The marketing concept completely relies on their size, target market, customer needs and by using the right **marketing mix** marketing teams can make decisions that will results in customers satisfaction.

4. **Societal concept** – This management direction tends to focus on satisfying the needs of the fashion consumer and demonstrating a long-term concern for societal welfare to achieve company objectives and attend to its responsibilities for society by finding a balance between company profits, social welfare and consumer needs.

The marketing mix

The marketing mix is a well-established marketing theory, developed in 1953 by Neil Borden.

Considering every element of the marketing mix, it is often referred to as the 4 Ps. Some companies will extend this to 7 Ps, enabling a company to establish an effective and appropriate marketing strategy. These are as follows:

Product

What is the product? What is its USP (unique selling point)? In other words, what makes this product different?

Place

This represents where the product will be sold, such as in a retail stores or online. Again, the organisation must consider where their competitors sell their products.

5.3
The 7 Ps. The marketing mix, or the 7 Ps, is a well-established theory developed by Neil Borden in 1953 (American Marketing Association).

Place
– Retail
– Wholesale
– Mail order
– Internet
– Direct sales
– Peer to peer
– Multi-channel

Product
– Design
– Technology
– Usefulness
– Value
– Quality
– Packaging
– Branding
– Warranties

Price
– Strategies
– Skimming
– Penetration
– Psychological
– Cost-plus
– Loss leader

Physical evidence
– Smart
– Run-down
– Interface
– Comfort
– Facilities

Target market

Promotion
– Special offers
– Advertising
– Endorsements
– User trials
– Direct mailing
– Competitions
– Joint ventures

Process
– Especially relevant to service industries
– How services are consumed

People
– Employees
– Management
– Culture
– Customer service

Price

The price of the product takes into account manufacturing prices as well as the final price paid by the customer. The business must also consider prices of competitive products.

Promotion

Promotion represents the type of communication used to promote the product to the consumer. Companies will also consider the promotional methods used by their competitors.

Some companies, depending on their products, may extend and use a further 3 Ps. See below.

People

This includes everyone involved in the product, from the target customer and their consumer profile, to those who work for the company.

Process

This refers to the process of providing the product, from conception to manufacture to end consumer.

Physical evidence

This refers to the physical evidence of a satisfied customer; good customer feedback should be used as part of a company's marketing strategy.

NOTE: The marketing mix should only be established after a **target market** is clarified.

In the classroom, the 4 Ps marketing mix has become a straightforward, introductory framework through which to think about fashion marketing. There are many other frameworks available, but the 4 Ps are a simple starting place. It is important not to be too rigid within any one framework, however; in fashion, having an amazing product is the essential foundation of a strong business. In the classical marketing framework, 'product' is described as an item or service that meets the consumer's need or desire. It is worth making a note that in fashion, designers usually create fashion products that consumers don't yet know they want. It's up to marketers to then use the appropriate marketing strategies to unleash their desire.

Traditional vs. integrated marketing

It is important to understand the two different approaches a brand may use when it is launching a new fashion product into the marketplace: the traditional approach and the integrated marketing approach. In order to grasp the fundamentals of marketing, the differences in traditional and integrated approaches to marketing are outlined next.

Generally, there are five different departments involved in the product during the creation process and launch: development, prototyping, manufacturing, marketing and distribution.

If a brand decides to use the **traditional approach**, all of the departments will function as separate entities.

> ### Traditional marketing
>
> Methods employed by marketers with proven success rates, such as print advertisements in newspapers or on billboards.

For technical change to prototyping, the development process will involve the sketch up of the design, and then it is passed to the technical department for pattern cutting and developing a prototype to create the toile/sample. Once the sample has been approved for design and fit this will be passed to production to mass-produce. After this stage, it is passed to the marketing team, which will then move the collection for the launch.

If a brand chooses to use an **integrated marketing approach**, it is the responsibility of all of the departments to work together as a single unit. The technical department will not develop the collection without checking that production has the capabilities to produce it. Development as a department would check with marketing to make sure the product correlates with the brand's image and approach, and each department at some point in the process will integrate their work with all the other departments.

Table of marketing approaches and outcomes

Concept	Focus	Means	Ends
1. Product	Products	A quality product at a reasonable price requires very little marketing effort	Achieves profits or objectives by fashion products generating consumer demand
2. Selling	Products	Aggressive advertising and selling efforts by the brand	Achieves profits or objectives by generating sales volume
3. Marketing	Customer needs	Integrated marketing approach	Achieves profits or objectives through customer satisfaction
4. Societal-Marketing	Customer satisfaction and long-run public welfare	Constant search for better fashion products: terms of appeal and benefit	Satisfies business goals and responsibilities for society

Integrated marketing

Methods employed by marketers that unify different departments in a company to increase sales, such as PR, social media, advertising and so on. The aim is to create a consumer experience with a brand.

It could be said that the integrated process is the better approach. Though it may take longer, this approach is more likely to lead to success. The traditional approach is considered an outdated mode of marketing, as it provides opportunities for conflicting interest and it often ignores the need of the customer. The integrated marketing approach provides a similar style that will reinforce the brand message aimed at the customer.

In summary, the term 'marketing' has a very specific context within fashion and is commonly used to describe communication linked to the promotion of products, services, and the creation and maintenance of a brand identity. This means the operational function called 'fashion marketing' has a narrowly defined role in the industry compared with the scope of general marketing. Fashion marketing is more of a science than its more creative counterparts – promotion, public relations and advertising – but it is important to understand some of the basic marketing theories. This understanding will help to contextualise the more creative aspects when putting together a marketing plan, and it is also helpful when attempting to make effective business decisions.

Fashion marketing as a career

The fashion marketer must know about brand equity, marketing techniques and consumer buying habits, as they are principally responsible for coordinating the product development team and departmental buyers in line with the company's marketing strategy: excellent communication skills are essential. In addition, they should have good mathematical and analytical skills in order to determine profit margin and pricing strategies. They must also have the skills to understand consumer psychology and social trends.

A marketing role can include a variety of responsibilities, from attending fashion shows and appointments in designer showrooms through to visual design, advertisement campaigns, promotions and maintaining brand strategy. A fashion-marketing professional should ideally have a degree in marketing or fashion marketing, management, communication or promotions.

It is important for the fashion marketer to recognise fashion trends before they happen in order to bring them to their customers; it is about showing off the product to its maximum advantage, but the marketer must understand the behaviour of the customer it is targeting. In order to do this, the fashion marketer needs to undertake research about the customer to ensure that they will be able to communicate the message to the customers they have identified. The following section covers the fashion consumer and what would need to be taken into account when developing a marketing plan.

The fashion consumer

Defining the target market is essential to running a successful fashion business. Without taking the time to define its target market, a brand is likely to waste precious time and money marketing to the wrong customers by trying to communicate to those who are not interested in its products.

Fashion begins and ends with the consumer; the primary task is to satisfy the consumer and their needs. Fashion provides us with a means of expressing ourselves, our identities and personalities through our clothing, in order to become part of a larger social group and society as a whole. By understanding and identifying what motivates and drives fashion consumers, designers and marketers can begin to target their products more effectively and efficiently. Basic human behaviour provides a number of concepts that help fashion marketers think about and understand their customers. Market research, which is undertaken by fashion companies and marketers, involves the study of consumer behaviour, drawing heavily on psychology, sociology and anthropology as well as our cultural history.

Consumer behaviour

Consumer behaviour is the investigation of individuals, groups or businesses and the processes they use to today's society. This includes the fashion goods and services they are attracted to, how they behave in relation to the efforts of companies to offer goods to them, and how they respond to the different media used to market these goods. In the study of customer behaviour, a distinction should be made between complex decision-making situations and the ones where little or no consideration is made to the purchase. Where a product is expensive and may be technologically complex, prospective purchasers most likely will go through a complicated search and evaluation process prior to making a purchase.

It is useful to study the buying decisions of consumers, both individually and in groups, in order to identify what the consumer will want to buy. In a fashion context, it helps designers and businesses to improve their marketing strategies by identifying the effects of socio-economic and demographic patterns of consumer fashion upon consumers' buying habits. It considers the consumer as an individual, looking at motivation, personality, perception, attitudes and communication; as well as groups of consumers within different social and cultural settings, such as family, social class and subculture.

There are various models for consumer behaviour analysis. Over the years, we have seen these develop with models reflecting different buying behaviours and situations that consumers find themselves in. Fashion brands undertake market research as a way of helping to determine why a customer will buy or not buy a product or service. Market research also provides information for

selecting the appropriate marketing mix (pricing, product, distribution and promotion) decisions. Specialist market research companies do both in-house and external research, tailored to the company's requirements or can be bought 'off the peg' so to speak. The research process involves defining the problem, looking at company records, analysis of published data sources, making decisions as to whether field work would be required, and what the best method would be if that were so. Specifics of the sample, location/size and type of sample, data collection analysis and evaluating the results and setting actions are all part of consumer behaviour research. A variety of methods and models are used in marketing research including surveys, experiments and observational methods.

There are four key factors influencing consumer behaviour: cultural factors, social factors, **personal factors** and **psychological factors**.

1. **Cultural factors:** Culture is one of the most critical factors when attempting to understand the needs and behaviours of the individual, as an individual is influenced throughout his or her existence by their family, friends, cultural environment and society. This teaches an individual their values, preferences and common behaviours to their own culture.

For a brand, it is important that the market researcher take into account and understand the cultural factors inherent to each market or situation, so that the marketing strategy and product can be adapted, as these play a role in the perception, habits, behaviour or expectations of consumers.

2. **Social factors:** Among the factors influencing consumer behaviour significantly are social factors, which fall into three categories: reference groups, family, social roles, and status.

The social groups that the fashion consumer belongs to have a direct influence on them, and membership to the groups is normally related to his or her social origin, age, hobbies, work and so on. The influence level may vary depending on groups and individuals, but it is generally observed as common consumption trends among the members of a same group.

Understanding the specific features (mindset, values, lifestyle, etc.) of each group allows a brand to clearly target its advertising message.

3. **Personal factors:** Buying behaviour and decision making is influenced by consumer characteristics, age and way of life. The consumer will not buy the same products at seventy that they bought at twenty. Lifestyle, hobbies, interests and values will evolve as life is lived. For example, a consumer could change their diet from unhealthy products (like fast food or cigarettes) to live a healthier lifestyle during mid-life with family to avoid health problems later in life by adhering to a low-cholesterol diet or giving up smoking.

Personal factors

Personal factors are also known as psychographics – the study and classification of people according to their attitudes, aspirations and other psychological criteria, especially in market research.

4. **Psychological factors:** Psychological factors can be divided into four categories: motivation, perception, learning, and attitudes and beliefs.

   - **Motivation** is what drives consumers to develop a purchasing behaviour. It is the expression of a need leading the consumer to make a purchase. This works on a subconscious level and as such is difficult to measure.
   - **Learning** is through action. We learn when we act; it implies changes to behaviour as a result of the experience.

Learning alters the behaviour of a person as they acquire information and experience.

   - **A belief** is a conviction that an individual has about something through the experiences they acquire, learning and external influences (family, friends, etc.). A person develops beliefs that will have an influence on their buying behaviour. An attitude can be defined as a feeling, the inclination to act in a certain way towards an object or a situation. Beliefs and attitudes are normally weighted down in the mind of the individual and are difficult to change. For many people, their beliefs and attitudes are part of their personality and who they are.

By identifying and understanding factors that influence their customers, brands have the opportunity to design strategies and marketing messages; in other words, unique value propositions, advertising campaigns and more efficient ways to meet customers' needs providing a way of targeting consumers and increase sales.

Segmenting, targeting and positioning

Segmentation, targeting and positioning (STP) is a strategic approach to marketing, and it is a common model applied in marketing practice. The STP model aims to develop and deliver personalised appropriate messages with the aim of engaging with different audiences.

STP is also relevant to digital fashion marketing where marketing personas can be applied to help develop more relevant digital communications. In addition, STP focuses on commercial efficiency by selecting the most valuable segments for a brand then developing a marketing mix and product positioning strategy for each segment.

Segmenting

Market segmentation is the process of separating different categories that are based on distinguishing characteristics. The idea around market segmentation is to help retailers identify the customers that are likely to purchase their products.

Retailers use segmentation to better reach their non-buying customers through adverts and other marketing efforts.

Small clothing retailers, manufacturers and wholesalers focus their research on the demographics, personalities and needs of that segment of their market. There are several types of key market segments used in retailing and clothing markets, and these companies can further differentiate their clothing products from their key competitors.

Segmentation, targeting and positioning can all have a positive affect on the revenue of a brand by accepting the fact that there are different demands in the marketplace.

There are several different market segments in fashion, although the information here is not exhaustive.

Gender-related segments

Some of the smaller clothing retailers would segment their offer by selling gender-specific fashion products. For example, menswear or ladieswear.

Age-related segments

Age is another distinctive factor or demographic that helps determine the audience of the clothing retailer. Many retailers target the 'trend-led' teenage market, focussing on new fashion lines, while others may look at focussing primarily on children's clothing as this is significant in size to be a segment in itself.

Geographic segments

Some clever retailers and marketers know that different geographical areas will have different preferences. For example, people living in warmer climates will wear shorts and swimwear for longer periods and the market for coats will be bigger in other geographical areas.

Lifestyle segmentation

Lifestyle is another segment that marketers will target and base their product selections on. For example, clothing manufacturers producing clothing for hunters or the military personnel sell camouflage and military products to meet their clients' lifestyle needs.

Some segments may be too small and therefore too competitive.

The first step is to research the market and identify how it might best be segmented into buying groups and work out how different they are in terms of each other in their buying behaviour and product or service needs. Market segmentation is a method for dividing consumers into different categories.

Positioning

A brand must be able to position itself in the correct place in the mind's eye of its customers so that its products and services stand out positively in the marketplace amongst its competitors. Differentiation is critical in fashion's crowded marketplace; the product/brand needs to make sure they position themselves correctly and in a way that it will attract the right customer and ultimately a larger market share. Brand positioning is a crucial element of the business's success and as such requires a lot of careful thought and consideration.

Simply put, positioning is defining your brand's products or services in the minds of your customers; it refers to the 'target customer's' reason to purchase the products you offer over another brand. The creation of an image or identity for your product expresses its position in relation to your competitors in the marketplace. It makes it important that your brand's activity is consistent with a common goal and focuses all of its points of contact with the customer.

Positioning a brand/organization's product or service is basically defining in the customer's eye just who you are. For example, marketers for the company would attempt to create an identity or brand image for a brand or company and usually express positioning relative to other competitors in the market.

Brand positioning involves identifying and determining points of likeness and differentiation to decide the right brand identity. A strong brand position enables the brand to stand out; it directs the marketing plan and communicates the brand details. It is this individual feature that sets your products or service apart from your competitors.

To summarise: marketing is currently accepted as a general management function or strategic discipline and, with this in mind, must care for the future health of the brand or company, particularly against competitive influences. Successful marketers therefore should be concerned with every aspect of their business, including future projects and the other areas of the fashion industry. Successful companies plan five or ten years in advance and generally know as much about their competition as they know about themselves. Marketing is not just a series of business-related functions but is more wide-ranging than this. It is a business viewpoint considered to widen an attitude of mind, which should be collective within the organisation. Every company relies on its customers for continued existence, and those who best meet customer needs will always survive a period of change.

The marketing function is consequently a vital component of business strategy, and therefore the marketing focus should be conveyed through strategic marketing planning into all aspects of the brand's business activity.

Customer profiles

A successful marketing strategy starts with the customer profile, which is used to market products to fulfil the needs of the consumer. Fashion marketers use a variety of research methods to compile customer profiles. Class is one of the most reliable indicators of consumer values, attitudes and lifestyles, but developing a customer profile will involve research into a variety of things that paint a visual picture of the customer, such as the magazines and newspapers they read, the food they eat, where they shop and so on. Customers are also profiled according to age, gender, career, education and values.

Pen portraits are sometimes used to define an audience; it is a technique that involves drawing a fictitious character to enable you to speak to them directly. To create this character, you need to **imagine who they are, what they are like and what drives them**. Manipulate and add to the picture until you are happy with the image and use that to target.

> ### Pen portrait
>
> A pen portrait can be used to informally describe a person or a group of people. They can be used as an informal qualitative research method when doing market research and consumer profiles.

Primary and secondary research methods

The two main approaches to marketing are primary and secondary research. Primary research is research that you would design and conduct yourself. For example, you may need to find out whether consumers would rather have their soft drinks be sweeter or tarter. This can be undertaken by asking the appropriate consumer groups how they like their drinks. It is important to realise that while research will never take risk away, it can reduce risks associated with a new product or fashion line. Secondary research, on the other hand, involves using the information that others have already researched and collated. For example, if you were thinking about starting a business making clothes for tall people, you wouldn't need to interview people about how tall they are to find out how many tall people exist – that information will have already been published by the UK or US governments and will be available online or in libraries. For the marketer, as with most business of creative projects, research is paramount when starting and developing a solution to solve the design or marketing problem set.

Consumer trends

Understanding and the application of consumer trends and insights will forever be the Holy Grail to business and marketing professionals. Consumer behaviour and preferences change on a global scale and at a faster speed than ever before, which means that tracking consumer trends is critical for marketers and fashion predictors. Consumer trends are constantly evolving. The ability to identify trends in consumer behaviour through trend watching should ultimately lead to profitable innovation. A fashion company may develop a team of trend forecasters in-house or they will buy the information from a forecasting agency; either way, it is the application of consumer trends that is key to success. Does the trend have the potential to influence or shape the company's vision; to enable it to develop a new business concept, a new venture or a new brand? Does the trend add something new for a certain customer segment: for example, a new product, service or experience? Does the trend speak the language of those consumers already living the trend; to communicate to them through marketing, advertising and PR? Above all else, the company must utilise consumer trends to competitive advantage: to continually create exciting new products and services.

'Consumer behaviour affects all aspects of the fashion industry . . . psychology, sociology and culture all influence the how, what, when, where and why of the buy.'

Rath, Bay, Petrizzi and Gill

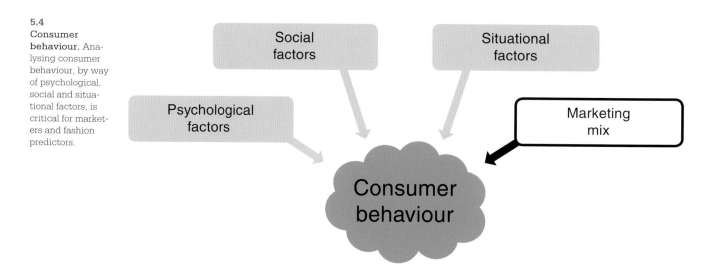

5.4
Consumer behaviour. Analysing consumer behaviour, by way of psychological, social and situational factors, is critical for marketers and fashion predictors.

Fashion promotion

Promotion is arguably one of the most important components of the marketing mix (see page 114). These include advertising, public relations (PR) and promotional strategies. Advertising includes any form of paid communication that appears in the cinema, on TV, in print and on billboards (see page 128). PR includes any form of communication that is not directly paid for, such as press releases, trade fairs and events. Other promotional strategies include viral marketing, informal communication via the internet or word of mouth from satisfied customers or people specifically employed to raise brand awareness.

It is important to consider all forms of promotional tools in order to use those best suited to reach the target consumer. Above all, the main objective of fashion promotion is to increase brand and product awareness. From large mass-market retailers to the small niche brands and independent designers, all companies in the fashion industry will need to use fashion promotion techniques to be successful.

Fashion PR

PR involves communicating a message to one or more target audiences, influencing them in a positive way. Fashion PR agencies are employed by brands and retailers to build and maintain a favourable public image. Because they do not pay for publicity or media coverage, PR specialists must find creative ways to keep the company's brand name in the public eye. PR specialists communicate the brand message through a number of channels, such as television, newspapers, radio and direct mail. They write up press releases, conduct press conferences and are also responsible for interacting with media when questions or crises arise from outside sources. As such, PR specialists must maintain strong professional relationships with media personnel.

The PR specialist is usually responsible for answering enquiries from individuals, journalists and organizations; preparing press releases and articles; organizing press briefings, conferences, exhibitions, receptions and tours; writing and

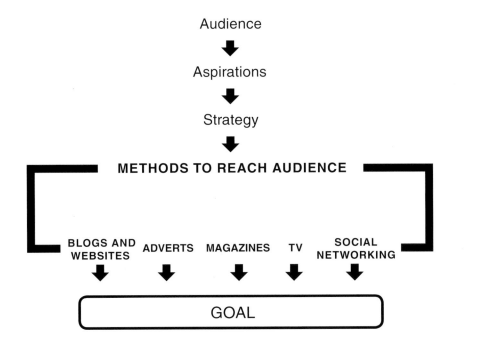

5.5
Define your audience. Promotion is one of the most important components of the marketing mix. It is important that all promotional tools are considered as part of company strategy.

editing in-house journals; creating and maintaining useful contacts; planning and initiating PR campaigns.

To succeed in PR, you need to have excellent written and verbal communication skills and the ability to deal with a number of different tasks at one time; as well as to be creative, determined, persuasive and persistent. Competition for entry-level posts is fierce. Many people enter PR after experience in journalism, advertising or marketing.

Press campaigns

Press releases and media kits are information kits that are sent out to generate positive press on behalf of the brand or fashion company. Other tools include traditional brochures and newsletters and, increasingly, interactive social media outlets, such as fashion blogs, Facebook and Twitter. The press release is developed to introduce a new product, collection or line of fashion clothing to the media. By sending press releases to relevant media such as fashion magazines, newspapers and blogs, the target consumer is kept informed about the brand's activities, such as new and upcoming products and launches, fashion shows and events, successes, product awards and newsworthy stories about the brand.

5.6
Louis Vuitton.
Large-scale, iconic Louis Vuitton luggage was placed around the Paris store for its 150th anniversary in 2004.
Alamy Stock Photo

Smaller brands or companies will often use a public relations agency to help reach larger audiences.

Product placement

Product placement, also known as embedded marketing, is used to raise brand awareness and increase sales by featuring fashion items and products on television, in the movies and on celebrities. In today's celebrity culture, this form of marketing is increasingly effective. Fashion houses gain a lot of free publicity by having their clothes worn by certain celebrities, who may be photographed at a key awards ceremony, movie premiere or simply walking down the street. The photographs are published in newspapers, magazines and online with the designer name often mentioned in the piece as a footnote – providing that important piece of publicity.

Innovative promotion

Today's fashion consumers are trend conscious and information savvy, and fashion marketers need to be up to date with the latest marketing trends so that they can target their customers in the most effective way. Brands are always looking for new and interesting ways of getting the attention of consumers.

Viral marketing

Social media is increasingly being used to stimulate consumer interest in a brand and build brand loyalty via viral marketing. Traditional advertising has been abandoned by some brands in an effort to save costs, yet there must be a balance between traditional and innovative marketing methods. Savvier brands use both in order to maintain market share, reinforcing brand credibility and appeal.

Most would consider social media and viral marketing to be here to stay, with consumers playing a greater role in determining whether or not a brand can survive. Today we can see that most major fashion brands have a Facebook fan page

and maintain a Twitter presence because, for now at least, online consumer communication has a big part to play in promoting events, sales and consumer trends.

Online fashion retailer ASOS is one of the most socially savvy brands in the contemporary fashion industry. At the time of writing, the company has around 5.5 million followers on Instagram, over 4 million followers on Facebook and over 1 million followers on Twitter. These numbers are not only an indication of the scope of ASOS's customer engagement but they also allow them to interact directly with fashion royalty.

While it is important for fashion brands to embrace new means of communication, most experts would agree that it couldn't replace traditional and more formal methods; it takes more than viral communication to build a brand. Social media is a form of consumer-driven communication and publicity that makes up one component of a brand's marketing strategy. In the case of ASOS, **buzz marketing** has been used to complement a well-executed marketing campaign, essential for reaching its target consumer market of fashion-forward sixteen to thirty-four-year-olds.

Buzz marketing

This is the interaction of consumers to emphasise the original marketing message by building excitement or anticipation about a product or service. Positive 'buzz' is often the goal of viral marketing, PR and advertising.

5.7
ASOS. Online fashion retailer ASOS is one of the most social savvy of brands in the contemporary fashion industry.
NurPhoto via Getty Images

'Editors love when I have knowledge of a product, even beyond things they may actually need to know about for their purposes, but it makes them realise what a great resource I am and how passionate I am about the brand. I couldn't do PR well for a brand I wasn't passionate about.'

Janna Meyrowitz, president of Style House

Fashion communication

Fashion communication is the way in which products are advertised and promoted. Innovation and originality are fundamental to the success of fashion communication and the key characteristics of the people working in the industry.

We are all aware of the power of the brand and logo, both of which are obvious forms of fashion communication. A brand message has to be clear and direct in order to be understood by the largest number of consumers. It is important to get the message across and speak louder than others. The message can be delivered in non-verbal and verbal ways to the consumer. However, successful brand communication will not happen overnight; it has to be built up over time.

Forms of fashion communication: Branding

According to the American Marketing Association (AMA) a brand is a 'name, term, sign, symbol or design, or a combination of them, intended to identify the goods and services of one seller or group of sellers and to differentiate them from those of the competition'. In order to build a successful brand, the company has to understand and address the needs and wants of its customers. It is essential to integrate brand strategies throughout the company to ensure brand loyalty. Successful branding must be based on a forward-looking positioning strategy that takes into account the brand, the competition and the entire sector. It is important to understand what rival brands are doing, even to learn from their mistakes and successes, in order to differentiate from the competition.

Fashion brands

The branding process starts with the name, and the naming strategy of a company will depend on whether the position of the brand is the product

Fashion communication involves the following sequence:

Who is the communicator?

This could be the brand, for example Gucci or Prada.

What is the message?

The message is what the communicator has written, spoken or shown; for example, an image or advertisement.

What is the channel?

This could be a magazine or billboard, for example.

To whom is the message being communicated?

This refers to the person receiving the message or the receiver, generally the target consumer.

Communication is a huge sector within the fashion industry and it is highly competitive. If you are looking at this area of fashion as a career, it is important that you are visually literate, with strong communication skills. You need creative problem-solving skills in order to develop a strong brand message and an in-depth understanding of the relationship between design, communication, retail and business – this is key to the success of any fashion brand.

of a designer or not. In the fashion industry, the designer's name is used most often. It is interesting to note that the use of the designer's full name, such as Calvin Klein or Tommy Hilfiger, retains a strong link with the designer; for those brands that use only the surname, such as Prada and Gucci, the brand transcends that link.

There are many powerful fashion brands that don't depend on a particular designer, such as Nike and Fila. However, it has taken a long time and a lot of money for them to become the household names we all recognise. The designer's name is usually the best way to go beyond current fads and trends that will date quickly.

'When you think of the blur of all the brands that are out there, the ones you believe in and the ones you remember, like Chanel and Armani, are the ones that stand for something. Fashion is about establishing an image that consumers can adapt to their own individuality. And it's an image that can change, that can evolve. It doesn't reinvent itself every two years.'

Ralph Lauren

5.8
Gucci. Gucci is a strong and recognisable brand with a trademark logo. It began as a mark on leather goods produced in Florentine workshops for the young Guccio Gucci. The characteristic double G motif printed on the canvas was introduced after World War II due to the shortage of leather. The Gucci Logo has become one of the most copied in the world.
© Marie Simonova via Getty Images

Forms of fashion communication: Advertising

Fashion advertising is the paid communication of fashion and lifestyle images to sell everything from garments and accessories to perfume. It is impossible to imagine our lives without advertising; it is everywhere: on the TV, in movies, on billboards and public transport, in newspapers, in magazines and online.

The key to effective fashion advertising is made up of a few simple things: knowing who the customer is; what it is that they like; and how to grab their attention. If, for example, a fashion label is marketing to a young, fashion-forward consumer, the advertising must appeal to this specific market. It is important to use the same intelligence used to create the product in order to place the advertising in the most effective way.

Big fashion houses have huge advertising budgets and employ fashion advertising agents to develop their campaigns. Lower-end stores will also use fashion advertising to capture their end of the market; irrespective of market and budget, all fashion brands have the same aim: to present consumers with images of a specific lifestyle, to tell a story

**5.9
Fashion
advertising.**
Fashion
advertising is all
about attracting
consumer
attention and
convincing them
to buy the
garments, which
means that
advertisers have
to make the
campaign as
enticing as
possible to the
target audience.
© Jie Zhao via Getty
Images

that appeals to them and in turn encourage them
to buy the products.

Forms of advertising

The most common and widely-used form of fashion
advertising is in print, which fills the pages of
glossy magazines such as *Vogue* and *Harper's
Bazaar*. Print advertising also includes billboards,
which are commonplace in cities such as LA, New
York and London. Big fashion houses such as
Prada, Gucci and Chanel spend a significant
amount of money on their ad campaigns.

Websites are another effective form of advertising; having an online presence is like having a
store that is always open. Successful web advertising ensures that traffic is generated to the
busines's site and, in addition, websites can link
to one another to draw in more customers.

AIDA

There are a number of theories about fashion
advertising and the thought process of the target
consumer. AIDA is a simple, effective tool used
extensively in fashion advertising, which was pioneered by American advertising and sales expert
E. St Elmo Lewis in 1898. The acronym stands for:

**A – Attention
I – Interest
D – Desire
A – Action**

The AIDA model states that the advertisement
must first attract the attention of the customer.
The advantages, benefits and features of the
product must be demonstrated to raise the customer's interest. Interest is followed by desire,
which is convincing the customer that they want
and desire the product, that it will satisfy their
needs. Action is the successful outcome of the
advertisement – the customer having taken
action to purchase the product.

Forms of fashion communication:
Visual merchandising

Visual merchandising could be considered the art
of attracting customers with visual cues. Visual
merchandising emerged during the early twentieth
century, when department stores began using theatrical set design and lighting to create exotic displays to entice customers. Today, stores are
carefully designed to take into account the location
of the escalators, the lighting, the changing rooms
and so on, all of which is planned to earn the store
more sales per square foot. Visual merchandisers
use lots of different elements when creating displays, including colour, lighting, space, product
information and music, as well as technologies
such as digital displays and interactive installations. They can be employed across a range of
retail channels, from bricks-and-mortar high street
stores to boutiques and online fashion stores.

The visual merchandiser's role

The visual merchandiser is responsible for the
following: the development of creative and artistic
concepts for in-store displays; the visual appeal of
the store; implementation and execution of effective merchandising strategies; creating and maintaining different visual displays; and the
conceptualization of new and fresh store design
ideas. The role of the visual merchandiser
requires a mix of creative flair and commercial
awareness. Promoting new stock and managing

brand standards requires regular liaison with other departments; therefore, the role also requires excellent team and communication skills. If you are thinking of entering the world of visual merchandising, try gaining relevant field experience through an **internship programme.**

Design concepts

The design and layout of a store is an important way of communicating brand image to the consumer. Understanding consumer behaviour is critical in order to design a user-friendly shopping layout; merchandise displays are only effective marketing tools if designed with the customer in mind.

A well-designed shop window has the power to inspire potential customers, compelling them to come in-store and spend money. A window display will hold the customer's attention for three to five seconds, so a successful window display must have instant impact, conveying a strong visual message. Creating distinct window displays with an artistic theme will lure the customer in a shopping mood into the store. A store window makes the first impression with customers; it is the easiest way to draw attention away from competitors.

'Anything we do in advertising is controversial. If it's provocative and sensual and related to what we're selling, I'm willing to take the chance. I have fun with the ads.'

Calvin Klein

**5.10
Futuristic flowers.** A skilled visual merchandiser will use innovative ideas to transport customers into a different world. This is Futuristic Flowers, by RCA graduates Hsiao-Chi Tsai and Kimiya Yoshikawa, a series of seven large-scale art installations, commissioned by Harvey Nichols for its SS07 window display.

Case study: ZARA marketing strategy

Zara was established in 1974 by Amancio Ortea Gaona and is Spain's best-known fashion brand. Zara has become one of the world's most popular, fastest-growing and affordable retailer of fashion since its start up. Zara currently has over 2,169 retail stores in over 88 countries, which include China and India, and the numbers are forecast to double in the next few years. Zara started its Indian operations in 2010 and has grown to over eighteen stores in that country, with the number still rising since its debut. Zara became the first apparel brand in India to cross the $100-million sales mark, only five years after it opened its first shop there.

The fashion group also owns brands Massimo Dutti, Pull & Bear, Uterique, Stadivarious, Oysho, and Berksha. Zara was described by Louis Vuitton fashion director Daniel Piette as 'possibly the most Innovative and devastating retailer in the world'.

Product in the marketing mix of Zara

The popular store uses a very clever marketing strategy in order to achieve its business goals and is described as the 'Coca Cola' of fashion, with fashion enthusiasts clamouring for its

products. The ability for the brand to respond very quickly to the changing needs of its customers is one of the major strengths of the company. The company manufactures products itself rather than using outsource suppliers, making it fully in control of its products and production. Its focus in imitation and creation of the latest trends is Zara's unique selling proposition (USP). Generally, new styles are on the sales floor within two weeks and a maximum of four, and a product will be immediately pulled from the stores if it is not selling.

However, consideration has to be made when it comes to some of its global stores. For example, Zara has had a few problems to sort out with its Indian stores with the lack of seasonal variations to the product range. In addition, the need to cope with and address the cultural needs of local customers by developing designs that integrate the local traditions with modernism are important.

Pricing in the marketing mix of Zara

Zara's concept is to provide fashion products to its customers at affordable prices, and as such customers find the process affordable. Zara is well known for its high fashion, low-cost business model, and as a fashion brand Zara has cheap labour, cheap materials and fast production schedules, enabling Zara to adopt a low pricing strategy. The pricing strategy allows its products to be affordable to most customers, giving Zara its strong position in the global market.

Promotion in the marketing mix of Zara

Zara's 'Zero investment in marketing' is its unique marketing policy, and the company uses the money it would have normally used for advertising to open new stores. The interesting thing about Zara is that it has identified the differences that resonate with its customer base and uses that to differentiate them from their competitors. In simple terms, Zara's key

5.11
New styles are normally available on the sales stores within two weeks.
© Kay-Paris Fernandes via Getty Images

marketing strategy is based on exclusivity, differentiation, experience and affordability.

Zara relies heavily on '**word of mouth**' advertising. Its target market is the eighteen- to forty age group living in cities, as these are the more fashion conscious than any other group. The market segment is made up of 65 per cent women, 25 per cent men and 15 per cent children, all fashion conscious and educated in the middle classes.

Zara's commitment to their customers is visible in the attention paid to each and every detail of the showrooms, the way their sales staff are groomed and the way their windows are laid out. Everything is worked out to plan and is very precise, providing each store with free access to speak to counterparts in Spain about marketing and improvement strategies.

Regular and small product deliveries are designed to keep the stock fresh and up-to-date, encouraging customers to buy quickly and often and encouraging regular visits to the store to check out the new stock. Methods designed to make the brand global include bar coding, aided purchases and online shopping.

Place in the marketing mix of Zara

Zara is a vertically integrated retailer, making it stand out as a unique brand. By vertical integration, we mean that the brand designs, manufactures and distributes all its products.

The approach is clearly successful as Zara is one of the world's leading brands operating stores in over eighty-eight countries with expansion continuing.

The Zara Company owns 90 per cent of its stores with the other 10 per cent owned as joint ventures or franchises, meaning that no matter where a customer may walk into a Zara store they will have the same shopping experience as if they were to walk in the Zara store in London, New York, Rio de Janeiro, Paris or New Delhi. The design of the stores is modern, predominantly white with wall-to-wall mirrors and good lighting.

The culture of the company is what many people say is its real strength; they employ young designers and train them to make good decisions, and while good decisions are welcomed in any business, Zara don't punish bad ones.

Finally, and astonishingly, Zara's designers develop at least 500 new designs each month. The company's design strategy involves updating collections, often allowing Zara's unconventional business model to eliminate risk of markdowns.

Word of mouth

Where customers who are pleased with a product or service tell others, becoming unofficial marketers.

Chapter summary

The chapter covered the functions of marketing, promotion and communication with its combined elements of promotion, advertising, design and business administration. You have learnt how the fashion marketer is responsible for ensuring a new clothing line gathers attention in the marketplace in order for the new product to be successful with its target audience.

The key aspects of fashion marketing have been outlined in addition to how to focus on the target market the products will be aimed at to determine where the products will sell and how to attract customers to generate profit.

With much of fashion marketing happening behind the scenes, staying abreast of and identifying the latest trends and consumer buying habits is a marketer's job. Being aware of the latest style innovations, and the fashion industry as a whole, in order to put together advertising campaigns that target specific consumer groups and appeal to their tastes is key to the role.

Through understanding the basics of fashion marketing and the connection the brand has with the customer, you will now be aware that the story behind the garment is fundamental in the marketing message of the designer, and the company intends to do more than purely increase sales. Marketing encourages brand loyalty among its consumers, which can have a massive effect on the company's image in the public domain.

The marketing strategy uses various models to help in the process; the classic 4 Ps marketing mix is one of them. This is a pretty straightforward, introductory framework that can be used to think about marketing. As outlined, there are many other frameworks available, but the 4 Ps are an easy approach.

We need to remember that, in fashion, having the essential foundation of a strong business means having an amazing product to meet the 'desire' of the customer and encourage them to 'buy'. Brands can select to work with a traditional approach to marketing where all departments involved in the activities operate as separate entities, or they may use an integrated marketing approach making it the responsibility of all the department to work together and simultaneously.

Core marketing activities involve areas such as promotion and communication, among others, with promotion arguably one of the most important components of the marketing mix. And in order to create a strong promotional plan, defining the target market has to be a key part of the plan, as this is essential to running any successful fashion business big or small. See Chapter 7 for more information. Without taking the time to define its target market, a company is likely to waste time marketing to the wrong customers.

Fashion marketing is a large, highly specialised, exciting and to some degree scientific part of selling products, making this is a very interesting and challenging area of the fashion industry in which to operate.

Case study and chapter reflection

Q. Where and when did the fashion brand Zara first establish its fashion stores?

Q. Explain what is one of the major strengths of the company and its USP?

Q. What contributes to Zara's low pricing strategy and how is this achieved?

Q. What does vertical integration mean in the context of Zara's marketing mix?

CHECKLIST

1. Explain some of the key marketing activities for a fashion brand today.

2. Outline the 4 Ps marketing mix.

3. Explain the difference between the traditional and integrated marketing.

4. Defining your target market and consumer are important for marketers. What is consumer behaviour? List three issues that are important to study.

5. How would you build a visual picture of the customer?

6. Explain what fashion promotion activities would achieve for a brand?

7. What is viral marketing?

8. Communicating fashion is very important for any brand; provide a brief description of the communication sequence.

9. What is AIDA in communication?

10. Describe in a few short sentences some of the key forms of communicating for fashion brands and how they work.

EXERCISE

Five steps to the perfect target market

One of the main elements of a marketing strategy is the development of your ideal target customer profile. Understanding who makes your ideal customer allows you to build your perfect business: its message, product or services, sales and the support around attracting and serving this narrowly outlined customer group.

This exercise, while designed as a theoretical one, could be used to identify the need of a start-up or business with very little customer experience. The five steps below can help you discover your ideal target customer.

Step 1: Start with the smallest market possible

Find a group of customers that think what you have to offer them is unique. The key is to find a very narrow group with very particular demographics or a very definite problem or need and create enthusing fans out of this group. It is important to remember you can always expand your reach after you gain a grip. However, you can also become a key player in this smaller market as your offer grows.

Step 2: Create an initial value proposition

You must create a 'why us' value proposition and use that as your theory for 'why us'. You are probably thinking that this is sounding a bit like science: that's because it is. You must always stay in the test-and-perfect mode in order to move forward.

Step 3: Get the truth in customer interaction sessions

Thriving businesses that are established have the opportunity to learn a great deal every day from customer interaction. New businesses have to create ways to test their initial theories. The key to both making and affirming your initial assumptions is to undertake what I call **customer interaction sessions** with potential customers that might easily fit into your initial smallest market group. These are essentially staged one-on-one meeting or focus groups. The main thing is that you start talking to potential customers about what they need, what they think, what works, what doesn't and what they don't have now. This is how you will evolve the plan and the business, your features and your assumptions based on serving your narrowly defined target customer.

Step 4: Draw an ideal customer pen portrait

Once you've worked out and tested your theory with your narrow group, the next thing is to work on learning about and outlining everything you can about your ideal target group. Some of this information will be understood (for example demographics) but a lot of it will be determined in your test sessions and additional research will be gained in more behaviour-oriented places such as social media. Who is the ideal customer? What do they look like? Draw them using the **pen portrait**!

Step 5: Add strategy model elements

The final step is to apply this new ideal customer approach to other sections of your marketing strategy.

When you discover your initial ideal client, it should impact the development of your basic business model and overall business strategy. Great business models are fundamentally customer-focused, and now that you have a picture of your customer this will allow you to consider how this alters the other aspects of your business. For example, you could test your revenue streams, distribution channels and even pricing against this customer picture. Consider how to reach this customer, and what resources you need to have in order to make an impact in this market.

Interview:
Jamie Holloway

Communications manager at COS, Los Angeles

Q: What was your first job role and how long did it take to become a communications manager?

A: My first role was an internship ten years ago. As soon as I finished university, I moved down to London and took an unpaid internship in a fashion PR agency Monday to Friday and then worked in retail on Saturday and Sunday. I did this for three months and it was exhausting, but at the end of my internship I was offered the position of junior account executive at the agency, which was my first step on the career ladder. Everywhere has a slightly different way of defining job titles, but I would say it took me three and a half years to get to a manager-type level.

Q: How and when did you start your career at COS (LA)?

A: I started this position in March 2016. I was told about the role by several friends and contacts in the fashion industry that alerted me to it and thought I should apply. I applied and interviewed for the position with the head of communications and several other team members.

Q: Can you tell us a little about your main day-to-day communication activities? What does your average nine-to-five day at COS look like?

A: It's such a cliché, but there is no 'average day' in fashion communications. It really does vary so much, which is why I love it. However, in a general sense, I manage the LA showroom, which is where we keep a sample set of both our current season collection and the collection for the upcoming season. I work with stylists, bloggers and fashion editors to loan them pieces for photo shoots and dressing opportunities. I also work closely with the head office team in London on special projects and events that we have coming up.

Q: What part of the job do you like the most?

A: I love interacting with so many different creative people, and building relationships with them, and I also still get a huge thrill when I see a piece of coverage that I have generated. There is nothing like seeing your hard work come to fruition in a tangible way.

Q: Would you let us know what has been your biggest achievement as a communications manager?

A: In every job I've had, I've definitely had moments where I've had a particular sense of achievement, whether it's pulling off a big event like a London Fashion Week show or the launch of a new brand, or seeing a big feature on my brand come out in print in a magazine or newspaper.

Q: What methods of communication do you use in your work today and has that changed in the last few years?

A: When I first started, the phrase of the office was very much 'get on the phone'. We would call the fashion desks on a daily basis to chat with the teams and find out what their stories were. Nowadays everything is done by email. People really don't pick up their phone, and with everyone's schedule being so busy it's much more convenient to communicate via email.

Q: Can you give us your opinion on the bloggers' role in promoting and communicating fashion brands today?

A: I feel like I came into the industry right before a huge moment of change. In one sense, I am quite old-school in that I really value print media and I still think there is nothing that beats seeing something in print. However, I also love Instagram and have personally bought things after seeing them on an influencer's account. Ultimately, there is room for everyone, and I enjoy working with both fashion press and digital influencers, as they all have the power to help a brand convey their products and messaging to a wider audience.

Q: With the changes taking place in the fashion industry today, such as the shifts in the fashion cycle etc. . . . do you think it will affect the role of the communicator, if so, what do you anticipate that would be?

A: It's certainly been interesting the last few years to see all the changes that have been taking place, and I think what we are seeing is that there is no one way or right way for a brand to do things. In some ways that creates more challenges, but it's also an exciting opportunity. For me as a publicist, I always choose to align myself with brands that I truly believe in and that have a unique perspective and strong brand identity. If there is a core brand DNA, the communications strategy grows from there. The key is to be flexible in your thinking and continue to evaluate if a certain approach or action makes sense for the specific brand, rather than just using the same approach because you have done so previously.

Q: Do you have any advice for those starting a career as a fashion communication professional?

A: I think the thing most people want to know is how hard is it to 'break into' the fashion industry? My answer has always been the same: on one level, it is hard because it's a specialist industry and there can be some elements of elitism to it. But on the other hand, everyone is actually crying out for hard-working entry-level candidates! So if you are willing to put in the work at the beginning, you can actually land an entry-level role within six months I would say. The key is to make yourself indispensable as an intern, so that even if the company you are with cannot keep you they will recommend you elsewhere, and may also call you back to join them further down the line. I can't tell you how many of my interns I have found jobs for throughout the years, and equally a lot of my opportunities were created through impressing someone at an earlier point in my career.

The fashion machine

In this chapter, you will learn about the important dates and events taking place every year in the fashion industry. Each year fashion retailers and designers work to a calendar of seasonal selling, shipping and delivery dates. You will find out that most work to the guidelines of the traditional calendar that has been in place for decades and combines buy dates with delivery dates and involves months of lead times between the presentations (shows) and the delivery of collections into stores. In addition, you will learn about the huge changes taking place in the industry – the timing, the development of fashion products and the way brands focus their promotional events to sell their products to the buyers.

The chapter will help you:

- Understand the current and long-established fashion calendar.
- Appreciate the changes taking place in the fashion system.
- Understand how fashion shows are a fundamental part of the industry and its buying cycle.
- Understand what part the fashion press plays in the industry.
- Appreciate the emerging role of the fashion curator and curation as a new discipline in the communication of fashion products to an audience.

**6.1
Backstage at London Fashion Week, February 2018.** The smooth running of the fashion industry is the meticulous planning and detailed precision of the well-oiled machine that is the fashion calendar and its activities.
© Ian Gavan/BFC/ Getty Images

The fashion calendar

The fashion calendar is a key component in the organisation of the fashion industry. It is the tool that facilitates the smooth running of the global fashion network, ensuring that events do not overlap but are also close enough together to enable a buyer to make an extended trip each season to see what is on offer in the fashion capitals of the world. Today, many companies now publish their information online and provide their own versions of fashion calendars, but these are primarily tailored to particular specialisms, such as menswear, sportswear or shoes, and specific market levels.

As the fashion industry is made up of lots of different kinds of companies including retailers, designers, marketers and image-makers, to name a few, the smooth running of such a complicated industry is crucial and down to the detailed planning that takes place each season, including key dates such as the fashion weeks for the upcoming season.

The fashion calendar has been under siege for a while, and it has to be recognised that advances in social media have meant immediate access to new fashion and has made change inevitable. Instant access the public have to catwalk images has led some to conclude that consumers get bored by the time the collections reach retail stores; the way 'fast fashion' retailers can have catwalk-inspired collections in store within weeks has added to this concern. The traditional process of design to store includes many stages, from the design process itself, production sourcing, the presentation of the collection to buyers, manufacture of the orders and finally delivery to store, all have been challenged by new, faster production methods shortening the calendar. But it is important to realise the shortened calendar has risks attached, and rushing the creative process is a key concern for some, particularly the designer, as this increases pressures to produce collections in factories that may not provide safe and ethical working conditions for its employees. In addition, smaller design brands do not have the resources to work to a shortened fashion calendar. This movement to instant purchasing is leading to a massive industry shake up. Outlined later in the chapter are some of the designers changing their approaches to the fashion calendar.

Fashion week

While we are seeing changes to the industry and its calendar, the traditional model is still the mainstay of the fashion industry. This means there are the four weeks of runway shows, known as Fashion Week, held each season in New York, London, Milan and Paris. New York Fashion Week is the first of the four each season; NY was also the world's first fashion

6.2
Chanel haute couture AW11.
Chanel couture shows are often held in spectacular venues around Paris, such as here at the Grand Palais.
© Dominique Charriau via Getty Images

week, which was organised by publicist Eleanor Lambert in 1943 to showcase American designers. Next to show is London, with London Fashion Week, then Milan and finally Paris. The shows traditionally run over February and March for the following autumn/winter season and throughout September for the following spring and summer. However, we are now seeing changes to this pattern with many brands and designers adopting different approaches to their fashion calendars and opting for more modern methods and timescales. Nevertheless, most designers are still showing in the four key fashion capitals using the original calendar of events.

The 'big four' are the foundation of the fashion industry and the most well-known, but there are now fashion weeks held at different times across the world, from Stockholm to Seoul to Sydney. Alongside each fashion week, the less commercial, more edgy or directional designer shows, often described as 'off-schedule', are held in alternative venues such as warehouses, train stations, galleries, gardens, museums or even in private homes.

Designers organising fashion shows can find it very costly and time consuming, and there is a great deal of hard work involved. It is not a task for one person alone and many designers will employ a team to work together to get the best results.

The right combination of aesthetics, encouraging participants in the planning stages and pulling together the show will ensure that it is an exciting and successful event. Fashion shows are all about the right organisation, planning, energy, excitement, location, music, selection of models, choreography and much more. Catwalk shows are increasingly

complex productions, and there are now many specialist production companies that organise everything from show logistics through to selecting models and music.

Before detailing some of the activities involved in the organising of a fashion show, attention needs to be paid to the changing nature of the fashion show. The following section on the future of the fashion show outlines some of the reasons why we are seeing the shift.

The future of the fashion show

The format of the fashion show has remained fundamentally the same since the 1940s. Collections are shown on the runway every six months in advance of the season when they would be 'worn'.

In the past, trend forecasters predicted colours, fabrics and the styles fashion consumers would be wearing years in advance. The trickle down of trends from forecast to catwalk to manufacturer to retail store was a seamlessly-paced conveyor belt in the fashion machine. However, as it has been

6.3
The right combination of aesthetics, encouraging participants and organised planning stages will ensure an exciting show.
© Andreas Rentz via Getty Images

identified in previous chapters, high street fashion today is a completely different beast, with retailers like Zara and Topshop updating their stock on a continuous basis, sometimes daily, in order to keep up with the lightning-fast speed with which fashion trends are changing. In the high-end fashion world, the fashion cycle has increased in speed, too. We have seen the introduction of more ranges and more justification to refresh designs with Resort, Pre-Fall and capsule collections, all popping up in between the traditional spring/summer and autumn/winter shows.

**6.4
Victor & Rolf
AW11.** Viktor &
Rolf present at
Paris Fashion
Week. The runway
shows are a suc-
cessful continua-
tion of the label's
design aesthetic.
© Pascal Le
Segretain via Getty
Images

The future of the fashion show is currently under discussion within professional and academic circles alike. With digital and technological shifts, a rise in the number of new brands, the power of pre-collections and the way brands are attempting to directly target their customers, the industry is at a point where huge changes are inevitable.

In February 2016, Burberry announced changes to its runway and retail calendar, and now only holds two seasonless annual shows, making its collections available immediately online and in stores. This, in addition to the cancellation of Tom Ford's New York show in September 2016, suggests an adoption of a see-now-buy-now model that will have an effect on other designers and brands, the way they follow the fashion calendar and how they present their collections to the buyers and the public.

With some brands trying the new model, other models are also emerging: appointment-only presentations, online shows and the combining of both menswear and womenswear collections into a single presentation have emerged in the last year or so. Nevertheless, however people feel about trends and the urge to indulge in conspicuous consumerism, a fashion show is a fashion show: the inspiration and escapism is still there whenever you like it. The 'big four' fashion weeks, once the domain of fashion editors, buyers and wealthy clients, currently attract more than 230,000 attendees, and they now have a huge real-time online audience.

But can Fashion Weeks be updated to contend with all this? At the time of writing, we are seeing a number of designers that are already doing just that. As mentioned, Burberry and other large brands such as and Tommy Hilfiger are initiating similar changes, making their designs immediately available for purchase. In February 2016, designers including Proenza Schouler and Michael Kors sold capsule collections instantly during New York Fashion Week. With the move to the new model, the fashion landscape is undergoing momentous transformation, but Paris federation in charge of Paris fashion week markedly disagreed with the changes and opted for the traditional timeline, careful supply chain and the slow gratification of the luxury industry.

Planning a fashion show

Step 1: Respect the designer's vision

From the start, it is important to understand that the show is an event to showcase the designer's vision. Having to create sometimes more than three collections a year, each show can be a massive task that is exciting, exhilarating and expensive. The designer wants the best scenario for the show and it will be your job to present it. Research the designer's work, past shows and look for a preferred style in music, décor and lighting. Attention to the designer's choice in models will help you make an informed and effective presentation to the designer.

Step 2: Know fashion history

You have to love fashion to produce fashion shows, and it is important to know the names of some of the key players, such as editors, photographers, models and other designers. It's important to understand trends, fabric colour and fit.

There is a complete language around fashion, and some of it changes by the second – particularly with the advent of social media – so it's best to study up on fashion history and know the difference between an appliqué and an A-line.

Step 3: The importance of PR and marketing

It is more than likely that a PR person or the marketing professionals will contact you before you meet the designer, as it is their responsibility to hire the professionals. They will be looking for someone with experience, passion and the ability to think creatively. They will also look for someone who understands and loves fashion, and gets the work of the designer. Someone who is an expert at organisation, timing and can stay on budget.

Step 4: Models' agents are your best friends

If you're new to the fashion show business, it is unlikely that you will secure a big designer name show to produce. Those designers have people that they will have worked with for many years. If you're lucky enough to produce a show for a small design house or new designer, although smaller, the production has all the same elements and will need just as much attention and expertise as one of the larger shows. You will need models, and that is why your best friend will be the agent. The relationship between a fashion show producer and model agent should be a close and wonderful thing.

Step 5: Organise

Get organised! Fashion shows are events on steroids; it is critical that you hire excellent people to work with you – people who are prepared to work hard and keep their opinions to themselves. They need to stay quiet, calm and collected. As the producer, it is your job to orchestrate, delegate and assign specific tasks to people best suited to complete them efficiently, with deadlines and regular progress reports.

You have to keep everyone motivated, focused and informed along the way so that there is a seamless, cohesive creative effort with the goal of respecting the designer's vision.

The team

A fashion show is a team effort; the team will often be comprised of the following roles:

Show producer: knowing what everyone is doing is the responsibility of the show producer; it is their job to keep everyone briefed on changes, times and rehearsals.

Backstage manager: this is an exciting but stressful job, which suits those who can work well under pressure. The backstage manager ensures that everything goes exactly to plan on show day.

Hair and make-up artists: these individuals work creatively and closely with the designer and show stylist to create an image for the models based on the overall look.

Casting manager: looking after the models is the core responsibility of the casting manager. Their role is to ensure that all models know what they are doing and that they attend rehearsals. This role relies heavily on good interpersonal and organisational skills.

Show stylist: develops the look for the show in consultation with the designer. Inspiration from magazines and trend prediction intelligence are all considered in the selection of the right 'look'. Tear sheets are often compiled as a look book for communicating the inspiration.

Promotional manager: this person organises tickets and invitations and is responsible for raising awareness of the event through the media.

Organising a show involves a lot of money and hard work, and for many designers, it will involve sourcing sponsors. Many designers are reliant to some degree on contributors to make the whole event work, and this is where students and interns can help. Being involved in raising funding and general show organisation duties can be a challenging but fantastic experience.

6.5
Backstage at New York Fashion Week. Hair and make-up artists and stylists are a creative part of the production team.
© Ilya S. Savenok via Getty Images

'Coming together is a beginning, staying together is progress, and working together is success.'
Henry Ford

The fashion press

The fashion sector is covered by a wealth of fashion press, a collective name for a variety of media such as trade journals, magazines, TV and radio. Trade journals such as *Women's Wear Daily* (US) and *Drapers* (UK) are focused on the business side of the fashion industry, such as market and industry news. As consumer awareness of designer fashion has increased over the last twenty years, there is now a huge range of fashion magazines catering to different fashion consumers, from the fashion-forward independents such as *V Magazine* and *POP* to the well-established glossies, such as *Vogue* and *Harper's Bazaar*. Reporting on fashion shows is a major part of the role of the fashion press; typically, fashion shows are held to promote a fashion label's clothing lines to the international press as well as to retail buyers.

Fashion journalism

Fashion journalism refers to all aspects of published fashion media, from fashion features in magazines and newspapers to books about fashion, fashion-related reports on television as well as online fashion magazines, websites and blogs. The work of a fashion journalist is varied and has changed quite a bit over the years; it can include anything from writing and editing articles to organising and styling fashion shoots. Researching and conducting interviews are a major part of the role of a fashion journalist, and it is essential to have good contacts with people in the fashion industry, including photographers, designers and PR specialists.

The role of fashion journalist will typically involve the following:

- Communicating the constantly changing fashion market to a wide audience
- Reviewing new ranges, designers and trends
- Building contacts with relevant PR companies
- Attending press open days, trade and consumer shows
- Researching the fashion media
- Interviewing designers
- Organising and attending fashion shoots
- Writing and editing features and news stories

Writing about fashion is a creative outlet; a good fashion journalist can skilfully translate fabrics, colours, style and image into words. In addition to excellent communication skills, the fashion journalist must have a love for fashion, to enjoy writing about runway shows, celebrity sightings, fashion events and trend spotting.

'I think consumers expect a great deal more from magazines now. There's so much free content online that people need a good reason to part with their money, and rightly so. There's a move towards magazines with more originality, with a real voice.'

Rob Nowill

Careers in journalism

Fashion journalists may work full-time for a newspaper or magazine, but more often than not they will work in a freelance capacity, whether for print or online. Due to the increased prevalence of blogs and online magazines, it is easier than ever to start out as a freelance fashion journalist; writing a blog is a great way to gain experience and get into the field.

Online press

The biggest impact on fashion journalism in the twenty-first century has been the internet, but print is most certainly not dead. Traditional

magazines have had to adapt and provide online versions. Internet technology has changed the way we view and consume fashion, enabling us to see images of the collections at home and abroad, read capsule reviews within hours of a catwalk show, receive live satellite feeds and view video conferencing with designers.

The internet has proved valuable for designers eager to see what the competition is doing; for consumers eager to see for themselves what lies ahead; and for journalists and magazine editors, accustomed to making their own runway sketches as notes, it is a great back up. The internet revolution has offered the fashion professional a multitude of career choices and directions.

Moving image

It used to be recommended that if you wanted to progress in the fashion industry, you needed to learn French; today, however, things have changed and some say that it is sensible to 'learn film' to get ahead in fashion. The fashion film has earned its place in the communication of the fashion collection. Practitioners of fashion communication need to be multi-lingual and able to communicate across a range of different platforms and media with film officially labelled the new 'French' of media production.

Fashion Film is an extremely exciting and dynamic area of the fashion industry. As the

world of fashion has been democratised through the development of online and live streaming, we are going to see this used in many different ways.

It could be argued that moving image is the future of fashion communication, bridging the gap between the traditional worlds of print and film. This exciting medium has started to change the way designers and marketers communicate and promote fashion. Today there are screens wherever you go, and most people now have mobile phones that can download film, making the possibilities exciting, more immediate and quite different to anything that has gone before.

In 2000, Nick Knight established his website SHOWStudio at the height of the online boom, and it was his intention to build an online home for fashion film. Over the past few years we have seen a growth in digital video consumption; according to Cisco (a technology conglomerate), by 2020 video will account for 82 per cent of internet traffic. However, present-day success has been inhibited by distribution constraints and budgetary constraints, among other things. It is important for aspiring fashion communicators and marketers to realise the potential of film in the future of fashion and to use the fantastic work of directors such as Spike Jonze ('The New Fragrance', Kenzo), Steven Klein ('Wolves', Balmain) and Glen Luchford (Gucci Autumn/Winter 2016) for inspiration to break the mould.

Fashion editorial

There is a lot of work involved in fashion editorial, and each and every shoot needs careful planning. Usually a photographer will be working two months ahead of publication; for example, a deadline in March would need to be planned in January. The editor will normally provide the brief, which can be exciting and provide a lot of free reign.

One of the best ways to get into the industry is to intern at a fashion magazine. However, internships are typically unpaid and the job is likely to be menial and unglamorous; it may involve steaming clothes, for example, or cleaning up after shoots. Nevertheless, most fashion editor's start from the bottom and work through the ranks. Anna Wintour, editor of American *Vogue* and one of the most influential people in the fashion industry, began her career as an editorial assistant.

The photographer

The photographer's influence and communication skills are key to the success of a photo shoot. A good photographer knows how to make the model comfortable and how to direct them. When given a particular assignment, the photographer should be able to use their creativity and skills to portray what the client wants in one shot.

It is not essential to obtain a degree in fashion photography; the skills required can be developed by learning on the job, whether as a photographer's assistant or through an apprenticeship. It is, of course, a competitive sector, and it is essential to build up a portfolio to showcase technical skills and a distinctive, creative perspective.

The stylist

Creating visual images is a key part of the role of the fashion stylist; photographs used in magazine articles or videos used in the music industry are a part of this process. Working from a design brief, stylists work with teams of people such as photographers, art directors, designers, lighting technicians and set builders to ensure a creative approach to the job in hand.

The fundamental part of the job involves planning creative solutions to a design brief. The fashion stylist is responsible for selecting clothing and accessories and putting them together in outfits that fit the visual expectations of the client. The stylist will meet with the client, producers and photographers to agree on what types of colours, garments or costumes will be needed to create outfits or 'looks'. They may sketch up their ideas onto mood boards to provide a visual example of the idea, with examples of outfits or costumes to ensure everyone is in agreement.

To re-emphasise a theme in this book, the stylist's job is about hard work and determination, complemented by a love for fashion. Typical work activities include contacting PR companies, manufacturers and retailers; and sourcing the best range of merchandise to be used in a shoot. Hours are often long because work continues until a photo shoot or the filming is finished.

Being employed as a fashion stylist is usually a freelance job, often developed through word of mouth and gaining contacts through work projects. Stylists must demonstrate competency by showing prospective employers the composition and editing skills of previous assignments within a portfolio. It can take one or two years to build up a comprehensive styling portfolio. As well as creative vision and staying ahead of trends, the stylist should have excellent organisational and time-keeping skills. If you were to consider a career as a fashion stylist, it is essential to network as much as you can while you're learning. It's the contacts that will get you a job. Many fashion stylists have a background in fashion design, which aids the transition between the three-dimensional garments and the two-dimensional image. However, there are other routes into fashion styling: a great way is to assist a stylist or a photographer. It's an opportunity to learn first-hand what goes on during a shoot, while assisting can also lead to personal commissions.

Fashion curating, online exhibition and the trade show

Fashion products are exhibited to customers at each stage of the fashion cycle through catwalk collection, international trade fairs and online presentation methods. Examples of trade fairs include the Pitti Filati yarn fair; Première Vision, a fabric trade show; as well as garment trade shows such as Bread & Butter or Prêt à Porter Paris. The presentation of fashion products as static exhibitions is something we are seeing as a growth area. Exhibitions to consumers and fashion audiences through retail exhibitions and historical events at museum and galleries are areas under development. In addition to the physical exhibition, online exhibitions are being explored, which is forming a growing discipline and creating a new role for the fashion communicator interested in the fashion story: this is the role of the fashion curator.

Fashion curation

'Curation' is a word that describes the work done in galleries and museums around the world and is the collecting of objects to research and how to display them. Curators can be specialised or have a wide variety of work to cover, and one of the areas of specialism is fashion. Fashion curation, however, deals with the presentation of 'dress' but can also deal with 'fashion' in its widest sense, including areas such as elaborately presented fashion shows, photography, fashion film, objects and accessories and all sorts of cultural materials relating to fashion.

Fashion design has seen a rapid growth in exhibitions around the world and has become much bigger than in the past. Massive exhibitions are not uncommon, for example, 'Savage Beauty – Alexander McQueen', broke visitor record numbers at the Victoria and Albert museum in London in 2015. 'China Through the Looking Glass' for the Metropolitan Museum of Art was the fifth most popular exhibition ever.

Fashion exhibitions and presentations are becoming a key part of the national and international landscape of contemporary society, and they attract some of the largest audiences to major museums and fashion exhibitions. They are also increasingly visible in department stores, galleries and the wider community. Fashion is starting to peer out from behind the curtain, with designers creating their own archives and retail stores organising exhibitions and thought-provoking window displays. Fashion curation is becoming a discipline with a lot of potential, both economically and educationally.

The curator

The shift and recent developments in exhibition design, primarily contemporary fashion as exhibited in museums and public gallery spaces, represent the growing status of the curator role as a central cultural mediator in the process.

Extensive research that comes before a fashion exhibition is a key part of the role of the curator, as it is their job to give meaning to the objects and pieces being exhibited, whether it's researching a particular designer's work, setting a contemporary fashion collection in a retail store or private collection, or placing a collection in cultural history.

Online curation

Online curation is a growing field, and in an era when organisations are expected to proactively interact and engage with their audiences through a range of media, it makes absolute sense that fashion curators embrace the potential of the internet and online communication. Recently we have seen the rise of the online museum collection, offering new ways of engaging with audiences, including the ability to exhibit items too fragile to show in a physical display, as well as the use of microphotography to show detail that could not otherwise be seen unless the garment was handled.

Other benefits include the ability to capture stories connected to a garment's maker or wearer and allowing the viewer to see behind-the-scenes museum and preservation practices. This also provides opportunities and mutual advantages for viewer engagement, with online displays offering an audience the opportunity to contribute their own stories, collections and image archives.

The trade show

Designer runway shows aside, the fashion industry is largely structured around the trade show. As the name suggests, trade shows are not open to the general public; these shows are aimed at bringing together designers and retailers to sell fashion products. The important trade shows are held around the same time each year, and they will be advertised in the industry press.

Booking a stand at a trade show can cost a lot of money, so exhibitors need to know that it's worth their while at the planning stage. An exhibitor would need to research the show carefully and check the official list of buyers attending to ensure the show will be suitable for their products and market.

The importance of trade shows

Fashion trade shows are an essential part of the fashion industry, as buyers and suppliers flock to them to discover new business opportunities. Trends change at a fast pace and businesses will look to trade shows in the fashion capitals such as Milan, Paris and New York to research the latest trends. Suppliers attend the shows in the hope of making new deals and gaining new clients. Many will also attend the events to scope out the competition. Buyers attend trade shows to discover the hottest styles at first glance. It also provides them with an opportunity to check out new businesses.

Trade shows prove to be a cost-effective means of business because so many people within the industry attend at once. It is easier to arrange meetings at a trade show than to arrange countless meetings in different places.

Money and goods will rarely change hands at trade shows; the aim is for stand holders to generate sales leads, which will be followed up at a later date. Exhibitors should collect business cards and contact details from buyers in order to contact them after the show closes. It is essential that they act promptly: buyers see lots of designs at shows, and if the connection is not made quickly, they can easily forget.

Trade stands

Setting up for a trade show event can be time consuming and expensive, yet the benefits that can be gleaned should make it well worth the time, money and effort.

For most exhibitors, the emphasis should be the display and maybe curation of their products. Key to the success of a trade show display is having strong designs that look good together, using a range of visual merchandising techniques. Most will have lookbooks, catalogues or brochures available to take away.

It is important to create the right atmosphere and display a strong brand message, such as a banner and logo; this is how the buyers will remember their stand.

Innovative promotional methods may be used to make buyers visit the stand, such as plasma screens playing fashion films to attract attention. However, buyers will not like gimmicks as they have limited time to do their sourcing: and time is money.

6.7
Bread & Butter, 2011, Berlin, Germany. The trade show stand needs to look professional and inviting to draw people in.
© Sean Gallup via Getty Images

Case study:
The future of New York Fashion Week

There have been many discussions on the changes taking place in the fashion weeks, and in March 2016, the Council for Fashion Designers America (CFDA) conducted a report to try and understand the future of New York Fashion Week. The group partnered with more than fifty designers, editors and fashion insiders, in addition to industry stakeholders and fashion executives, to discuss the current fashion system, seasons, their relevance and vision for the future. In the last few years, the fashion system has gone through a number of changes, with technological advances making the fashion show, once restricted to a

trade audience, accessible to a global audience. Today we are seeing fashion shows streamed in real time, and the hype about a new collection occurs often months before the products hit the stores. Many designers (for example, Tom Ford, Burberry and Paco Rabanne) are beginning to embrace a new model labelled: Direct-to-consumer. In addition, as many fast fashion companies have the advantage over the luxury collections and their long lead times, allowing companies such as H&M and Zara to imitate them and get them into store and to their consumers at a fraction of the cost, and way ahead of the

6.8
Designers such as Burberry are beginning to embrace the direct-to-consumer model.
© Bloomberg via Getty Images

original products, designers are having to rethink the way they show their collections.

The report as commissioned by the CFDA suggests there isn't a one-size-fits-all solution to the changes taking place and there are many challenges taking place within the industry. Immediacy was one of a few areas outlined as a factor, with consumers looking to buy products quicker, resulting in the retailer being out of sync with the season, inhibiting the full price potential.

Technological advantages have made it much easier to expose new collections to consumers well before they are available, resulting in customer fatigue and out-of-date trends, damaging the potential of full-price sales. Finally, the confusion and complex nature of the production cycle has created a difficult situation for designers and retailers to keep up with, which in turn hinders artisanship and the creative process.

New approaches

In addition to the changes mentioned above, there are a number of designers working on different approaches to the problem of what some are saying is an antiquated fashion system. Appointments and presentation is one suggestion that is being considered by Michael Kors. Michael Kors is a popular high-end fashion brand set up in 1981. The brand specialises in fashion products aimed at women in the twenty- to thirty-five-year-old age group. With over thirty years in the industry and setting trends, the brand had to reinvent itself in the 1990s when it filed for bankruptcy. At the time, the lower-priced KORS range was the way for the company to continue. The line, which still exists today, became the face of the brand.

Kors discussed the direct-to-consumer presentation trend sweeping the international fashion industry with *Women's Wear Daily* (WWD). The designer only released five images of his 2017 resort collection after showing the complete collection – which was presented to press after and no social media was permitted. The rest of the looks were released in October when they became available in stores and online.

A Michael Kors Resort 2017 lookbook was distributed for long-lead editorial requests, WWD reported. *'The value lies in creating a sense of fashion immediacy,'* Kors.

In an interview with the magazine, Kors explained that this approach for the pre-collections, as they were not large, staged events like the show created for fashion weeks, was that by only releasing a sneak preview of five images on the day of the presentation, he is able to provide their customers with a little teaser into what is to come without swamping and confusing them by presenting products that are not yet available. In a world of instant gratification, the aim is to show the full range of looks closer to the time they are available to purchase.

'I don't think there is any one right answer. Each fashion house is going to have to find what works for them.'
Michael Kors

Chapter summary

In this chapter, we have seen that fashion retailers and designers work each year to a seasonal calendar of selling, delivery and shipping dates, with many working to the traditional calendar that has been in place for decades. We are, however, seeing changes taking place, and the future of the fashion show is currently under discussion. With digital and technological shifts, the rise in the number of new brands and the way brands are attempting to directly target consumers, some say that so many things bombarding customers has created what is described as customer fatigue and has had a damaging effect on the potential of full-price sales. Finally, the confusion and complex nature on the production cycle has created a difficult situation for designers and retailers to keep up with, which in turn hinders artisanship and the creative process.

As the fashion industry is made up of lots of different company types, including retailers, designers, marketers and image-makers, the smooth running of this complicated industry is down to the detailed planning that takes place each season. The fashion show remains a popular form of presentation to both the public and fashion professionals and requires many people to pull the show together, particularly with the new selling and communicating opportunities for the brands.

Key to getting the message out and reporting the work from the shows are the bloggers and the magazine journalists. And as consumer awareness of designer fashion has increased over the last twenty years with the huge range of fashion magazines catering to different fashion consumers, from the fashion-forward independents such as *V Magazine* and *POP* to the well-established glossies, such as *Vogue* and *Harper's*. It is evident that we are in a transition period with many things evolving, and it is important that fashion professionals in all areas of the system are plugged in; flexible and open to change in order to meet the changing needs of the industry.

Case study and chapter reflection

Q. Outline reasons for the changes taking place in the fashion weeks discussed.

Q. Why are designers rethinking the way they show their collections?

Q. How has technology changed the way collections are shown to the customer?

Q. Michael Kors only released five images of his 2017 resort collection. What were his reasons for doing this?

CHECKLIST

1. Who developed the first fashion show and what year was that held and where?

2. What is the fashion calendar and why is it important for the industry?

3. The fashion show format is evolving. Explain the details of the see-now-buy-now model.

4. What are the key roles in a fashion show team?

5. The press are important contributors to the industry. Explain the different reporting formats a journalist may write for and what the role may involve.

6. Moving image is an exciting area of presentation. Describe how this is being used in communication fashion collection.

7. Explain the different contributors in the fashion editorial.

8. What is curating fashion?

9. Explain why presenting work at a trade fair is important and what happens?

10. Why is the fashion calendar different for luxury and high street fashion?

EXERCISE

Organising a fashion shoot

Fashion shoots in the fashion magazine industry will be done by hiring a photographer and team. However, as a student you may be required to do your own shoot for lookbooks or project portfolios and blog posts. The following exercise will help you organise a shoot, from coming up with the concept to the final shoot day.

Step 1: The idea or concept

It is important that you have an idea of what you want: a look, feel and mood you want to achieve. Think about what ideas you have of clothing, hair and make-up, as planning will help you get the best result. You could be a little vague at this point, it could just be a 1970s vibe or glamour, trashy . . . your call. It is important at this point that you get an idea or concept to start the ball rolling.

Step 2: The storyboard

You might want to use something like Pinterest at this point, as it is one of the greatest ways of collating images. Sign up, and once you do, you can pin to your heart's content. Alternatively, you could explore some of the websites or magazines you might find online for ideas. The more images you find, the more inspiration you will get and be able develop a clearer idea of what you want to achieve. This isn't just for you to get your head around; it is to communicate your idea to your team so they can get behind it too!

Step 3: Finding your team

This sometimes can be the hardest part particularly if you are a student. But the team members should be as follows:

1. A make-up artist
2. A hair stylist
3. A garment stylist

Where do you find these people? As a student, you may want to contact other students in your college or university. Most universities will have other creative courses where you could find fellow students to collaborate with to shoot your fashion story. You could send emails through your tutors to get the message out. Most courses have Instagram and Facebook sites – ask professors or tutors to add your details and make a connection that way. You could post a casting which will be visible to all the above and wait for responses. If the courses aren't geared towards clothes, make-up or beauty, there are usually colleges in your town that will specialise in hair and make-up that may be able to help as they will be looking for potential projects for their students too. When seeking out a team, remember to add your mood-board link. This will be where you sell the idea! You want the team to be as invested in the idea as you are.

Step 4: Models

Sourcing models from your fellow students is a way you can do this on the cheap. However, sometime these volunteers can be unreliable, so it might work best if you club together with another student working on a similar project to share the cost for the day and approach a model agency. You may get a new model, as they will be cheaper, need the practice and the photos. Agency models is really where you want to be, as on the whole they will turn up and know what they're doing. You will probably have to shoot tests with friends at first to build up a portfolio. This way, when you contact the agencies, you can include the images to give them an idea of what you want to do.

Step 5: Location

You now have a team and you will need to figure out where you're going to take the photos! Good locations can tell stories, reveal fantastic light and bring out the best in you and your camera. For an indoor location, think of friends' houses or local buildings of interest. It is important that they are visually interesting (e.g. your local town hall or public library. . .etc.). Sometimes wedding venues and country houses will let you shoot for free. Shooting outside, your biggest problem will be the weather. Think carefully about this and plan your day accordingly.

Step 6: The date

You will need to arrange a date that everyone can commit to. It is important that you also keep in mind that hair and make-up can often take a couple of hours longer than the other things.

Step 7: The shoot

Everyone is with you at the location, so remember to keep your mood-board out to remind everyone to keep up the theme of the day, including yourself. Also, communicating your idea and your vision is important, so it is crucial that you spend time explaining this to everyone in order to do everything you can to make it happen.

6.9
You will need models, and that is why agents should be your best friends.
© Uriel Sinai via Getty Images

If you are shooting an editorial, it means that you are aiming for a magazine style. Keep this in mind, and remember not to shoot too many landscape images. Nearly always keep your camera in portrait. It's about the clothes, so try to remember that when shooting. Keep the hair stylist, make-up artist and garment stylist on hand as well. Ask them to monitor the shots and if a dress hem is up or a stray hair has gone array get them to dart in and out to fix these things. Communicate with your team for the best outcome.

Interview:
Charmone Diane Williams

Freelance production assistant and fashion stylist, New York

Q: You are a fashion management graduate; tell us about how you got into your work after graduation.

A: My senior year of college I was constantly thinking about my plans for after graduation. I wrote out all the things I enjoy doing within the fashion industry and narrowed down my skills into three categories: marketing, fashion show production and styling. I shortly realised that I wanted to move to NYC, so I planned a trip to visit and meet with industry leaders. I went on countless interviews and met people over coffee. I reached out and sent thank-you cards and I was offered a freelance position to work for NYFW as a production assistant for spring/summer 2017 for Tory Burch, Victoria Beckham, Tommy Hilfiger and Thom Browne. From there, I began freelancing for different brands and building connections in the industry.

Q: Your work covers three main areas of fashion management: event planning, marketing and show production. Can you tell us a little bit about each and what is your favourite area of work.

A: For me, marketing consists of social media management, press releases, sample coordination, creative ways of gaining more consumers and building brand relationships. Fashion show production is basically handling pre- and post-production work for a show. So scouting a venue and finalising it, model castings, staff for day of show, lighting, music, seating and clothing coordination. Styling consists of creating looks and an image for a client or magazine. My favourite area of work varies; amongst all three changes from project to project, but I love show production the most because it allows me a chance to be involved in so many different things from start to finish. I love watching a show from concept to finish and finally being unveiled to the masses.

Q: You were wardrobe stylist on *Circus Magazine Photo-shoot*. Can you take us through what you had to do?

A: Styling is the most creative-driven skill I enjoy. It comes so natural to me. I have a colleague who started her own magazine and she wanted to create fresh editorials to be featured, so she asked me to style a shoot for it. I collaborated with a photographer and make-up artist for the shoot. I bought six different looks and styled the shoot. I thought of the theme, found and sourced all the clothing, steamed all the garments and discussed with the team what type of images we were going for. I'm always seeking new ways of expressing my creativity as a stylist. I save images on my phone; I take photos of possible locations to shoot, etc. My mind is so free when I have a shoot to conceptualise and style.

Q: In September of 2016 you moved to New York City to work as a production assistant for NYFW. Can you tell us a little bit about what you do?

A: As a production assistant for NYFW, I assist with the pre- and postproduction of several fashion shows per season. Depending on the company, I freelance with, I work weeks before fashion week begins. I help with the model castings, clothing coordination in prep for the show, organising model comp cards and serve as a liaison between designers and executive producers when they aren't on location. The day of show, the team and I arrive at least four or five hours before the show starts to make sure the stage is properly built, the collection arrives safely, hair and makeup is on time and that each model is prepped and ready.

Q: What would you say are the three key attributes the fashion show producer should have today?

A: As a fashion show producer, you must be organised to stay on top of all the components that are required to have a successful show. It's important to be reliable because you work with so many people that you should always be on call and stay on top of things. There are countless production companies and producers, so you have to be mindful of your clients' time and be there for them no matter what. Most importantly you have to be strategic because when things go wrong (in which they always do), as the producer you have to think fast to create an alternative way to proceed.

Q: In recent months, we have heard a lot about the fashion business and the changes to the system. What are your thoughts on the future of runway shows?

A: Runway shows are just as important as the legendary design houses we see and admire today. Though things may change and certain trends may come, such as the see-now-buy-now that customers can buy instantly, runway shows are more than just unveiling the next collection. It has become a way of self-expression for the designers and chosen audience. Having a runway show allows designers to communicate their inspiration behind the clothing for a given season and to be the utmost creative without worrying about the sales of a garment and trying to appeal to a certain audience. That's why so many designers have 'marketable pieces' separated from what's shown on the runway, because the runway is where the real creativity and art is allowed to shine.

Q: If you could change anything about fashion shows now, what would it be?

A: I would change the instant gratification of social media. I do enjoy that you can live stream a show and that you can watch some shows on your phone. However, there has to be a balance between keeping the genuine art of it and not focusing so much on being the most Instagrammed show.

Q. You believe that your education is important to have longevity in the fashion industry. Do you have any advice for future fashion management graduates?

A: My advice would be to take your time in college to learn what you do and do not like. Experiment different areas of the industry and be honest about what you want to do. Intern as much as possible, build connections with your professors and fellow graduates because those are the people you will see again while working in the industry. Never stop learning and perfecting your craft, read articles and stay up to date with how things are going. Stay focused and inspired to succeed.

'Opportunity wastes no time with those who are unprepared. Always stay ahead of the game'.

Charmone Diane Williams, 2016

Fashion entrepreneurship and management

This final chapter covers the area of fashion management in the context of the micro business. As fashion entrepreneurship serves as a vehicle for economic developments, the next chapter will introduce you to the idea of developing management and business skills for the small and micro business. Fashion entrepreneurship is about developing new fashion concepts through to the commercialisation of these, and we look at this in the chapter as a step-by-step guide to working them out. The chapter will also provide you with some ideas on new opportunities and business models available to the fashion entrepreneur in the twenty-first-century global fashion industry.

Throughout the chapter, we will be covering areas such as entrepreneurial practice, new business models, the planning and management of the creative fashion enterprise. The chapter will cover other important aspects such as the management of intellectual property, copyright, design rights and how to raise funds for start-up using crowdfunding.

The chapter will help you:

- Develop an awareness of what entrepreneurial practice is.
- Test your design concepts and ideas you may want to take through to commercialisation.
- Develop an understanding of the changes taking place in the global fashion industry and how the small fashion business and new business models are emerging.
- Understand how to plan and manage a small-scale fashion business.
- Think about the value and importance of protecting your ideas.
- Raise financing through crowdfunding.

7.1
Dino Alves SS18.
The fashion industry is not just about designer frocks; it is a serious business that contributes billions to the world economy.
© Estrop/Contributor via Getty Images

Entrepreneurial practice

The definition of a fashion entrepreneur can be described as someone whose primary work activities are that of operating within the fashion industry. For example, it would most likely be a fashion designer who would use entrepreneurial principles to organise, create and manage ventures within and connected to areas in the fashion industry.

Current practice

In today's fashion industry, fashion entrepreneurs focus on core business practices such as creativity and innovation, developing business plans, raising finance, sales and marketing of fashion products in addition to possessing small business management skills needed to run a creative company. In other areas, fashion entrepreneurs may operate and deliver fashion business expertise to retailing, manufacturing and marketing.

In the twenty-first century, we have seen the explosion of organisations and award ceremonies supporting, inspiring and stimulating online entrepreneurship by drawing attention to the enterprising attributes, creativity, innovation and the success of modern entrepreneurs along with the desire and contribution of giving back to society in areas such as ethical fashion and sustainability. The following chapter will cover some of the key areas that are necessary for anyone thinking of setting up a small fashion business or looking at how small fashion enterprise contributes to the industry as a whole, and how there is a place in the industry for the micro business and its manager.

Starting a fashion business

Starting any kind of business requires tenacity, endurance and dedication; setting up a fashion business, even small scale, is all the more challenging because it is such a complex and competitive industry. Fashion companies can very quickly find themselves with customers and suppliers scattered all around the world, which requires a lot of coordination and organisation. All of the raw materials (fabrics, trims, haberdashery and so on) must be supplied to the manufacturer to start production and the finished garments supplied to customers in different global locations. Even those designers with excellent forward planning and trouble-shooting skills will find it a challenging experience.

Many young designers dash into setting up a business, attracted by the perceived glamour and fun that is fashion. But it doesn't matter how talented you are as a designer, if you are going to run a successful fashion label you also need to know about the business side of the industry (it is even said that setting up a fashion business requires 90 per cent business acumen and 10 per cent design capabilities). When setting up a business, you will be involved in everything from manufacturing to marketing and PR, and, of course, sourcing the money to finance it all. It takes hard work, creativity and a true passion for a fashion designer to achieve success, but you can break into this career much more quickly and easily if you are aware of the pitfalls, processes and skills you will need to succeed as a fashion entrepreneur.

Entrepreneur

An entrepreneur may be defined as a person who identifies an opportunity or new idea and develops it into a new venture or project. As such, a fashion entrepreneur can be defined as someone who sets up a new fashion venture or starts a new fashion label. Entrepreneurs are acknowledged as being the driving force behind innovative change in our society, and the fashion and textile industry is no exception.

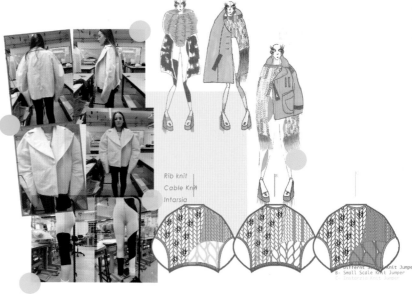

7.2
Design boards.
It is essential to
learn about the
business side of
the industry if you
are planning to set
up a fashion label.

Developing new concepts through to commercialisation

Small enterprises have been described as leaders in innovation, mostly when it comes to re-engineering products or processes or when trying new approaches. Developing new concepts through to commercialisation is a fundamental part of the role for new business managers to stay ahead of the game and its visionary managers, designers or product specialists, particularly in the fashion industry, that very often lead small organisations. The small scale of these companies allows for flexibility in the design of new concepts that will address the needs of the ever-demanding fashion consumer. This type of activity is crucial for a new business to succeed in turbulent and diverse economic market conditions.

As covered in Chapter 2, product development can be defined as designing, creating, manufacturing, introducing and delivering new fashion products or services to the consumer. The activities of the micro-business manager when developing new concepts for products or services are no different to those developed in a larger brand context. The process is undertaken in both business contexts with the view to addressing customer need, providing fresh user experiences, increasing the customer base or market share in addition to driving sales and growing profit for the company.

In a larger company, the different business or management areas would be the sole responsibility of a specific fashion manager, while in a micro enterprise, all of this may be the responsibility of a single person or a few at most. The fuel and growth of the fashion industry depends a lot on the small fashion business and the process of developing new products, concepts and the commercialisation of these, and therefore this is the industry's essential life-blood, as fashion consumer demands are in a constant state of flux and the demands of customers are ever changing.

In order to start a successful micro fashion business, understanding the customer needs is the first part of the start-up strategy. It is no good thinking that you can set up a business without truly identifying what consumers need or want. The following will cover concept development in a step-by-step approach to help in the process of working out what you would need to consider before launching a fashion business and moving into the business plan stage.

A step-by-step approach to developing concepts for commercialisation

1. Generating the idea for a product/service

The need for new product development within the fashion industry may come from a number of places. These could include but are not limited to:

- Awareness of a need or gap in the market
- A demand by the consumer for new or improved fashion products
- Product innovation drive
- New products introduced into the market by the competition
- Developments in technology
- Trends and seasonal requirements and changes.

Methods for generating concepts for products that will sell vary, and can be formal or informal but generally should involve coming up with ideas through brainstorming exercises, focus group discussions and your own market research. Starting a new business will require research into your selected market and customer base, and although you may have limited funds, you will still be able to direct your research into your selected customer base through interviews and questionnaires, using either online or offline methods. Research is key to identifying your market, customer and products, and by understanding what they want, you can then start generating ideas for the new product/range/collection/service.

2. Concept screening

Concepts generated in the idea-generating step above should go through a procedure involving thorough screening and scaling based on the following criteria.

The feasibility of the concept/idea

You would need to make sure you have a clear idea of the market you will be operating in and your market feasibility should cover the following: Is there a demand for your products or services? Who are the customers that will buy your products or services? What are the numbers involved? Will your products appeal to your potential customers? How will you sell to them? Do your products or services fill a gap? What are the differences in your products compared to your competition? Are there any barriers to you entering the market?

Consideration to the design and development time

You would need to estimate how long it would take you to develop your products. This would need to be done at first by looking at what you have done in the past. Use this and time it by your planned project; this will then be your estimate. The more you do, the better and more accurate your estimate will become.

Estimated cost of producing the product

In a similar method to above, you will need to look at what you have done before, work out the material costs, the time and the overhead costs that would need to be paid regardless. Calculate as a rough estimate how many you would need to produce and sell in order for the business to be viable.

The estimated return on investment

You need to consider the costs of producing the product or service you're selling. In marketing, you need to calculate your return on investment (ROI) on your gross profit for the product/service you're selling, not on your gross revenue. But in business, you would need to consider what it costs to produce what you're selling and subtract that cost from your gross revenue.

The benefit to the consumer

You will need to work out your product's key benefit to your customer. A benefit is a true solution to a specific need. Think of your product as a solution and understand what issues it addresses.

Competitor analysis

The first part of the competitive analysis process only requires some basic research. By looking up and making note of easy-to-find facts about your competitor's business, you will need to have some idea about who your competitors are, where to find their website and social media pages, and perhaps have access to their offline marketing materials such as brochures, ads and posters. You would need to compare your brand to these and the products to your competitors'. What is unique to you and or your competitors?

Your competitors market share

You would need to estimate their market share by calculating their sales measured as a percentage of the market total revenue. To do this, divide its sales by the market's total sales over a financial period, such as one year. This can be used to get a basic idea of the size of your competitor relative to the industry.

Identifying your target retailers

Research the retailers you have targeted, look at which brands they stock and what the average retail price point is. It is also critical that you determine the type of product they offer and that your product sits in their range. Make sure you spend plenty of time physically on the shop floor of your key retailers so you can talk knowledgeably and ask pertinent questions about the store.

Setting your prices

The prices you set will be one of the most important business decisions you will make, so it is important that prices of your products/services are not too high or too low as this will limit your business growth. Make sure when setting them that you set them at a price that will allow your business to be profitable. Remember to take note of where your product or service sits compared with you competitors.

Time to market

You will need to work out the length of time it would take you to get your product from conception to becoming available for sale. It is particularly important in fashion as products can go out of fashion very quickly.

Manpower and technological requirements

You would finally need to work out whom you need to operate in the business to make it work, along with the machinery or digital technology to enable the business to function. This process is critical in the development stage for the new products/business as only products and ideas that can get through this stage should make it to production and finally into the market and to your customers. By undertaking this process, you can work out which are the commercial concepts that will be the basis of your business idea/product/collection/service.

3. Testing the concept

Where possible, it is important that you test out your concepts on your potential customers. It is essential you find out consumers' response to the business idea/product/collection/service. Where necessary, this will create a route for further improvement of the product/service. As a new business manager, getting a small group of targeted customers may be difficult, but where possible this should be a crucial part of the process. The best way at first would be to think about your extended personal network; you could reach out to people you know via social media as another option and you might have to offer some kind of fee or incentive. In this step, you will sample consumer opinion on how your idea will fare in contrast to others in the market. Concept testing will also provide information on pricing options. It is at this point too that attention is given to design details and any legal technicalities (i.e. branding or design rights where necessary). As a fashion and design business, for example, testing may take the form of a fashion show, private viewing for buyers and stockists and to the press.

It is important to realise that setting up a creative fashion **enterprise** in addition to developing the products and holding fashion shows and press days will also involve setting goals, writing the business plan and setting time aside for the marketing, promotion and selling of your fashion collection. Success can only be achieved by addressing the underlying issues that merge the passion for fashion with practical business skills.

Without the managerial tools and leadership skills needed to manage the business itself, you are likely to experience short-lived success. Managerial tools in the context of the micro business encompass financial, marketing, business development models and strategies.

Setting up a business after leaving fashion education is daunting, yet the business aspects can be developed just as creatively as the development of concepts for a collection. You can be creative about how you think things through, how you approach and solve problems – they can be challenged and resolved in surprising and unconventional ways. It is important to think creatively around your practice, assess and analyse the business idea in the same way as you develop your design concepts to make the most of the opportunities that exist, and provide yourself with the skills to develop a successful business model.

Identifying market opportunities in the 21st-century global fashion industry

There are many opportunities for fashion entrepreneurs today with the internet, as we have discovered it has changed the way we do business. The internet has provided the smaller fashion operator with the opportunity to work within the industry alongside larger business enterprises. The idea of the fashion entrepreneur for most people will inevitably conjure up the vision of the fashion designer or retailer, but following are many options for other types of businesses that the fashion entrepreneur could start. Next is a list of potential ideas for fashion businesses that can be operated by a sole trader or small number of people.

> **Enterprise**
>
> An enterprise is an organisation created for business ventures. A growing enterprise must have a bold leader.

1. **The fashion influencer (blogger):** If you have a keen eye for trends and have a passion for fashion, this is a business that can be set up with no capital and can make you some money as long as you put in the time and energy to keeping it up with regular posts.

2. **Set up a fashion magazine:** You can set up your own magazine; though a traditional style mag will require capital, you may want to consider an online version and upload to places like ISSUU or Wordpress for your readership. The mag can focus on fashion, lifestyle and trends, but the main task will be keeping fashion enthusiast abreast of what is going on in the industry.

3. **Become a celebrity manager:** This can be a viable business in the industry. The work you would be involved with is to manage the contracts of fashion celebrities including sourcing jobs and negotiating contracts on their behalf.

4. **Become an author or information marketer:** Once you have some experience in one area of the industry, you may want to think about how you can pass on that information to others. Becoming an author with a focus on fashion and lifestyle is one way and if this is not for you, you may want to stick with being an information marketer and make money by selling this information on the Internet. Information products can be written on a wide variety of fashion subjects, the only difference is, information products such as audio and ebooks, etc. are digitally downloaded rather than being a physical product.

5. **Start a fashion TV show:** You could start up your own online fashion or lifestyle TV

company. Online resources like YouTube and Vimeo are a way of getting your video online.

6. **Fashion boutique or retailing outfit:** If you're not a designer, you can still sell fashion products by setting up a retail outlet, online or offline. Working with other designers and product developers, such as accessories and shoes, is a way of selling fashion to the public. You can start a fashion boutique for women, men, children, etc.

7. **Fashion photography:** This is one of the most difficult and sought-after professions, and for every professional photographer that gets their work on the cover of a top magazine, there are many more working in other areas of the industry. You may find your niche such as advertising, art photography and fashion celebrity portraits or paparazzi work.

8. **Organise fashion events, expos and trade shows:** You may have some financial backing available to you. So as long as you have the organisational skills and the ability to attract corporate sponsors, then organising events such as trade events, fashion competitions, and so on could be your calling.

9. **Set up a modelling agency:** Setting up an agency that represents models is another option. Such agencies earn their income through commission, generally through the deal made between the model and the agency for jobs done with shows, magazines, and so on if you have the competency to source modelling deals and models.

In conclusion, it is worth emphasising that the fashion industry is huge, and as such there are many opportunities for the fashion entrepreneur to make a living – whether that is working for someone else or working for himself or herself. The self-employment route is becoming more popular, and the opportunities for start-up are available if you are prepared to think creatively, work hard and plan. There are more opportunities outside of the designer/maker route with many new and emerging ways to make money.

An example of an emerging small fashion business model: The microbrand

The following describes one area of the industry and how fashion designers are working on a small scale that is changing the way some people, including celebrities, are supporting new microbrands.

For a long time, fashion has been about the big names, designers and brands that are renowned across the globe and endorsed by the rich and famous. It has been about showing that you had money and how you hung about with the jet setters. To some extent, little has changed. However, as we get further into the twenty-first century, the fashionistas we so often emulate are starting a brand new trend that will be very difficult to replicate unless you have some idea of where to go. The newest trend in the fashion industry is the emergence of the micro designer. Micro designers, also known as underground or 'indie' fashion houses, are on the rise. Once considered as outcasts of the fashion industry, micro designers are now rapidly becoming the fashion houses that the rich and famous are running to. Some of the designers offering options for the wealthy are MY Theresa Ginger & Smart and the Designer Forum. Unlike mainstream brands that may end on the sale rack in stores, the 'indie' brands or micro designers rarely have their name plastered on the clothing. The micro designers, often locally focused, are starting to get the attention they deserve, which is adding to the appeal.

In other words, Australian lovers of fashion would look to microbrands in Sydney or Melbourne, whereas in the US, people would most likely find 'indie' designers' brands in New York City.

We are seeing a lot of change when it comes to the traditional versus the emerging business model. As outlined there are many options for fashion entrepreneurs to develop ideas for commercialisation. The next section covers some of that in more detail.

Micro design house

Micro design houses are mall enterprises, often comprising just one or two key persons (mostly women).

New and emerging business models

There are many small businesses in the United States, with more than 543,000 or more started every month. In the UK, research from Startup Britain, a Government-backed enterprise campaign, showed that 342,927 new businesses were registered between January and June 2016 compared with 608,110 for the whole of 2015. Therefore, if you have a business idea, it is crucial that you stand out from everyone else to succeed. In addition to the many opportunities for fashion entrepreneurs, there are equally many new business models that could be adopted for the business you want to start.

When embarking on a new business venture, designers must make decisions about the kind of business they would want to build. This is from the type of products they develop to how they want to sell them and all the stages in-between. Many designers today are creating their own rules and building businesses that are unique to their own life goals and personal values. The following trends are some of the new models we are seeing in fashion businesses today.

Sharing personal values as brand identity

The best part of being an entrepreneur is the control you have over your own future. However, this only works if you have managed to build something that complements your life and does not work against it. If your work competes with you every day, then you have no control. However, if the model works with the kind of life you are leading, then you are in the driver's seat. A major part of building a business that compliments your lifestyle is building it based on your personal values. We are seeing businesses based on what matters to the entrepreneur as a human being, what values they hold and the personal message they want to convey to the world; this has become the basis of so many independent and emerging brands.

Rather than adhering to the old-school version of what you think a fashion brand is, you can build a lifestyle brand that has purpose, meaning and is fulfilling not only for you but for the people that buy from you, write about you and collaborate with you.

Selling direct-to-consumer

There are opportunities to be had by utilising the direct-to-consumer sales model. The channel is growing fast and has been adopted by some of the larger brands. Smaller designers are now finding creative ways to get their brands recognised and drive customers to their websites by picking up this new business model.

Individual versions of success

Money has long been a driver and a measure of success, and to an extent, we need to make money to be financially secure. However, we are now seeing designers stepping back and reflecting on what makes them happy in their lives and their work and are redefining what success is for themselves. Some of this is money, but we are seeing designers state that freedom and time are indicators of personal success rather than money.

Ignoring seasons

The fashion industry has been amending the seasons for years now. We have seen resort, pre-fall and winmmer (a merging of seasons as described on social media) develop over time, all in the name of 'new stuff'. One of the new models emerging recently is the way designers are refusing to join in. The old models of autumn/winter and spring/summer are hard enough to deal with, without the addition of more. The changes being made to the industry are interesting to watch, whether it is dropping seasonal collections or simply focusing on the two key seasons, the new fashion business model means 'making up your own production rules'.

Redefining collections

In addition to ignoring seasons is the concept of what a collection has to be. Many designers work to a thirty-, fifty-, eighty-piece collection model that is fully merchandised in order to provide the buyer with a rich, well-rounded collection to display. Currently, we are seeing emerging brands launch a single hero piece to test the market and provide them with the capital to progress. There are brands that have introduced one or two styles every three months, and others developing collections of five to eight pieces and having fun with one, limited-edition additional style launched every month and this is totally unique to the brand!

Finding value in niche press

Once upon a time, it used to be that if you weren't picked up from the core fashion press, you really had not made it in fashion. Now so many designers have stopped looking at that as the only way to become recognised as a good designer. It would still be important for a brand to have a write up in *Vogue*, but designers have stopped letting this dictate whether they are on the road to success. Many designers have realised the power of tapping into social media, connecting with bloggers, doing interviews for podcasts and working hard to tell their own narrative – with many seeing the positive impact on their businesses both in terms of brand awareness and cash flow.

Location

Today's designers are not restricted to working in a major city. While the key cities are still major fashion hubs, such as New York, Milan, Paris and London, it is now feasible for a designer to be running a business out of a studio in Birmingham or Denver, and it makes them no less a member of the global fashion industry. Participating in the seasonal fashion weeks matters a lot less to designers today.

The common theme in all the models discussed is that new and independent brands are no longer waiting to be 'picked'. Many designers are taking success into their own hands; they realise that the industry is changing, that their values matter, rules can be broken and they have the power to create and mould their businesses to the lives they want to lead. There is nothing wrong with working to the traditional model either. What is exciting for anyone entering the fashion industry today is that there are so many opportunities available. If the model is not there currently, a new one can be designed to suit you.

Planning and management of the creative enterprise

In order to build a successful fashion business, you need to think like an entrepreneur from the outset. That means understanding how the business works and putting together a plan to lay out the short-, medium- and long-term goals for the business is crucial. The following section will go through the key stages to business start-up and creative management and planning of a small business.

Key stages to a business start-up

Starting a fashion business can be broken down into key stages:

Decision time: deciding what type of fashion business to open, whether it is designing clothes, selling clothes at a retail store or providing fashion services such as promotions. Going through the research stage will have provided you with your concept for products and or services. In your plan, you will need to be explicit about what you want, and you will need to do some comparison-shopping in addition to your book research to confirm your idea.

Planning: this includes researching ideas that suit your skills, support and capabilities. Developing this research into a business plan will help indicate if the business will be profitable. Whatever the business, a thorough business plan must be created, including the name of the business, location, costs and marketing ideas (see page 171 for more information on how to create a business plan).

Legal structure: although there are many different types of business set-up, a small fashion start-up will generally fit into one of two formats: sole proprietorship (also known as sole trader) or partnership. Sole proprietorship is the simplest format. This is a for-profit business consisting of a single owner. The owner may operate on his or her own or may employ others. Keeping records is more straightforward, but the owner of the business has unlimited liability for the debts incurred by the business. A partnership is a for-profit business owned by two or more people, and this format can work well for fashion graduates who are looking to pair different skills. In most forms of partnerships, each partner has unlimited liability for the debts incurred by the business.

7.3
Be explicit about what you want, and do some comparison-shopping.
© Gareth Cattermole via Getty Images

'There will always, one can assume, be the need for some selling. But the aim of marketing is to make selling superfluous. The aim of marketing is to know and understand the customer so well that the product or service fits him and sells itself.'
Peter Drucker

Money

The financial side of setting up a fashion business is usually the area most designers fear. However, it is critical to the plan to make projections for how the business will grow, in terms of profits and revenues, and what financing you will need to make it happen.

A carefully thought out projection of how your business will grow starts with an income statement, which will also project the costs of delivering that growth. The income statement does not tell you how much money you will need to raise, as it does not reflect the timing of cash inflows and outflows; for this, you will need a cash flow statement.

The cash flow statement shows the peaks and troughs of the cash situation on a monthly basis and identifies what funding will be needed to make it through the troughs. Think of the cash flow statement as a monthly account of cash coming in and cash going out. The difference between these two figures is the funding that will be needed for that month. It is always better to know funding needs in advance, rather than finding out when the bank account is empty and

suppliers are asking for payment before they release goods. This is particularly important in the fashion business where many costs are incurred upfront (such as designing, sampling, sales efforts) before revenues come in.

Offering the market something new

The following question must be addressed before setting out: can you offer the market something new? Defining and identifying a unique selling point (USP) will give focus and enable the formulisation of a business direction. Looking at the different types of fashion products and services in the fashion **marketplace** will provide a starting point for the fashion entrepreneur. Opening a fashion store or e-business will involve all aspects of the business from concept to promotion.

> ### Marketplace
>
> The fashion marketplace is the commercial world of buying and selling fashion products.

7.5
Supermarket Sarah. This online store has a unique boutique concept: the buyer views a wall of products; each wall featuring one-off offerings. Sarah's 'walls' started in her living room but have now spread into public spaces, galleries, shop fronts and bars.
Images courtesy of Supermarket Sarah

Creative business planning

Once the product or service is identified, the next stage is to develop a business plan and to regularly monitor progress and make adjustments along the way. This is called 'strategic planning' and it means to develop a clear, workable plan to take you forward in business. While it does take time to create and consider the development of a creative business plan, it is time well invested; not having one will cost far more in lost time, mismanaged resources and the frustration and stress caused by lack of planning.

This section guides you through the process of creating a strategic plan that can be used in the set-up of a fashion business or in the development of fashion projects.

Objectives

Creating a plan for a fashion business includes the following steps:

1. Consider the purpose of the business.
2. Analyse your business opportunities in the competitive landscape (SWOT – see diagram).
3. Research those non-variables identified in the SWOT analysis, minimising weaknesses and capitalising on your strengths.
4. Determine the outcome desired for the business over the first twelve to eighteen months.
5. Create smart objectives, strategies and tactics.
6. Organise the objectives, strategies and tactics into a timeline that can be used to track the plan.
7. Consistently monitor progress and document results.
8. Refine the plan if necessary.

7.6
SWOT analysis. SWOT analysis is a strategic planning method used to evaluate the strengths, weaknesses, opportunities and threats involved in a project or in a business venture.

S	W	
Strengths	**Weaknesses**	**Internal factors**
– Technological skills – Leading brands – Distribution channels – Customer loyalty/relationships – Production quality – Scale – Management	– Absence of important skills – Weak brands – Poor access to distribution – Low customer retention – Unreliable product/service – Sub-scale – Management	
O	**T**	
Opportunities	**Threats**	**External factors**
– Changing customer tastes – Technological advances – Changes in government politics – Lower personal taxes – Change in population age – New distribution channels	– Changing customer base – Closing of geographic markets – Technological advances – Changes in government politics – Tax increases – Change in population age – New distribution channels	

Positive

Negative

Strategic planning

The big picture can be overwhelming, so a strategic plan will help break down goals into manageable chunks to be tackled day by day, enabling decisions to be made in an ever-changing business landscape. Failure to spend time thinking and researching leads to wasted time and loss of money, which unfortunately is one of the most common reasons why fashion companies fail. The following table illustrates why it is important to have a strategy in place.

Creating a business plan

A good business plan should be clear and accurate and will clearly illustrate why the business would be successful. It provides a picture of how the business will be run and must be based on fact or research that has been carried out specific to the fashion industry and business direction. Potential funders, such as bank managers or grant providers, will see lots of business plans and the

Firefighting

In a business context, firefighting is an emergency allocation of resources required to deal with an unforeseen problem immediately. A frequent need for emergency action reflects poor planning or a lack of organisation.

main questions they will need answering before they will part with any money are as follows:

1. Who will the customers be?
2. Why will the target customers buy from the business?
3. How will target customers find out about the business?
4. Who are the business's competitors?
5. How will the business beat the competition?

Defining strategy

Successful business	Unsuccessful business
Sees the bigger picture	Resorts to **firefighting**
Sees patterns and their relationships	Reactive rather than proactive
Has a process to deal with uncertainties	Fears the unknown
Gathers facts, feedback and information from many sources	Vague about what success looks like
Has a plan to accomplish short-term and long-term objectives that are monitored and adapted	No plan in place

'Strategy is the direction and scope of an organization over the long-term, which achieves advantage for the organization through its configuration of resources within a challenging environment, to meet the needs of markets.'

Johnson and Scholes

There are three primary parts to a business plan. The first is the business concept, which takes into account the industry, business structure, particular product or service and how to make the business a success. The second is the marketplace section, which should offer an analysis of potential customers: who and where they are, what makes them buy and so on. The marketplace should also include the competition and how to position the business to beat it. Finally, the financial section contains income and cash flow statement, balance sheet and other financial ratios, such as break-even analyses.

Forecasting fashion sales

Forecasting sales is probably the most difficult and yet most important part of a business plan. First, it will involve establishing the size of the overall market. It is useful to research a similar company to estimate the proposed company's market share, how many garments or units it aims to sell or capture from the competition. Unless the business venture is something totally new – in other words, a new market is being created – it is likely that the market share will start small and grow slowly. It helps to know what the competitors' revenues and unit sales are; forecast sales can then be calculated as a percentage of this overall figure.

Setting prices

The simplest way to calculate price is to work out the cost of the general business **overheads** and assign a percentage to each garment. Work out how many garments the business can produce in a day, then calculate the running costs of the business for a day and divide the second number by the first. When paying for ongoing costs that aren't used on non-business days (for example, if you take weekends off but still have to pay for a website), add a fraction of this cost to the price of each item as well.

It helps to check the cost of similar garments in the marketplace. Include all material and trims, such as buttons and thread, as well as the fabric. Account for the time it takes for garments to be made up; ensure that you charge a reasonable amount. (The national minimum wage is a good place to start. Make sure that you can earn enough to live on!)

Overheads

Overheads are the ongoing costs of running a business, such as rent, electricity, wages and so on.

Raising finance for creative projects

One of the biggest challenges an entrepreneur faces is the challenge of raising finance and funding the business. As covered in the money section earlier, you will need to know where your funding is coming from and you will need to keep your finances under control. There are different ways of raising finance; taking investment can mean losing some of control over your business. Therefore, we are seeing new methods of financing your business without giving too much away.

What is crowdfunding?

Crowdfunding can be described as a way to raise money, awareness and support for a project from the people around you. It is a way of funding where an individual uses the power of the crowd to make their ideas a reality. People with great ideas can get backing from the general public through the internet to raise the money that they need to make a project work. The public can back an idea with pledges of cash and the project owners can 'thank' their backers with rewards that reflect the money contributed.

By asking a large number of people for a small amount of money, you can raise the finance needed for the project. In the past, the main way of raising finance was the opposite; it mainly involved asking a few people for a large sum of money. Crowdfunding switches this idea around by using the internet to communicate with thousands – sometimes millions – of potential funders. Those looking for funds set up a profile of their project on a website such as Crowdfunder, Crowdcube and others. They can then use social media, alongside the traditional networks of friends, family and work colleagues and acquaintances, to raise the money needed for the project.

A little bit of history

It is thought that the first online crowdfunded project occurred in 1997. The rock band Marillion is reported to have been unable to afford their tour after the release of their seventh album *Brave*. The term was not yet coined, but American fans used the internet to raise 60,000 dollars so the band could play in the US. At the time, music fans only had minimal access to the internet but that didn't stop Marillion from pioneering the funding method to support their tour. The band has since used the same techniques to fund the production of their following three albums.

There have been many other creative projects that soon followed suit, such as the production of films. The year 2001 saw the first crowdfunding website; by 2012, there were over 500 crowdfunding platforms online. In February of that year, the first crowdfunded project to raise over £1,000,000 was published.

There are three different types of crowdfunding: donation, debt and equity.

Donation/reward crowdfunding

Most people will invest in this type of fundraising purely because they believe in the idea or cause. Rewards are offered, such as an acknowledgment on an album cover, free gifts, tickets to an event, etc. Returns are considered intangible and donors have social or personal reasons for putting their money into the project and expect nothing in return except to feel that they have contributed to doing good by helping the project. UK sites include: www.buzzbnk.org; www.crowdbnk.com; www.crowdfunder.co.uk; www.gambitious.com; www.justgiving.com; www.peoplefund.it; hubbub.net.

Debt crowdfunding

In this type of crowdfunding, investors will receive their money back with interest. This method is also called peer-to-peer funding (p2p lending). This method allows the lending of money and bypasses the traditional banking system. The returns are financial, and investors also have the advantage of having contributed to an idea they believe will be a success. In the case of micro finance, no interest is paid, this is usually where very small sums of money are leant to the very poor in developing countries and the lender is rewarded by doing social good. Sites include: www.abundancegeneration.com; www.banktothefuture.com; www.buzzbnk.org; www.trillionfund.com.

Equity crowdfunding

This method is where people will invest in an opportunity in exchange for equity. In this case, money is exchanged for shares, or a small stake in the venture, project or business. As with other types of shares, if the project is successful, the value will go up; if not, it will go down. Sites include: www.angelsden.com; www.crowdcube.com; www.ethex.org.uk;

www.gambitious.com; www.microgenius.org.uk; www.crowdmission.com; www.seedrs.com; www.sharein.com; www.indiegogo.com.

How crowdfunding is changing fashion business

In the past, a garment was not produced until a customer placed an order. Now, however, the industry has moved past bespoke to mass-produced fast fashion and online retailers, such as Gustin and the Petite Shop, are bringing decision-making and production back to the customer in the US with faster turnaround and lower minimum quantities.

These retailers used an 'in-house' crowdfunding model for their business – it is like a private Kickstarter for a single designer or retailer. In this model, a product is listed with its own campaign and only if the product gets enough backers is it produced. Compare this with the current-day retail model where a brand will design the complete season's collection of ten to fifteen styles, try to estimate the demand based on past season's performance or wholesale orders and produce thousands of pieces abroad. Once done, these mass-produced pieces are presented to customers at inflated prices to take into account the inevitable markdowns, as time and excess demand will devalue them.

How it works

This is seen as a new business model for those willing to trade a little more time to get better quality and the same price as before. In Gustins's case, the campaign runs for approximately two weeks and six to eight weeks for production. In return, the customer will get high-quality, limited-edition American-made goods using excellent Italian and Japanese fabric, with almost no wasteful production as every piece is reserved before it is made. All at wholesale prices – as the brand Gustin does not have to take into account the cost of holding stock – products are shipped as each run is finished.

The changing nature of the industry, the business models and the way we use the internet to support entrepreneurship is paving the way for new designers to enter a very large and complex industry. It is providing a low-risk way for designers to enter the industry and provides customers with more variety in a cost-effective way, as the designer is not investing in lots of stock that may or may not sell. This type of approach allows designers access to new revenue streams. It also serves as a data-driven fashion laboratory in which the designer and retailer can better understand what their customers are looking for in order to guide future offerings.

Understanding IP and protecting design work

It is important for any fashion company to ensure that their brand and product designs are protected from being copied by rivals or from counterfeiting. Intellectual property laws enable fashion companies and designers to separate themselves from their competitors and ensure that their designs and ideas are protected. Fashion companies can utilise a network of government laws to defend and protect their works, including copyright, trademark, unfair competition law and design patents.

An essential starting point for any business or designer in seeking to keep competitors at bay is a package of registered rights, such as trademark and design registrations, which are easier to enforce than copyright, together with unregistered designs or unregistered trademark rights.

A design constitutes the appearance of a product; in particular, the shape, texture, colour, materials, contours and ornamentation. To qualify as a new design, the overall impression should be different from any existing design. Typically, the creator of the design owns any rights in it, except where the work was commissioned or created during the course of employment, in which case the rights belong to the employer or party that commissioned the work.

Copyright in fashion

Copyright law provides limited protection for a designer's work. Copyright includes original artistic work such as sketches and patterns but does not encompass ideas, information, styles, techniques and names. One-off fashion designs, such as haute couture or jewellery, may be protected as copyright works if they can be shown to be 'works of artistic craftsmanship'. Anything that is mass-produced, however, should rely on design law rather than copyright law.

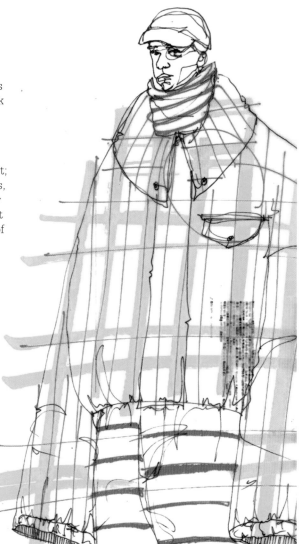

7.7
© Hattie Crowther

Design rights in fashion

Design rights can be bought, sold or licensed in a similar manner to copyright. Design rights exist independently of copyright; they focus more on the shape, design and structure of a product. In order to qualify for design protection, the design must be new and unique. A comparison must be made between the design and what is already in the public domain. The clothing industry has been calling for stronger worldwide intellectual property protection for fashion designs because of potential losses from counterfeiting. Unregistered design rights protect the shape or configuration of a marketable (or potentially marketable) product and are used to prevent unauthorised copying of an original design.

Trademark brand protection

Trademark law protects the marks (logo) by which goods or services are recognised in commerce. A trademark owner may claim against anyone who produces or distributes products with marks or logos that are similar and may cause confusion or dilute the value of the original.

Fashion licensing

Licensing can offer designers and manufacturers additional revenue streams and marketing opportunities. It can enable a fashion company to expand into new geographical territories or product categories.

Design patents

Design patents protect the ornamental design of a functional item. Anyone holding a design patent can seek an injunction and damages against a party who makes, uses, copies or imports a substantially similar design.

'It is argued that copying benefits the industry because it creates diffusion of designs, promotes creativity and innovation, anchors trends and helps burn those trends out so the next season is ready to receive new designs.'

Stuart Vandermark

Case study:
Nabil Nayal

Nabil Nayal is a designer currently attracting a lot of attention. Nabil has his own RTW brand, Nabil Nayal, that melds traditional craftsmanship with new technology. I met Nabil four years ago when he was working as a specialist-visiting lecturer at Sheffield Hallam University on the fashion design course where I am currently principal lecturer. Nabil has his own RTW brand, Nabil Nayal, that melds traditional craftsmanship with new technology. Nabil Nayal was born in Syria and moved to England at the age of fourteen. After studying a BA in fashion design at Manchester Metropolitan University, he went on to win many prestigious awards including the Graduate Fashion Week 'Best Womenswear' Award, the Royal Society of Arts Award, and the British Fashion Council MA Scholarship Award; which enabled him to study his craft at the Royal College of Art.

Nabil has taken his approach to fashion entrepreneurship very seriously; from when he left university and entered the fashion industry, his route to self-employment was supported by some creative and professional experiences in some key areas to build his business on, including, being invited to work with Creative Director Cristopher Bailey at Burberry Prorsum in 2008 to work as researcher. In 2009, Nabil was commissioned by River Island to develop a capsule collection, which took only three days to sell out. Nabil's MA collection was picked up by Harrods as part of the 2010 Harrods Launches platform, and in 2011, Nabil Nayal made its London Fashion Week debut. It was a pivotal point for the brand, attracting high-profile supporters such as Florence Welch, Rihanna, Claudia Schiffer and Lady Gaga.

Being shortlisted for the prestigious LVMH Prize came next along with an invitation to show at Paris Fashion Week in 2011. There he was praised for his creative work and the innovative processes that keep the designer's brand modern and future-facing. His work has been described as 'disrupting' traditional craftsmanship with cutting-edge technologies. Nabil's interest in Elizabethan craftsmanship has profoundly informed his practice; the development of new techniques makes his work stand out from other designers and his use of pleats, dramatic construction and strong silhouettes and the utilisation of historical references remain at the heart of the brand identity. To keep his work future-facing, Nabil is also conducting extensive research into ways the techniques can be applied to his collections using the latest and emerging technologies. He is currently undertaking a research doctorate in how 3D scanning can become integral to the design process and uses 3D printing in the development of his garments.

Nabil has attracted attention from many of the industry's key players including Karl Lagerfeld who first saw a white shirt by the designer in Paris 2015 in the collection that was shortlisted for the LVMH Prize. He asked, "How did you do this?" And then exclaimed, "I love it! I love it! I love it!" Lagerfeld bought it there and then for Lady Amanda Harlech, his muse, friend and collaborator. He later shot it for 100th issue of Vogue Magazine on Jerry Hall.

All of this creates a lot of hard work for Nabil as an entrepreneur and researcher, as he is solely in charge of his brand, the development of his collection, as well as the management and promotion of his company.

7.8
Paris Fashion Week 2015. Karl Lagerfeld meets Nabil Nayal, LVMH shortlister and RCA graduate.

Nabil uses a variety of social media platforms to communicate activities to his audience. On Facebook, we see regular post from the designer promoting his work, his involvement in photo shoots, fashion weeks, etc., alongside posts of his academic research study. His dedication and commitment to his brand and making it in the industry shows in regular posts promoting his work and the interaction he has with the media. His microbrand demonstrates the forward-thinking nature of the new designer to the industry and all he is involved in.

Nabil is a fashion entrepreneur who is creating a brand using new methods and processes and in addition works tirelessly on his academic study, too. This merging of fashion, technology and academic study describes how new designers are working to break the rules within the fashion industry and work in different ways. This interesting approach to his craft sets Nabil Nayal, the brand, apart from some of the more traditional collections on the market and it will be interesting to watch what happens in the young entrepreneur's/ designer's journey.

At the time of writing, Nabil has been shortlisted again for the LVMH Prize came next along with an invitation to show at Paris Fashion Week in 2017.

Chapter summary

This chapter on fashion entrepreneurship brings together many of the same issues around the management of a fashion brand that would be undertaken in a much larger organisation. The focus of the chapter, however, was on amalgamating those activities for a small or 'micro' enterprise.

The Internet is contributing to changes taking place in the industry, resulting in the creation of additional opportunities for fashion graduates wanting to enter the fashion industry by setting up their own fashion brands competing on a global scale with some of the larger brands. This chapter outlined how, in today's fashion industry, small fashion entrepreneurs are as important as the big names. We are also seeing the development of new small business models contributing to the success of modern entrepreneurs along with their desire to contribute and give back to the society in areas focusing on new ways to produce and sell ethical fashion and sustainable products. In order to start a successful micro fashion business, whatever the model, the first part is the start-up strategy, by understanding the customer, working out what is needed, before launching the business and by developing the business plan the fashion entrepreneur will be more likely to succeed.

Small enterprises have been described as leaders in innovation, and the development of new concepts through to commercialisation is a fundamental part of the role for small business managers to stay ahead of the game. The flexibility of a small business allows for this to happen, and this type of activity is crucial for a new business to succeed in turbulent and diverse economic market conditions.

There are many small businesses set up each year globally; therefore, having a business idea that allows you stand out from everyone else to succeed is crucial. There are many opportunities for fashion entrepreneurs today thanks to the internet and many new business models that you could adopt for the business you want to start up. Deciding what type of fashion business to open, whether it is designing clothes, selling clothes at a retail store or providing fashion services such as promotions, requires research and planning skills.

A good business plan should be clear and accurate and will clearly illustrate why the business would be successful. It must provide a picture of how the business will be run and must be based on fact or research that has been carried out specific to the fashion industry and business direction. Potential funders, such as bank managers or grant providers, will see lots of business plans and lots of questions will be asked, so clarity and consideration to this is key.

Raising finance will be something to consider early on, but with new opportunities like crowdfunding, you may be able to bypass traditional ways of finding cash by developing a crowdfunding pitch that will allow you to gain support from the creative community to launch your business.

Finally, there is no point in going through all of the planning without protecting your ideas. Depending on the type of business you are involved with, you will need to look at protecting your work either through design rights or copyright. Many small design companies fail to recognise the value of their ideas, and it is important that you understand where you stand on this.

The next section will aid you in reflecting on the chapter through some questions.

Case study and chapter reflection

Q. What fashion educational routes has Nabil undertaken to gain his skills as a fashion entrepreneur?

Q. What fashion companies has Nabil either worked for or had his work sold through?

Q. Which key designer showed attention to Nabil's work, and what was his response to the collection?

Q. How does Nabil's work differ from other designers?

CHECKLIST

1. Explain in a sentence or two how you would describe entrepreneurial practice.

2. Describe the three steps in developing concepts for commercialising products.

3. List at least four different fashion businesses that a fashion entrepreneur can set up if not a designer.

4. Describe what a microbrand is.

5. Outline some of the different small business models in the current industry.

6. Outline some of the key stages to starting a fashion business.

7. Explain the main point in creating a business plan.

8. What is crowdfunding?

9. Explain what IP is.

10. What is at the centre of Nabil Nayal's work?

EXERCISE

Five steps to a crowdfunding pitch video

The most important thing in the pitch is the first impression you make with your video. This is essentially your elevator pitch in a short video format, and this will be your one-time-only chance to sell your idea and yourself, so make it count. The following exercise will take you through the five important steps of making a strong crowdfunding pitch and really get in touch with the viewer in order to get them to donate. In addition to the platforms listed on pages 174 and 175, some of the most popular platforms include rockethub.com, Indiegogo.com and kickstarter.com.

Step 1: In your own pitch video. . .. show yourself!

You must show yourself in the pitch, don't make the mistake many pitchers make by not showing who they are. People donate to people, not to projects. The personal connection is important at this stage, as this is what will raise the cash.

Step 2: Demonstrate that you've thought about the tone and mood of your pitch.

Find a location that enhances your project and the mood of the pitch, this should instil a cosy and warm feeling to your audience and make them, as potential funders, feel at ease. Remember, the film is an extension of you and if you come across as cold and uninteresting to the viewer, they won't reach into their pockets.

Step 3: Even in a pitch, you must show you care about production value.

You don't have to have an expensive camera; you can shoot this on a smartphone and still make a good impression. But whatever you shoot it on, ensure you put thought into the production value of your pitch. Think carefully about your lighting, audio recording, and all other things you need to pay close attention to when making the film you're crowdfunding for. Make the pitch something you'd be proud to share with the world.

Step 4: Demonstrate you can pitch with conviction.

Don't be over sentimental or beg. You want to evoke a sense of empathy that will empower the viewer to want to contribute to making it happen. Try to pitch with conviction, be passionate about your project, excited about what you are offering to potential funders, and remember, always make the pitch about the funders, never about you.

Step 5: Show potential funders their money is in safe hands.

Your funders will want to be reassured that you'll know exactly how to use the money you are raising. A brief showcase of your previous work is the easiest way to do it. Stories speak louder than a shot of a paper award on the wall; tell the viewer what it was and how you achieved it and how this has contributed to your current work. And if this is your first project you're crowdfunding for, tell them that in your pitch, outline the amount you're looking to raise. The bottom line is to be honest with yourself and your potential funders. Good luck!

Interview:
Nabil Nayal

Q: Could you let the readers know what made you want to be a fashion designer?

A: Wanting to be a designer happened gradually; I began making clothes at the age of three/four. I never labelled it as fashion – I was just very much into fabric, construction and found that through this medium, I was able to project my creative vision, which has obviously evolved over time. I have never wanted to be anything else – I am quite single-minded about what I want to do so I have pursed my ambitions and I love what I do. I have never been drawn to the celebrity culture aspects that surround fashion – I get excited by the creative potential of my work.

Q: When did you think, 'I want to start my own label'?

A: Probably around the age of fifteen/sixteen. By then, I knew I was going to be a fashion designer and had already begun researching where I was going to study my first degree. But of course, I was very naïve to think it would just 'happen'. It doesn't just happen. I finally set up my business in 2014, after my MA studies at the Royal College of Art and a few years' work-experience.

Q: Who are the team behind NABIL NAYAL the brand ?

A: Myself, my business partner, my seamstress, my pattern cutter, my production unit and my PR.

Q: Please tell us about the current collection?

A: My SS17 collection is the third instalment of six Elizabethan sportswear collections. The collections draw from the Elizabethan period

(1558–1603) and contemporary sportswear technology. I spent a week in the archives of the Prato Museum in Italy studying Elizabethan linens – construction techniques, fabrication, embellishment and silhouette. These findings informed the collection through laser-cutting, smocking techniques and silhouette.

Q: What is the business model of the brand NABIL NAYAL?

A: We provide high-end garments that are rich in craft-techniques drawn from the Elizabethan era, which we contemporarise and re-contextualise for a new audience. Our numbers are deliberately small – we want to be niche and have learned the value of saying no before saying yes to stockists/collaborators. We manufacture in England and take sustainability very seriously.

Q: How do you promote your brand to the industry and your potential customers?

A: We have a PR agency who promote us via the obvious routes. But we also use social media outlets – especially Instagram. After meeting the Instagram team during our exhibition at the LVMH Prize in 2015, I was invited to New York to discuss our brand strategy on Instagram as we have become known for using the platform in an innovative way.

Q: What is next for NABIL NAYAL? Where do you see the brand heading over the next few years?

A: We have been showcasing our collections internationally during Milan Fashion Week and Paris Fashion Week. We will carry on this model and grow the business organically. For AW17, we will be showing our collection under the support of the British Fashion Council in Paris. The brand will always be involved in research of historical artefacts, which is disseminated through the collections thereby offering my audience garments that are informed by accurate historical construction techniques, juxtaposed against a modern backdrop. Research is at the kernel of the brand; I am currently undertaking a research doctorate on Elizabethan dress and the practice of contemporary fashion. No doubt, I will carry on actively researching archives around the world to inform my creative output.

Q: Any advice for a future fashion entrepreneur?

A: Hard work is not enough to get you to where you need to be; you have to be strategic. Think beyond the here and now and step out of your business – what advice would you give yourself in five years' time? It is cliché, but you have to trust your gut. Realise also that you cannot and should not do it all on your own – it is virtually impossible. I think being successful in this industry requires you to be good at acknowledging your flaws; no one is good at everything. Finally – design counts for around 10 per cent of the amount of time you'll spend on a collection. The other 90 per cent is spent running the business. Imran Amed gave me that advice and he was right. Oh and also, try your hardest not to borrow a penny – we have bootstrapped it all from the outset and never borrowed anything. That advice came from Jonathan Saunders – he was so right!

For every twenty emails you send out, you'll probably only get one reply. Don't give up hope – if you stick at it long enough, you'll get there!

Conclusion

The fashion industry is dynamic, extremely competitive and important to the growth and development of the global economy. The success of the multibillion dollar, global fashion industry is reliant upon the work and dedication of those working in fashion management, which is evolving at great speed. Fashion management encompasses the business side of fashion, and its continuing success is about responding effectively to the constant changes in consumer demand, technology and global economic challenges: one of the biggest challenges in today's global marketplace is managing fashion in an ethical, sustainable way.

Fashion is a competitive industry and graduates entering the industry are more innovative and creative than ever before, with excellent creative thinking, cross-communicative skills, technology awareness and critical skills. *The Fundamentals of Fashion Management* has explored the way the industry continues to evolve in response to changes taking place. It looks at the different roles within the fashion industry and how these play their part in the business. Offering an insight into these sectors helps to demonstrate how the fashion business is a much larger and broader industry than simply fashion design: each individual role is an important contribution in such a large and important industry. These roles may include researching trends, buying, selling and the art of persuasion through innovative and inventive approaches to presenting products to the fashion customer. There are opportunities in fashion buying, trend prediction, communication, marketing and entrepreneurialism.

It is hoped that this book has developed your understanding of the theoretical and practical issues relevant to fashion business and management, from designer to consumer. It should encourage you to explore fundamental principles inherent within the processes of fashion management. Take the time to investigate the huge variety of challenging and rewarding career opportunities, whether as a means to nurture your own entrepreneurial venture or to join the fashion industry in a managerial role.

Bibliography

Adair, J (2006) *100 Greatest Ideas for Effective Leadership and Management,* Capstone Publishing.

Ambrose, G and Harris, P (2010) *Packaging the Brand,* AVA Publishing.

Blundel, R (1997) *Effective Business Communication: Principles and Practice for the Communication Age,* Pearson Higher Education.

Boddy, D (2005) *Management: an Introduction,* Pearson Higher Education.

Burk Wood, M (2007) *Essential Guide to Marketing Planning,* Prentis Hall.

Butler, D (2000) *Business Planning: a Guide to Business Start-Up,* Butterworth-Heinemann.

Constantino, M (1998) *Fashion Marketing and PR,* Batsford.

Evans, C and Frankel, S (2008) *The House of Viktor & Rolf,* Merrell.

Evans, D (2007) *Coolhunting: a Guide to High Design and Innovation,* Southbank Publishing.

Evans, D (2008) *Coolhunting Green: Recycled, Repurposed and Renewable Projects,* Southbank Publishing.

Everett, J and Swanson, K (2004) *Guide to Producing a Fashion Show,* Fairchild Publications.

Goworek, H (2001) *Fashion Buying,* Blackwell Science.

Handy, C (1985) *Understanding Organizations,* Penguin.

Hess, J and Pasztorek, S (2010) *Graphic Design for Fashion,* Laurence King.

Hingston, P (2001) *Starting Your Business,* Dorling Kindersley.

Jackson, T and Shaw, D (2000) *Mastering Fashion Buying and Merchandising Management,* Palgrave Macmillan.

Kojima, N (ed) (1999) *Maison Martin Margiela Street: Special Edition Volumes 1 and 2,* Street Magazine.

Le Marinel, A (2005) *Start and Run Your Own Business: The Complete Guide Setting Up and Managing a Small Business* How To Books.

Levinson, J (2007) *Guerilla Marketing,* Piatkus Books.

Mackrell, A (2004) *Art and Fashion,* Batsford.

Marchetti, L and Quinz, E (2007) *Dysfashional: Adventures in Post-Style,* OM Publishers.

McKelvey, K and Munslow, J (2008) *Fashion Forecasting,* Wiley-Blackwell.

Morris, M (2005) *Starting a Successful Business,* Kogan Page.

Mullins, L (2004) *Management and Organisational Behaviour,* Pearson Higher Education.

Pakhchyan, S (2008) *Fashioning Technology,* O'Reilly Books.

Pettinger, R and Nelson, B (2007) *Managing for Dummies,* John Wiley and Sons.

Phaidon (ed) (2003) *Area: 100 Graphic Designers, 10 Curators, 10 Design Classics,* Phaidon.

Pie Books (ed) (2008) *Absolute Appeal: Direct Mail Design,* Pie Books.

Pie Books (ed) (2007) *Fashion Brand Graphics,* Pie Books.

Pricken, M (2004) *Visual Creativity,* Thames & Hudson.

Reuvid, J (2006) *Start Up and Run Your Own Business,* Kogan Page.

Ridderstrale, J and Nordstrom, K (2001) *Funky Business,* Pearson Professional.

Roscam Abbing, E (2010) *Brand-Driven Innovation: Strategies for Development and Design,* AVA Publishing.

Savoir, A and Diman, P (2008) *Invitation and Promotion Design,* Harper Collins.

Sheridan, J (2010) *Fashion, Media, Promotion: The New Black Magic,* John Wiley and Sons.

Toth, M (2003) *Fashion Icon: The Power and Influence of Graphic Design,* Rockport.

Tungate, M (2004) *Fashion Brands: Branding Style from Armani to Zara,* Kogan Page.

Waddell, G (2004) *How Fashion Works,* Blackwell.

Williams, S (2006) *The Financial Times Guide to Business Start Up,* Pearson Professional.

Index